AF560380

Pest Management
Principles and Practices

Pest Management:
Principles and Practices

Rajesh Ravi

ANMOL PUBLICATIONS PVT. LTD.
NEW DELHI - 110 002 (INDIA)

ANMOL PUBLICATIONS PVT. LTD.
H.O.: 4374/4B, Ansari Road, Darya Ganj,
New Delhi-110 002 (India)
Ph.: 23278000, 23261597
B.O.: No. 1015, Ist Main Road, BSK IIIrd Stage
IIIrd Phase, IIIrd Block,
Bangalore - 560 085 (India)
Visit us at: www.anmolpublications.com

Pest Management: Principles and Practices

First Published, 2007
ISBN 978-81-261-3411-3

PRINTED IN INDIA

Printed at Mehra Offset Press, Delhi.

Contents

Preface

The book comprises of several chapters deal intensively and extensively with pests and diseases caused by insects, nematodes, fungi, viruses, bacteria, mollicutes and viroids. These chapters present a comprehensive picture of diseases and pests with particular focus on symptoms, transmission, host range, production of diagnostic reagents, detection technology, taxonomy, ecology, epidemiology and effective management practices of the concerned pests or diseases. This immensely useful book is designed to update the knowledge of undergraduate and postgraduate students of economic entomology, mycology, nematology and plant protection. This book provides detailed information on the management of pests of almost all the tropical, subtropical and temperate horticulture crops. Ecological approaches and strategies of pest management which help in developing efficient and reliable techniques and tools required for pest management are discussed in detail. Different aspects of biological, cultural, mechanical and regulatory controls are also appropriately highlighted. Use of insecticides, status and scope of insect growth regulators and the role of semiochemicals for pest control are also dealt with. Keeping in view the recent scientific developments, indigenous technology knowledge and the genetic engineering techniques used for pest management have also been discussed.

This book is intended to provide a clear overview of the principles and practices of pest management and should serve as a useful source of information to the scientists as well as to orchardists and farmers alike. It will also serve as a text/ reference book to the teachers, postgraduate students and researchers.

Rajesh Ravi

Biointensive Integrated Pest Management

Fundamentals of Sustainable Agriculture

Abstract: This publication provides the rationale for biointensive Integrated Pest Management (IPM), outlines the concepts and tools of biointensive IPM, and suggests steps and provides informational resources for implementing IPM. It is targeted to individuals interested in agriculture at all levels.

"Conventional" and "Biointensive" IPM

Pest management is an ecological mattor. The size of a pest population and the damage it inflicts is, to a great extent, a reflection of the design and management of a particular agricultural ecosystem.

We humans compete with other organisms for food and fibre from our crops. We wish to secure a maximum amount of the food resource from a given area with minimum input of resources and energy. However, if the agricultural system design and/or management is faulty—making it easy for pests to develop and expand their populations or, conversely, making it difficult for predators and parasites of pests to exist—then we will be expending unnecessary resources for pest management.

Therefore, the first step in sustainable and effective pest management is looking at the design of the agricultural ecosystem and considering what ecological concepts can be applied to the design and management of the system to better manage pests and their parasites and predators.

The design and management of our agricultural systems need re-examining. We've come to accept routine use of biological poisons in our food systems as normal. But routine use of synthetic chemicals represents significant energy inputs into the agricultural system, and carries both obvious and hidden costs to the farmer and society. Attempting to implement an ecology-based discipline like IPM in large monocultures, which substitute chemical inputs for ecological design, can be an exercise in futility and inefficiency.

IPM, as it was originally conceived, proposed to manage pests though an understanding of their interactions with other organisms and the environment. Most of the 77 definitions for IPM listed in The Database of IPM Resources (DIR) Web site, despite some differences in emphasis, agree with this idea and have the following elements in common:

- A conception of a managed resource, such as a cropping system on a farm, as a component of a functioning ecosystem. Actions are taken to restore and enhance natural balances in the system, not to eliminate species. Regular monitoring makes it possible to evaluate the populations of pest and beneficial organisms. The producer can then take steps to enhance natural controls (or at least avoid or limit the disruption of natural controls) of the target pest(s).
- An understanding that the presence of a pest does not necessarily constitute a problem. Before a potentially disruptive control method is employed, appropriate decision-making criteria are used to determine whether or not pest management actions are needed.
- A consideration of all possible pest management options before action is taken.
- A philosophy that IPM strategies integrate a combination of all suitable techniques in as compatible a manner as possible; it is important that one technique not conflict with another.

However, IPM has strayed from its ecological roots. Critics of what might be termed "conventional" IPM note that it has been implemented as Integrated Pesticide Management (or even Improved Pesticide Marketing) with an emphasis on using pesticides as a tool of first resort. What has been missing from this approach, which is essentially reactive, is an understanding of the ecological basis of pest infestations. Also missing from the conventional approach are guidelines for ecology-based manipulations of the farm agro-ecosystem that address the questions:

Biointensive IPM incorporates ecological and economic factors into agricultural system design and decision making, and addresses public concerns about environmental quality and food safety. The benefits of implementing biointensive IPM can include reduced chemical input costs, reduced on-farm and off-farm environmental impacts, and more effective and sustainable pest management. An ecology-based IPM has the potential of decreasing inputs of fuel, machinery, and synthetic chemicals—all of which are energy intensive and increasingly costly in terms of financial and environmental impact. Such reductions will benefit the grower and society.

Over-reliance on the use of synthetic pesticides in crop protection programmes around the world has resulted in disturbances to the environment, pest resurgence, pest resistance to pesticides, and lethal and sub-lethal effects on non-target organisms, including humans. These side effects have raised public concern about the routine use and safety of pesticides. At the same time, population increases are placing ever-greater demands upon the "ecological services"—that is, provision of clean air, water and wildlife habitat—of a landscape dominated by farms.

Although some pending legislation has recognized the costs to farmers of providing these ecological services, it's clear that farmers and ranchers will be required to manage their land with greater attention to direct and indirect off-farm impacts of various farming practices on water, soil, and wildlife resources. With this likely future in mind, reducing dependence on chemical pesticides in favour of ecosystem manipulations is a good strategy for farmers.

Consumers Union, a group that has carried out research and advocacy on various pesticide problems for many years, defines biointensive IPM as the highest level of IPM: a systems approach to pest management based on an understanding of pest ecology. It begins with steps to accurately diagnose the nature and source of pest problems, and then relies on a range of preventive tactics and biological controls to keep pest populations within acceptable limits. Reduced-risk pesticides are used if other tactics have not been adequately effective, as a last resort, and with care to minimize risks.

This "biointensive" approach sounds remarkably like the original concept of IPM. Such a "systems" approach makes sense both intuitively and in practice.

The primary goal of biointensive IPM is to provide guidelines and options for the effective management of pests and beneficial organisms in an ecological context. The flexibility and environmental compatibility of a biointensive IPM strategy make it useful in all types of cropping systems.

Even conventional IPM strategies help to prevent pest problems from developing, and reduce or eliminate the use of chemicals in managing problems that do arise. Results of 18 economic evaluations of conventional IPM on cotton showed a decrease in production costs of 7 percent and an average decrease in pesticide use of 15 percent. Biointensive IPM would likely decrease chemical use and costs even further.

Prior to the mid-1970s, lygus bugs were considered to be the key pest in California cotton. Yet in large-scale studies on insecticidal control of lygus bugs, yields in untreated plots were not significantly different from those on treated plots. This was because the insecticides often induced outbreaks of secondary lepidopterous larvae (*i.e.*, cabbage looper, beet army worm, and bollworm) and mite pests which caused additional damage as well as pest resurgence of the lygus bug itself.

These results, from an economic point of view, seem paradoxical, as the lygus bug treatments were costly, yet the treated plots consistently had lower yields (*i.e.*, it cost farmers money to lose money). This paradox was first pointed out by R. van den Bosch, V. Stern, and L. A. Falcon, who forced a re-evaluation of the economic basis of Lygus control in California cotton.

Components of Biointensive IPM

An important difference between conventional and biointensive IPM is that the emphasis of the latter is on pro-active measures to redesign the agricultural ecosystem to the disadvantage of a pest and to the advantage of its parasite and predator complex.

At the same time, biointensive IPM shares many of the same components as conventional IPM, including monitoring, use of economic thresholds, record keeping, and planning.

How to Get Started with IPM

Good planning must precede implementation of any IPM programme, but is particularly important in a biointensive programme. Planning should be done before planting because many pest strategies require steps or inputs, such as beneficial organism habitat management, that must be considered well in advance. Attempting to jump-start an IPM programme in the beginning or middle of a cropping season generally does not work.

When planning a biointensive IPM programme, some considerations include:

- Options for design changes in the agricultural system (beneficial organism habitat, crop rotations).
- Choice of pest-resistant cultivars.
- Technical information needs.
- Monitoring options, record keeping, equipment, etc.

Blocks on the Pesticide Treadmill

Resistance: Pesticide use exerts a powerful selection pressure for changing the genetic make-up of a pest population. Naturally resistant individuals in a pest population are able to survive pesticide treatments. The survivors pass on the resistance trait to their offspring.

The result is a much higher percentage of the pest population resistant to a pesticide. In the last decade, the number of weed species known to be resistant to herbicides rose from 48 to 270, and the number of plant pathogens resistant to fungicides grew from 100 to 150. Resistance to insecticides is so common—more than 500 species—that nobody is really keeping score.

Resurgence: Pesticides often kill off natural enemies along with the pest. With their natural enemies eliminated, there is little to prevent recovered pest populations from exploding to higher, more damaging numbers than existed before pesticides were applied. Additional chemical pesticide treatments only repeat this cycle.

Secondary Pests: Some potential pests that are normally kept under good control by natural enemies become actual pests after their natural enemies are destroyed by pesticides. Mite outbreaks after pesticide applications are a classic example.

Residues: Only a minute portion of any pesticide application contacts the target organism. The remainder may degrade harmlessly, but too often water, wind, and soil will carry pesticides to non-target areas and organisms, affecting the health of human and wildlife populations. Public concerns over residues are deepened by the lack of research and knowledge about possible synergistic interactions between pesticide residues and the hundreds of other synthetic chemical residues now found in the environment.

The Pest Manager/Ecosystem Manager

The pest manager is the most important link in a successful IPM programme. The manager must know the biology of the pest and the beneficial organisms associated with the pest, and understand their interactions within the farm environment. As a detailed knowledge of the pest is developed, weak links in its life cycle become apparent. These weak links are phases of the life cycle when the pest is most susceptible to control measures.

The manager must integrate this knowledge with tools and techniques of biointensive IPM to manage not one, but several pests. A more accurate title for the pest manager is "ecosystem doctor," for he or she must pay close attention to the pulse of the managed ecosystem and stay abreast of developments in IPM and crop/pest biology and ecology. In this way, the ecosystem manager can take a pro-active approach to managing pests, developing ideas about system manipulations, testing them, and observing the results.

IPM options may be considered pro-active or reactive. Pro-active options, such as crop rotations and creation of habitat for beneficial organisms, permanently lower the carrying capacity of the farm for the pest. The carrying capacity is determined by factors like food, shelter, natural enemies complex, and weather, which affect the reproduction and survival of a species. Cultural controls are generally considered to be pro-active strategies.

The second set of options is more reactive. This simply means that the grower responds to a situation, such as an economically damaging population of pests, with some type of short-term suppressive action. Reactive methods generally include inundative releases of biological controls, mechanical and physical controls, and chemical controls.

Pro-active Strategies (Cultural Controls)

- Healthy, biologically active soils (increasing below ground diversity)
- Habitat for beneficial organisms (increasing above ground diversity)
- Appropriate plant cultivars

Cultural controls are manipulations of the agro-ecosystem that make the cropping system less friendly to the establishment and proliferation of pest populations. Although they are designed to have positive effects on farm ecology and pest management, negative impacts may also result, due to variations in weather or changes in crop management.

Farm Systems for Pest Populations

In a non-farm scaped system, where pests have fewer natural controls and thus reach higher average populations, they are more likely to approach or exceed the economic threshold level for the crop, making pesticide treatments likely. In a farm scaped system, greater and more consistent populations of beneficial organisms put more ecological pressure on the pests, with the result that pest populations are less likely to approach the economic threshold. In other words, the ecological carrying capacity for a pest will probably be lower in a farm scaped system.

Maintaining and increasing biological diversity of the farm system is a primary strategy of cultural control. Decreased biodiversity tends to result in agro-ecosystems that are unstable and prone to recurrent pest outbreaks and many other problems. Systems high in biodiversity tend to be more "dynamically stable"—that is, the variety of organisms provide more checks and balances on each other, which helps prevent one species (*i.e.*, pest species) from overwhelming the system.

There are many ways to manage and increase biodiversity on a farm, both above ground and in the soil. In fact, diversity above ground influences diversity below ground. Research has shown that up to half of a plant's photosynthetic production (carbohydrates) is sent to the roots, and half of that (along with various amino acids and other plant products) leaks out the roots into the surrounding soil, providing a food source for microorganisms. These root exudates vary from plant species to plant species and this variation influences the type of organisms associated with the root exudates.

Factors influencing the health and biodiversity of soils include the amount of soil organic matter; soil pH; nutrient balance; moisture; and parent material of the soil. Healthy soils with a diverse community of organisms support plant health and nutrition better than soils deficient in organic matter and low in species diversity. Research has shown that excess nutrients (*e.g.*, too much nitrogen) as well as relative nutrient balance (*i.e.*, ratios of nutrients—for example, twice as much calcium as magnesium, compared to equal amounts of both) in soils affect insect pest response to plants. Imbalances in the soil can make a plant more attractive to insect pests, less able to recover from pest damage, or more susceptible to secondary infections by plant pathogens. Soils rich in organic matter tend to suppress plant pathogens.

In addition, it is estimated that 75% of all insect pests spend part of their life cycle in the soil, and many of their natural enemies occur there as well. For example, larvae of one species of blister beetle consume about 43 grasshopper eggs before maturing. Both are found in the soil. (Unfortunately, although blister beetle larvae can help reduce grasshopper populations, the adult beetles can be a serious pest for many vegetable growers. Overall, a healthy soil with a diversity of beneficial organisms and high organic matter content helps maintain pest populations below their economic thresholds.

Genetic diversity of a particular crop may be increased by planting more than one cultivar. For example, a recent experiment in China demonstrated that disease-susceptible rice varieties planted in mixtures with resistant varieties had 89% greater yield and a 94% lower incidence of rice blast (a fungus) compared to when they were grown in mono-culture. The experiment, which involved five townships in 1998 and ten townships in 1999, was so successful that fungicidal sprays were no longer applied by the end of the two-year programme.

Species diversity of the associated plant and animal community can be increased by allowing trees and other native plants to grow in fence rows or along water ways, and by integrating livestock into the farm system. Use of the following cropping schemes offers additional ways to increase species diversity.

Crop rotations radically alter the environment both above and below ground, usually to the disadvantage of pests of the previous crop. The same crop grown year after year on the same field will inevitably build up populations of organisms that feed on that plant, or, in the case of weeds, have a life cycle similar to that of the crop. Add to this the disruptive effect of pesticides on species diversity, both above and below ground, and the result is an unstable system in which slight stresses (*e.g.*, new pest variety or drought) can devastate the crop.

An enforced rotation programme in the Imperial Valley of California has effectively controlled the sugar beet cyst nematode. Under this programme, sugar beets may not be grown more than two years in a row or more than four years out of ten in clean fields (*i.e.*, non-infested fields). In infested fields, every year of a sugar beet crop must be followed by three years of a non-host crop. Other nematode pests commonly controlled with crop rotation methods include the golden nematode of potato, many root-knot nematodes, and the soybean cyst nematode.

When making a decision about crop rotation, consider the following questions: Is there an economically sustainable crop that can be rotated into the cropping system? Is it compatible? Important considerations when developing a crop rotation are:

- What two (or three or several) crops can provide an economic return when considered together as a biological and economic system that includes considerations of sustainable soil management?
- What are the impacts of this season's cropping practices on subsequent crops?
- What specialized equipment is necessary for the crops?
- What markets are available for the rotation crops?

A corn/soybean rotation is one example of rotating compatible economic crops. Corn is a grass; soybean is a leguminous broadleaf. The pest complex of each, including soil organisms, is quite different. Corn root-worm, one of the major pests of corn, is virtually eliminated by using this rotation. Both crops generally provide a reasonable return. Even rotations, however, create selection pressures that will ultimately alter pest genetics. A good example is again the corn root-worm: the corn/bean rotation has apparently selected for a small population that can survive a year of non-corn (*i.e.*, soybean) cropping.

Management factors should also be considered. For example, one crop may provide a lower direct return per acre than the alternate crop, but may also lower management costs for the alternate crop (by reducing weed pressure, for example, and thus avoiding one tillage or herbicide application), with a net increase in profit.

Other Cropping Structure Options

Multiple cropping is the sequential production of more than one crop on the same land in one year. Depending on the type of cropping sequence used, multiple cropping can be useful as a weed control measure, particularly when the second crop is interplanted into the first.

Interplanting is seeding or planting a crop into a growing stand, for example over-seeding a cover crop into a grain stand. There may be micro-climate advantages (*e.g.*, timing, wind protection, and less radical temperature and humidity changes) as well as disadvantages (competition for light, water, nutrients) to this strategy. By keeping the soil covered, interplanting may also help protect soil against erosion from wind and rain.

Inter-cropping is the practice of growing two or more crops in the same, alternate, or paired rows in the same area. This technique is particularly appropriate in vegetable production. The advantage of Inter-cropping is that the increased diversity helps "disguise" crops from insect pests, and if done well, may allow for more efficient utilization of limited soil and water resources. Disadvantages may relate to ease of managing two different crop species— with potentially different nutrient, water, and light needs, and differences in harvesting time and method—in close proximity to each other.

Strip cropping is the practice of growing two or more crops in different strips across a field wide enough for independent cultivation (*e.g.*, alternating six-row blocks of soybeans and corn or alternating strips of alfalfa and cotton or alfalfa and corn). It is commonly practised to help reduce soil erosion in hilly areas. Like Inter-cropping, strip cropping increases the diversity of a cropping area, which in turn may help "disguise" the crops from pests.

Another advantage to this system is that one of the crops may act as a reservoir and/or food source for beneficial organisms. However, much more research is needed on the complex interactions between various paired crops and their pest/predator complexes.

The options described above can be integrated with no-till cultivation schemes and all its variations (strip till, ridge till, etc.) as well as with hedgerows and intercrops designed for beneficial organism habitat. With all the cropping and tillage options available, it is possible, with creative and informed management, to evolve a biologically diverse, pest-suppressive farming system appropriate to the unique environment of each farm.

Other Cultural Management Options

Disease-free seed and plants are available from most commercial sources, and are certified as such. Use of disease-free seed and nursery stock is important in preventing the introduction of disease.

Resistant varieties are continually being bred by researchers. Growers can also do their own plant breeding simply by collecting non-hybrid seed from healthy plants in the field. The plants from these seeds will have a good chance of being better suited to the local environment and of being more resistant to insects and diseases. Since natural systems are dynamic rather than static, breeding for resistance must be an ongoing process, especially in the case of plant disease, as the pathogens themselves continue to evolve and become resistant to control measures.

Sanitation involves removing and destroying the over-wintering or breeding sites of the pest as well as preventing a new pest from establishing on the farm (*e.g.*, not allowing off-farm soil from farm equipment to spread nematodes or plant pathogens to your land).

This strategy has been particularly useful in horticultural and tree-fruit crop situations involving twig and branch pests. If, however, sanitation involves removal of crop residues from the soil surface, the soil is left exposed to erosion by wind and water. As with so many decisions in farming, both the short- and long-term benefits of each action should be considered when tradeoffs like this are involved.

Spacing of plants heavily influences the development of plant diseases and weed problems. The distance between plants and rows, the shape of beds, and the height of plants influence air flow across the crop, which in turn determines how long the leaves remain damp from rain and morning dew. Generally speaking, better air flow will decrease the incidence of plant disease. However, increased air flow through wider spacing will also allow more sunlight to the ground, which may increase weed problems. This is another instance in which detailed knowledge of the crop ecology is necessary to determine the best pest management strategies. How will the crop react to increased spacing between rows and between plants? Will yields drop because of reduced crop density? Can this be offset by reduced pest management costs or fewer losses from disease?

Altered planting dates can at times be used to avoid specific insects, weeds, or diseases. For example, squash bug infestations on cucurbits can be decreased by the delayed planting strategy, *i.e.*, waiting to establish the cucurbit crop until over-wintering adult squash bugs have died. To assist with disease management decisions, the Cooperative Extension Service (CES) will often issue warnings of "infection periods" for certain diseases, based upon the weather.

In some cases, the CES also keeps track of "degree days" needed for certain important insect pests to develop. Insects, being cold-blooded, will not develop below or above certain threshold temperatures. Calculating accumulated degree days, that is, the number of days above the threshold development temperature for an insect pest, makes the prediction of certain events, such as egg hatch, possible. University of California has an excellent Web site that uses weather station data from around the state to help California growers predict pest emergence.

Some growers gauge the emergence of insect pests by the flowering of certain non-crop plant species native to the farm. This method uses the "natural degree days" accumulated by plants. For example, a grower might time cabbage planting for three weeks after the *Amelanchier* species (also known as saskatoon, shadbush, or serviceberry) on their farm are in bloom.

This will enable the grower to avoid peak egg-laying time of the cabbage maggot fly, as the egg hatch occurs about the time *Amelanchier* species are flowering. Using this information, cabbage maggot management efforts could be concentrated during a known time frame when the early instars (the most easily managed stage) are active.

Optimum growing conditions are always important. Plants that grow quickly and are healthy can compete with and resist pests better than slow-growing, weak plants. Too often, plants grown outside their natural ecosystem range must rely on pesticides to overcome conditions and pests to which they are not adapted.

Mulches, living or non-living, are useful for suppression of weeds, insect pests, and some plant diseases. Hay and straw, for example, provide habitat for spiders. Research in Tennessee showed a 70% reduction in damage to vegetables by insect pests when hay or straw was used as mulch.

The difference was due to spiders, which find mulch more habitable than bare ground. Other researchers have found that living mulches of various clovers reduce insect pest damage to vegetables and orchard crops. Again, this reduction is due to natural predators and parasites provided habitat by the clovers. Vetch has been used as both a nitrogen source and as a weed suppressive mulch in tomatoes in Maryland. Growers must be aware that mulching may also provide a more friendly environment for slugs and snails, which can be particularly damaging at the seedling stage.

Mulching helps to minimize the spread of soil-borne plant pathogens by preventing their transmission through soil splash. Mulch, if heavy enough, prevents the germination of many annual weed seeds. Winged aphids are repelled by silver-or aluminum-coloured mulches. Recent springtime field tests at the Agricultural Research Service in Florence, South Carolina, have indicated that red plastic mulch suppresses root-knot nematode damage in tomatoes by diverting resources away from the roots (and nematodes) and into foliage and fruit.

Biotech Crops: Gene transfer technology is being used by several companies to develop cultivars resistant to insects, diseases, and herbicides. An example is the incorporation of genetic material from *Bacillus thuringiensis* (Bt), a naturally occurring bacterium, into cotton, corn, and potatoes, to make the plant tissues toxic to bollworm, earworm, and potato beetle larvae, respectively.

Whether or not this technology should be adopted is the subject of much debate. Opponents are concerned that by introducing Bt genes into plants, selection pressure for resistance to the Bt toxin will intensify and a valuable biological control tool will be lost. There are also concerns about possible impacts of genetically-modified plant products (*i.e.*, root exudates) on non-target organisms as well as fears of altered genes being transferred to weed relatives of crop plants. Whether there is a market for gene-altered crops is also a consideration for farmers and processors. Proponents of this technology argue that use of such crops decreases the need to use toxic chemical pesticides.

Biological Controls

Biological control is the use of living organisms—parasites, predators, or pathogens—to maintain pest populations below economically damaging levels, and may be either natural or applied. A first step in setting up a biointensive IPM programme is to assess the populations of beneficials and their interactions within the local ecosystem. This will help to determine the potential role of natural enemies in the managed agricultural ecosystem. It should be noted that some groups of beneficials (*e.g.*, spiders, ground beetles, bats) may be absent or scarce on some farms because of lack of habitat. These organisms might make significant contributions to pest management if provided with adequate habitat.

Natural biological control results when naturally occurring enemies maintain pests at a lower level than would occur without them, and is generally characteristic of bio-diverse systems. Mammals, birds, bats, insects, fungi, bacteria, and viruses all have a role to play as predators and parasites in an agricultural system. By their very nature, pesticides decrease the biodiversity of a system, creating the potential for instability and future problems. Pesticides, whether synthetically or botanically derived, are powerful tools and should be used with caution.

Creation of habitat to enhance the chances for survival and reproduction of beneficial organisms is a concept included in the definition of natural bio-control. Farmscaping is a term coined to describe such efforts on farms.

Habitat enhancement for beneficial insects, for example, focuses on the establishment of flowering annual or perennial plants that provide pollen and nectar needed during certain parts of the insect life cycle. Other habitat features provided by farmscaping include water, alternative prey, perching sites, over-wintering sites, and wind protection. Beneficial insects and other beneficial organisms should be viewed as mini-livestock, with specific habitat and food needs to be included in farm planning.

The success of such efforts depends on knowledge of the pests and beneficial organisms within the cropping system. Where do the pests and beneficials over-winter? What plants are hosts and non-hosts? When this kind of knowledge informs planning, the ecological balance can be manipulated in favour of beneficials and against the pests.

It should be kept in mind that ecosystem manipulation is a two-edged sword. Some plant pests (such as the tarnished plant bug and lygus bug) are attracted to the same plants that attract beneficials. The development of beneficial habitats with a mix of plants that flower throughout the year can help prevent such pests from migrating *en masse* from farm scaped plants to crop plants.

Applied biological control, also known as augmentative bio-control, involves supplementation of beneficial organism populations, for example through periodic releases of parasites, predators, or pathogens. This can be effective in many situations—well-timed inundative releases of *Trichogramma* egg wasps for coddling moth control, for instance.

Most of the beneficial organisms used in applied biological control today are insect parasites and predators. They control a wide range of pests from caterpillars to mites. Some species of bio-control organisms, such as *Eretmocerus californicus*, a parasitic wasp, are specific to one host—in this case the sweet potato whitefly. Others, such as green lacewings, are generalists and will attack many species of aphids and whiteflies.

Information about rates and timing of release is available from suppliers of beneficial organisms. It is important to remember that released insects are mobile; they are likely to leave a site if the habitat is not conducive to their survival. Food, nectar, and pollen sources can be "farm scaped" to provide suitable habitat.

The quality of commercially available applied bio-controls is another important consideration. For example, if the organisms are not properly labelled on the outside packaging, they may be mishandled during transport, resulting in the death of the organisms. A recent study by Rutgers University noted that only two of six suppliers of beneficial nematodes sent the expected numbers of organisms, and only one supplier out of the six provided information on how to assess product viability.

While augmentative bio-controls can be applied with relative ease on small farms and in gardens, applying some types of bio-controls evenly over large farms has been problematic. New mechanized methods that may improve the economics and practicality of large-scale augmentative bio-control include ground application with "bio-sprayers" and aerial delivery using small-scale (radio-controlled) or conventional aircraft.

Inundative releases of beneficials into greenhouses can be particularly effective. In the controlled environment of a greenhouse, pest infestations can be devastating; there are no natural controls in place to suppress pest populations once an infestation begins.

For this reason, monitoring is very important. If an infestation occurs, it can spread quickly if not detected early and managed. Once introduced, biological control agents cannot escape from a greenhouse and are forced to concentrate predation/parasitism on the pest(s) at hand.

An increasing number of commercially available bio-control products are made up of microorganisms, including fungi, bacteria, nematodes, and viruses. Appendix B, Microbial Pesticides, lists some of the formulations available. Appendix C, Microbial Pesticide Manufacturers and Suppliers, provides addresses of manufacturers and suppliers.

Mechanical and Physical Controls

Methods included in this category utilize some physical component of the environment, such as temperature, humidity, or light, to the detriment of the pest. Common examples are tillage, flaming, flooding, soil solarization, and plastic mulches to kill weeds or to prevent weed seed germination.

Heat or steam sterilization of soil is commonly used in greenhouse operations for control of soil-borne pests. Floating row covers over vegetable crops exclude flea beetles, cucumber beetles, and adults of the onion, carrot, cabbage, and seed corn root maggots. Insect screens are used in greenhouses to prevent aphids, thrips, mites, and other pests from entering ventilation ducts. Large, multi-row vacuum machines have been used for pest management in strawberries and vegetable crops. Cold storage reduces post-harvest disease problems on produce.

Although generally used in small or localized situations, some methods of mechanical/physical control are finding wider acceptance because they are generally more friendly to the environment.

Pest Identification

A crucial step in any IPM programme is to identify the pest. The effectiveness of both pro-active and reactive pest management measures depend on correct identification. Misidentification of the pest may be worse than useless; it may actually be harmful and cost time and money. Help with positive identification of pests may be obtained from university personnel, private consultants, the Cooperative Extension Service, and books and Web sites listed under Appendix F at the end of this publication.

After a pest is identified, appropriate and effective management depends on knowing answers to a number of questions. These may include:

- What plants are hosts and non-hosts of this pest?
- When does the pest emerge or first appear?
- Where does it lay its eggs? In the case of weeds, where is the seed source? For plant pathogens, where is the source(s) of inoculum?

- Where, how, and in what form does the pest over-winter?
- How might the cropping system be altered to make life more difficult for the pest and easier for its natural controls?

Monitoring (field scouting) and economic injury and action levels are used to help answer these and additional questions.

Monitoring

Monitoring involves systematically checking crop fields for pests and beneficials, at regular intervals and at critical times, to gather information about the crop, pests, and natural enemies. Sweep nets, sticky traps, and pheromone traps can be used to collect insects for both identification and population density information. Leaf counts are one method for recording plant growth stages. Square-foot or larger grids laid out in a field can provide a basis for comparative weed counts. Records of rainfall and temperature are sometimes used to predict the likelihood of disease infections.

Specific scouting methods have been developed for many crops. The Cooperative Extension Service can provide a list of IPM manuals available in each state. Many resourcos are now available via Internet.

The more often a crop is monitored, the more information the grower has about what is happening in the fields. Monitoring activity should be balanced against its costs. Frequency may vary with temperature, crop, growth phase of the crop, and pest populations. If a pest population is approaching economically damaging levels, the grower will want to monitor more frequently.

Economic Injury and Action Levels

The economic injury level (EIL) is the pest population that inflicts crop damage greater than the cost of control measures. Because growers will generally want to act before a population reaches EIL, IPM programmes use the concept of an economic threshold level (ETL or ET), also known as an action threshold. The ETL is closely related to the EIL, and is the point at which suppression tactics should be applied in order to prevent pest populations from increasing to injurious levels. In practice, many crops have no established EILs or ETLs, or the EILs that have been developed may be static over the course of a season and thus not reflect the changing nature of the agricultural ecosystem. For example, a single cutworm can do more damage to an emerging cotton plant than to a plant that is six weeks old. Clearly, this pest's EIL will change as the cotton crop develops.

ETLs are intimately related to the value of the crop and the part of the crop being attacked. For example, a pest that attacks the fruit or vegetable will have a much lower ETL (that is, the pest must be controlled at lower populations) than a pest that attacks a non-saleable part of the plant. The exception to this rule is an insect or nematode pest that is also a disease vector. Depending on the severity of the disease, the grower may face a situation where the ETL for a particular pest is zero, *i.e.*, the crop cannot tolerate the presence of a single pest of that particular species because the disease it transmits is so destructive.

Special Considerations

Cosmetic Damage and Aesthetics

Consumer attitudes toward how produce looks is often a major factor when determining a crop's sale price. Cosmetic damage is an important factor when calculating the EIL, since pest damage, however superficial, lowers a crop's market value. Growers selling to a market that is informed about IPM or about organically grown produce may be able to tolerate higher levels of cosmetic damage to their produce.

Record-keeping: past is "prologue"

Monitoring goes hand-in-hand with record-keeping, which forms the collective "memory" of the farm. Records should not only provide information about when and where pest problems have occurred, but should also incorporate information about cultural practices (irrigation, cultivation, fertilization, mowing, etc.) and their effect on pest and beneficial populations. The effects of non-biotic factors, especially weather, on pest and beneficial populations should also be noted. Record-keeping is simply a systematic approach to learning from experience. A variety of software programmes are now available to help growers keep track of—and access—data on their farm's inputs and outputs.

Time and Resources

A successful biointensive IPM programme takes time, money, patience, short-and long-term planning, flexibility, and commitment. The pest manager must spend time on self-education and on making contacts with Extension and research personnel. Be aware that some IPM strategies, such as increasing beneficial insect habitat, may take more than a year to show results.

A well-run biointensive IPM system may require a larger initial outlay in terms of time and money than a conventional IPM programme. In the long run, however, a good biointensive IPM programme should pay for itself. Direct pesticide application costs are saved and equipment wear and tear may be reduced.

Chemical Controls

Included in this category are both synthetic pesticides and botanical pesticides. Synthetic pesticides comprise a wide range of man-made chemicals used to control insects, mites, weeds, nematodes, plant diseases, and vertebrate and invertebrate pests. These powerful chemicals are fast acting and relatively inexpensive to purchase.

Pesticides are the option of last resort in IPM programmes because of their potential negative impacts on the environment, which result from the manufacturing process as well as from their application on the farm. Pesticides should be used only when other measures, such as biological or cultural controls, have failed to keep pest populations from approaching economically damaging levels.

If chemical pesticides must be used, it is to the grower's advantage to choose the least-toxic pesticide that will control the pest but not harm non-target organisms such as birds, fish, and mammals. Pesticides that are short-lived or act on one or a few specific organisms are in this class. Examples include insecticidal soaps, horticultural oils, copper compounds (*e.g.*, bordeaux mix), sulphur, boric acid, and sugar esters.

Bio-rational Pesticides: Although use of this term is relatively common, there is no legally accepted definition. Bio-rational pesticides are generally considered to be derived from naturally occurring compounds or are formulations of microorganisms. Biorationals have a narrow target range and are environmentally benign. Formulations of *Bacillus thuringiensis*, commonly known as Bt, are perhaps the best-known bio-rational pesticide. Other examples include silica aerogels, insect growth regulators, and particle film barriers.

Particle Film Barriers: A relatively new technology, particle film barriers are currently available under the trade name Surround WP Crop Protectant. The active ingredient is kaolin clay, an edible mineral long used as an anti-caking agent in processed foods, and in such products as toothpaste and Kaopectate. There appears to be no mammalian toxicity or any danger to the environment posed by the use of kaolin in pest control. The kaolin in Surround is processed to a specific particle size range, and combined with a sticker-spreader. Non-processed kaolin clay may be phytotoxic.

Surround is sprayed on as a liquid, which evaporates, leaving a protective powdery film on the surfaces of leaves, stems, and fruit. Conventional spray equipment can be used and full coverage is important. The film works to deter insects in several ways. Tiny particles of the clay attach to the insects when they contact the plant, agitating and repelling them. Even if particles don't attach to their bodies, the insects may find the coated plant or fruit unsuitable for feeding and egg-laying. In addition, the highly reflective white coating makes the plant less recognizable as a host.

Sugar Esters: Throughout four years of tests, sugar esters have performed as well as or better than conventional insecticides against mites and aphids in apple orchards; psylla in pear orchards; whiteflies, thrips, and mites on vegetables; and whiteflies on cotton. However, sugar esters are not effective against insect eggs. Insecticidal properties of sugar esters were first investigated a decade ago when a scientist noticed that tobacco leaf hairs exuded sugar esters for defence against some soft-bodied insect pests. Similar to insecticidal soap in their action, these chemicals act as contact insecticides and degrade into environmentally benign sugars and fatty acids after application. AVA Chemical Ventures of Portsmouth, NH hopes to have a product based on sucrose octanoate commercially available by the end of 2001.

Because pest resistance to chemical controls has become so common, susceptibility to pesticides is increasingly being viewed by growers as a trait worth preserving. One example of the economic impact of resistance to insecticides has been documented in Michigan, where insecticide resistance in Colorado potato beetle was first reported in 1984 and caused severe economic problems beginning in 1991. In 1991 and following years, control costs were as high as $412/hectare in districts most seriously affected, in contrast to $35-74/hectare in areas where resistance was not a problem. The less a product is applied, the longer a pest population will remain susceptible to that product. Routine use of any pesticide is a problematic strategy.

Botanical pesticides are prepared in various ways. They can be as simple as pureed plant leaves, extracts of plant parts, or chemicals purified from plants. Pyrethrum, neem formulations, and rotenone are examples of botanicals. Some botanicals are broad-spectrum pesticides. Others, like ryania, are very specific. Botanicals are generally less harmful in the environment than synthetic pesticides because they degrade quickly, but they can be just as deadly to beneficials as synthetic pesticides. However, they are less hazardous to transport and in some cases can be formulated on-farm. The manufacture of botanicals generally results in fewer toxic by-products.

Compost teas are most commonly used for foliar disease control and applied as foliar nutrient sprays. The idea underlying the use of compost teas is that a solution of beneficial microbes and some nutrients is created, then applied to plants to increase the diversity of organisms on leaf surfaces. This diversity competes with pathogenic organisms, making it more difficult for them to become established and infect the plant.

An important consideration when using compost teas is that high-quality, well-aged compost be used, to avoid contamination of plant parts by animal pathogens found in manures that may be a component of the compost. There are different techniques for creating compost tea. The compost can be immersed in the water, or the water can be circulated through the compost. An effort should be made to maintain an aerobic environment in the compost/water mixture.

Pesticide Application Techniques

As monetary and environmental costs of chemical pesticides escalate, it makes sense to increase the efficiency of chemical applications. Correct nozzle placement, nozzle type, and nozzle pressure are very important considerations. Misdirected sprays, inappropriate nozzle size, or worn nozzles will ultimately cost the grower money and increase the risk of environmental damage.

If the monitoring programme indicates that the pest outbreak is isolated to a particular location, spot treatment of only the infested area will not only save time and money, but will conserve natural enemies located in other parts of the field. The grower should also time treatments to be least disruptive of other organisms. This is yet another example where knowledge about the agro-ecosystem is important.

With the increasing popularity of no-till and related conservation tillage practices, herbicide use has increased. One way to increase application efficiency and decrease costs of herbicide use is through band application. This puts the herbicide only where it is needed, usually in soil disturbed by tillage or seed planting, where weeds are most likely to sprout.

Baits and micro-encapsulation of pesticides are promising technologies. For example, Slam™ is an insecticide-bait mixture for control of corn root-worm. It is a formulation of a bait, curcubitacin B, and carbaryl (Sevin™) in micro-spheres. It is selective, and reduces the amount of carbaryl needed to control the root-worm by up to 90%. (Remember that crop rotation will generally eliminate the need for *any* corn root-worm chemical control.)

Another example of bait-insecticide technology is the boll weevil bait tube. It lures the boll weevil using a synthetic sex pheromone. Each tube contains about 20 grams of malathion, which kills the boll weevil. This technique reduces the pesticide used in cotton fields by up to 80% and conserves beneficials. It is most effective in managing low, early-season populations of the boll weevil.

Integrated Weed Management Systems

Weeds as competitors in crops present a number of unique challenges that need to be recognized when developing management strategies. The intensity of weed problems during a growing season will be influenced by weed population levels in previous years. The axiom "one year's seeding equals seven years' weeding" is apt.

Weed control costs cannot necessarily be calculated against tho current year's crop production costs. Weeds present a physical problem for harvesting. Noxious weed seed mixed with grain reduces the price paid to growers. If the seed is sold for crop production the weed can be spread to new areas. For example, the perennial pepperweed, thought to have been introduced to California in sugar beet seed, now infests thousands of acres in the state.

In addition, weed economic thresholds must take into account multiple species and variable competitive ability of different crops. For example, 12.7 cocklebur plants in 10 sq. meters of corn cause a 10% yield loss. Only 2 cockleburs in the same area planted to soybeans will cause the same 10% crop loss.

Sustainable Agriculture and IPM

Sustainable agriculture is a system of agriculture that is ecologically, economically, and socially viable, in the short as well as long term. Rather than standing for a specific set of farming practices, a sustainable agriculture represents the goal of developing a food production system that:

+ yields plentiful, affordable, high-quality food and other agricultural products
+ does not deplete or damage natural resources (such as soil, water, wildlife, fossil fuels, or the germplasm base)
+ promotes the health of the environment
+ supports a broad base and diversity of farms and the health of rural communities
+ depends on energy from the sun and on natural biological processes for fertility and pest management
+ can last indefinitely

IPM and sustainable agriculture share the goal of developing agricultural systems that are ecologically and economically sound. IPM may be considered a key component of a sustainable agriculture system. A premise common to IPM and sustainable agriculture is that a healthy agro-ecosystem depends on healthy soils and managed diversity. One of the reasons modern agriculture has evolved into a system of large monocultures is to decrease the range of variables to be managed. However, a system with few species, much like a table with too few legs, is unstable.

Tactics that can be integrated into weed management systems include:

- *Prevention:* The backbone of any successful weed management strategy is prevention. It is important to prevent the introduction of seeds into the field through sources like irrigation water or manure.
- *Crop Rotation:* A practical and effective method of weed management (discussed in previous sections).

"Rotation crops, when accompanied by care in the use of pure seed, is the most effective means yet devised for keeping land free of weeds. No other method of weed control, mechanical, chemical, or biological, is so economical or so easily practised as a well-arranged sequence of tillage and cropping."

Source: Leighty, Clyde E. 1938. Crop Rotation. p. 406-429. In: Soils and Men, 1938 Yearbook of Agriculture. U.S. Govt. Print. Office, Washington, DC.

- *Cultivation: Steel in the Field: A Farmer's Guide to Weed Management Tools* shows how today's implements and techniques can handle weeds while reducing or eliminating herbicides.
- *Flame Weeding:* Good for control of small weeds.
- *Delayed Planting:* Early-germinating weeds can be destroyed by tillage. And with warmer weather, the subsequently planted crop (depending on the crop, of course) will grow more quickly, thus competing better with weeds.
- *Staggered Planting Schedule:* This will allow more time for mechanical weed control, if needed. This also lessens the weather risks and spaces out the work load at harvest time.
- *Surface Residue Management:* As mentioned earlier, a thick mulch may shade the soil enough to keep weed seeds from germinating. In addition, some plant residues are allelopathic, releasing compounds that naturally suppress seed germination.
- *Altered Plant Spacing or Row Width:* An example is narrow-row (7–18" between rows compared to conventional 36–39" between rows) soybean plantings. The faster the leaves shade the ground, the less weeds will be a problem.
- *Herbivore:* Cattle, geese, goats, and insects can be used to reduce populations of specific weeds in special situations. Cattle, for example, relish Johnson grass. Weeder geese were commonly used in cotton fields before the advent of herbicides. Musk thistle populations can be satisfactorily reduced by crown-and seed-eating weevils. Goats may be used for large stands of various noxious weeds.
- *Adjusting Herbicide Use to Situation:* Herbicide selection and rate can be adjusted depending upon weed size, weed species, and soil moisture. Young weeds are more susceptible to chemicals than older weeds.

Weed Prevention

- Have a long, diverse rotation
- Sow clean seed
- Prevent weed seed formation
- Avoid imported feeds or manures
- Compost all manure thoroughly
- Control weeds in field borders
- Delay planting the crop (for faster crop growth and quicker ground coverage)
- Maintain good soil quality

Current Status of IPM

Crops with Developed IPM Programmes

In the last twenty years or so, IPM programmes have been developed for important pests in corn, soybeans, cotton, citrus, apples, grapes, walnuts, strawberries, alfalfa, pecans, and most other major crops. These programmes are constantly being revised or fine-tuned, and occasionally undergo a significant overhaul as the introduction of a new technology or new pest makes the present IPM programme obsolete.

The best source of information on conventional IPM is the Cooperative Extension Service (CES) associated with the land-grant university in each state. Booklets and fact sheets describing IPM programmes and control measures for a wide range of crops and livestock are available free or for a small charge. For the address of a state IPM coordinator, refer to the Directory of State Extension Integrated Pest Management Coordinators. A free copy can be obtained from the Cooperative State Research, Education, and Extension Service. The USDA Regional IPM Centres Web site includes a searchable database of state contacts for IPM.

Government Policy

In 1993, leaders from USDA, EPA, and FDA announced a goal of placing 75% of U.S. crop acreage under IPM by the year 2000. The IPM Initiative described three phases:

1. Create teams of researchers, Extension personnel, and growers to propose projects to achieve the 75% goal.
2. Fund the best of those projects.
3. Facilitate privatization of IPM practices developed in the process.

Although some progress is evident, the Initiative has not received full funding from Congress. In addition, the USDA's criteria for measurement have been criticized for not distinguishing between practices that are related to "treatment" and those that are "preventive," that is, based on altering the biological and ecological interactions between crops, pests, and beneficial organisms. Practices that constitute "treatment" with or contribute to the efficiency of pesticides are considered as "indicative of an IPM approach" by USDA's criteria, as are practices that draw upon and are most compatible with biological relationships on the farm.

The primary goal of biointensive IPM is to provide guidelines and options for the effective management of pests and beneficial organisms in an ecological context. This requires a somewhat different set of knowledge from that which supports conventional IPM, which in turn requires a shift in research focus and approach. Recommended actions to better facilitate the transition to biointensive IPM are:

- Build the knowledge/information infrastructure by making changes in research and education priorities in order to emphasize ecology-based pest management.
- Redesign government programmes to promote biointensive IPM, not "Integrated Pesticide Management."
- Offer consumers more choices in the marketplace.
- Use the market clout of government and large corporations.
- Use regulation more consciously, intelligently, and efficiently.

The Future of IPM

As this publication has highlighted, IPM in the future will emphasize biological and ecological knowledge in managing pests. Beyond that, specific areas are described here that will impact research and implementation of IPM in the future.

Food Quality Protection Act

The FQPA, the amended Federal Insecticide, Fungicide, and Rodenticide Act (FIFRA), requires the EPA to review all federally registered pesticides in the next 10 years and to use a more comprehensive health standard when allowing re-registration. The ultimate impact is unknown, but FQPA will most likely result in stricter regulations concerning pesticide residues in food, particularly with respect to organochlorines, organophosphates, and carbamates. Some of the most toxic pesticides have already been "de-registered" with respect to some of their former uses. These regulations may provide incentive for more widespread adoption of IPM

A convergence of technical, environmental and social forces is moving agriculture towards more non-pesticide pest management alternatives like biological control, host plant resistance and cultural management.

New Options

Pest control methods are evolving and diversifying in response to public awareness of environmental and health impacts of synthetic chemical pesticides and resulting legislation. The strong growth of the organic foods market—20% annual expansion for the past several years—may also be a factor in the accelerated development of organic pest management methods.

Agricultural pests are developing resistance to many synthetic agrichemicals, and new synthetic chemicals are being registered at a slower rate than in the past. This situation has helped open the market for a new generation of microbial pesticides

Research is proceeding on natural endophytes—fungi or bacteria that have a symbiotic (mutually beneficial) relationship with their host plant—and their effects on plant pests. This research might yield products that could be used to inoculate plants against certain pests.

Synthetic beneficial attractants such as Predfeed IPM™ and L-tryptophan may help increase the efficacy of natural controls by attracting beneficials to a crop in greater numbers than usual.

More Weed IPM

Weeds are the major deterrent to the development of more sustainable agricultural systems, particularly in agronomic crops. Problems associated with soil erosion and water quality are generally the result of weed control measures like tillage, herbicides, cultivation, planting date and pattern, etc. In the future, research will focus not on symptoms, such as soil erosion, but on basic problems such as how to sustainably manage soils. Weeds, as an important facet of sustainable soil management, will consequently receive more emphasis in IPM or Integrated Crop Management (ICM) programmes.

On-farm Resources

As farm management strategies become increasingly fine-tuned to preserve a profitable bottom line, the conservation, utilization, and development of on-farm resources will take on added importance. In the context of IPM, this will mean greater emphasis on soil management as well as on conserving beneficial organisms, retaining and developing beneficial habitats, and perhaps developing on-farm insectaries for rearing beneficial insects.

IPM Certification and Marketing

Certification of crops raised according to IPM or some other ecology-based standards may give growers a marketing advantage as public concerns about health and environmental safety increase. For example, since 1995, Wegmans has sold IPM-labelled fresh-market sweet corn in its Corning, Geneva, Ithaca, Syracuse, and Rochester, New York stores.

Wegmans has also added IPM-labelled corn, beets, and beans to its shelves of canned vegetables. One goal of the programme, in addition to being a marketing vehicle, is to educate consumers about agriculture and the food system.

Another goal is to keep all growers moving along the "IPM Continuum." Growers must have an 80% "score" on the IPM programme elements within three years, or face losing Wegmans as a buyer.

These "ecolabels," as they're known, are becoming more popular, with over a dozen brands now in existence. They may provide for a more certain market and perhaps a price premium to help growers offset any costs associated with implementing sustainable farming practices. A possible downside to implementing such programmes is that they require additional paperwork, development of standards and guidelines, and inspections. There is concern from some quarters that IPM labelling will cause consumers to raise more questions about pesticide use and the safety of conventional produce. Some advocates of organic farming worry about consumer confusion over the relationship of the ecolabel to the "Certified Organic" label.

Mothers & Others for a Livable Planet, a national, non-profit, consumer advocacy and environmental education organization, has partnered with apple farmers in the Northeast region to create a supportive market environment for farm products that are locally grown and ecologically responsible. The result is the Core Values eco-label:

A CORE Values Northeast apple is locally grown in the Northeast (New York and New England) by farmers who are striving to provide apples of superior taste and quality while maintaining healthy, ecologically balanced growing environments. Growers whose apples bear the CORE Values Northeast seal are accredited in knowledge-based biointensive Integrated Pest Management (IPM) production methods.

The Homegrown Wisconsin ecolabel is a result of a collaboration between the World Wildlife Fund (WWF), the Wisconsin Potato and Vegetable Growers Association (WPVGA), and the University of Wisconsin. Raising consumer demand for biology-based-IPM farm products is the goal of the programme.

There has been an IPM labelling programme casualty in 2000. Massachusetts's "Partners with Nature" marketing programme closed its doors after losing funding support from the Massachusetts Department of Food and Agriculture. The programme, which included IPM production guidelines, had operated since 1994, with 51 growers participating in 1999.

Plant Pest-management Curriculum Development

Indian agriculture has made significant progress in increasing crop production. Beginning with the first agricultural university at Pant Nagar in 1960, India now has one of the largest networking of agricultural education system today. It provides education to about 10,000 students in 11 undergraduate programmes of agriculture and allied sciences and about 6,000 students in post-graduate programmes in more than 60 disciplines. Human resource development is regarded as the most important factor to quickly popularize the latest technological development in plant protection among the farmers.

The Bachelor degree holders constitute the bulk of recruits for public and private sectors in agriculture. From time to time, the Dean's Committees of the Indian Council of Agricultural Research have recommended model curriculum to unify the curricula of agricultural universities. In the past, postgraduate education in Entomology and Plant Pathology has received little attention. But Plant Protection has become important recently because of global concern about environmental and health effects of pesticides, related issues of international trade and the need for Integrated Pest Management (IPM) approach. Re-orientation of formal education and extension methods becomes crucial as IPM assumes more importance. IPM courses for both the undergraduate and post-graduate levels have also been proposed.

In general, many graduates now in extension functionaries lack practical experience. Training to upgrade their professional competence is needed. Presently, the National Plant Protection Training Institute at Hyderabad and the Directorate of Plant Protection are generating trained manpower in IPM of rice, cotton, vegetables, and some oilseed and pulse crops. These involve season-long Training-of-Trainers programmes and other long and short training programmes. The curriculum, updated regularly, is aimed at developing IPM skills, and is augmented with panel discussions, special topics and group dynamics.

Since the Government of India and the State Governments are providing increasing support in IPM among farmers, it is envisaged that there will be a greater need for the introduction of IPM courses in the curricula of universities/institutes.

Agriculture is the backbone of the Indian economy. The most important goal in agriculture is to achieve higher productivity and production to meet the ever-increasing demand of food commodities/products. In order to achieve this, a number of scientific disciplines and diverse kinds of resources have to be deployed in a well-planned and systematic manner. The primary producers also must be made aware of the great potentials through the application of science in agriculture. Plant protection technology occupies an important position in agricultural crop production.

Most often, losses due to pests are the major limiting factor for sustaining the increase in crop productivity and production. On average, the avoidable crop losses caused by pests, such as insects, diseases, weeds and others in India, have been estimated to range from 10% to 30% of the total production. To keep pace with the demand for food commodities, adoption of appropriate strategies that include effective, economical, safe and environmentally sound plant protection technology in sustainable agriculture, is a critical requirement. Agricultural education caters to the needs of the country's manpower in utilizing research and extension appropriately for the country. Curriculum plays an important role in imparting knowledge and skill required for human resource development in any discipline.

Periodic revision of syllabi by all institutes of learning is an essential component of curriculum development to produce qualified and competent manpower to handle emerging situations in a rapidly changing agricultural scenario. The curriculum for plant pest management in agricultural universities and allied institutes is thus an integral part of agricultural education.

Natural Pest Management

Whether conventional or organic, all farmers are concerned with pests. They spend a lot of time and resources controlling them. However, in the organic "world view," pests — whether weeds, insects or diseases — are not simply scourges. They are indicators of how far a production system has strayed from the natural ecosystems it should imitate. Certain weeds, for example, tend to predominate when soils are too acidic or too basic; some become a problem when soil structure is poor and conditions become anaerobic; others may be stimulated by excessive fertilizer or manure salts.

Organic proponents also believe that insect pests are attracted to inferior or weak plants — the result of poor crop nutrition. Their logic continues by asserting that pests are naturally repelled by vigorous, well-nourished plants. This belief is often challenged, and significant research remains to be done. As scientific understanding has grown, insect pest outbreaks are also being understood as imbalances in the whole agro-ecosystem and how it is managed. In nature, massive pest outbreaks are relatively rare and short-lived, due to the presence of natural predators, parasites, and disease agents that quickly knock the pest numbers back down to a moderate level. In farming systems that inadvertently destroy or otherwise fail to support the natural control complex, pest problems are routine and, typically, worsen with time. The farmer becomes increasingly addicted to costly and extreme control methods to produce a crop.

Most organic growers consider pesticides to be a cause of agro-ecosystem imbalances and employ allowed natural pesticides as little as possible.

Integrity

Integrity refers to the systems in place and actions undertaken to assure that consumers of organic products get what they pay for. Consumers have a right to expect that the organic food they buy not only be raised by organic methods but be protected from contamination and from commingling with non-organic products.

While the responsibility for much of this rests with others in the organic marketing chain, many certified organic growers need to incorporate additional practices that work to assure the integrity of their products. Proper record keeping is very important in this regard, though growers are often reluctant to spend much time on it. Among the more important production practices in the field are buffer strips, which reduce chemical drift from neighbouring fields and roadsides, while also serving water and soil conservation objectives.

Tools and Practices

The tools and practices of organic agriculture include traditional alternatives — crop rotation, manuring, liming, etc.—long recognized as important to a sound production system. They also include more contemporary practices and materials that research and keen observation over time have contributed. The following list of tools and practices is not intended to be comprehensive, though the primary options are addressed. Note, too, that each farm operation will employ its own combination of tools and practices to build a working organic system. There is no simple cookbook formula for combining them in ideal proportions.

Planned Crop Rotation

Essentially a tool for annual cropping systems, crop rotation refers to the sequence of crops and cover crops grown on a specific field. Particular sequences confer particular benefits to long and short-term soil fertility, and to pest management.

Agronomic operations are especially dependent on crop rotations that include forage legumes. These provide the vast majority of the nitrogen required by subsequent crops like corn, which is a heavy consumer of that nutrient. Even when livestock are present to generate manure, the animals are largely recycling the nitrogen originally fixed by legumes in the system. An example of a basic agronomic rotation, typical of that found on midwestern organic farms.

The basic Midwestern rotation demonstrates the elegant way in which a whole farm system can function:

- Legumes fix nitrogen in the soil, providing for subsequent non-legumes in the rotation.
- Several insect pest cycles are interrupted, especially those of the northern and western root-worm species that can be devastating to corn.
- Several plant diseases are suppressed, in cluding soybean cyst nematode.
- Weed control is enhanced as perennial weeds are destroyed through cultivation of annual grains; most annual weeds are smothered or eliminated by mowing when alfalfa is in production.
- Livestock manures (if available) are applied just in advance of corn, a heavy nitrogen consumer.
- All crops can be marketed either as is or fed to livestock to be converted into value-added milk, meat or other livestock products.

Ralph and Rita Engelken, widely respected organic pioneers in the 1970s and 1980s, used a similar rotation that suited their hilly northeast Iowa farm and supported their main livestock enterprise, *backgrounding* beef cattle. (Backgrounding is confined or semi-confined feeding of young range stock to increase their size before final finishing in a feedlot.) The feed ration the Engelkens relied on consisted mostly of haylage, corn silage, and ground ear corn.

Green Manures and Cover Crops

Green manuring consists of incorporating into the soil a crop grown for the purposes of soil improvement. It is a practice with a long history. Green manuring has been ignored in recent years as a serious option for soil improvement because the traditional practice entailed planting a full-season cover crop. This removed the field from commercial production for a whole season. Interest has returned, however, since green manuring strategies have been combined with cover cropping schemes.

Cover cropping is growing a crop for the purpose of soil and nutrient conservation. It is a more contemporary concept than green manuring, in crop agriculture. The two concepts — cover cropping and green manuring — go well together, as most cover crops are easily used as green manures prior to the planting of a commercial crop. The combined benefits become economically feasible when the cover is grown during the off-season or inter-seeded with the main crop. It is made even more desirable when the cover crop includes nitrogen-fixing legumes.

Manuring and Composting

Livestock manures are the most traditional and widely recognized organic fertilizers. Under ideal circumstances, livestock enterprises are integrated into the whole farm operation, and manuring becomes part of a closed system of nutrient recycling. This is still strongly encouraged in organic operations. In reality, however, crops and livestock production are often divorced from each other, and manures must be imported.

This has created some concerns in the organic community, since much manure is now generated by large, industrial agriculture feeding operations called CAFOs (Confined Animal Feeding Operations). Not only are there concerns about contaminants (heavy metals, antibiotics, pesticides, hormones) but many in the organic community also object to any "partnering" with this segment of conventional agriculture, which is considered at odds with the environmental and social values represented by organic farming.

Nonetheless, the National Organic Programme does not differentiate between CAFO and other livestock manure sources. However, the NOP regulations do require that livestock manure not contain any synthetic substances not included on the National List of synthetic substances allowed for use in organic crop production. Another issue that has grown up around manure use in organic farming relates to food safety.

At a time when concerns about microbial contamination are high, there are questions about the risks associated with manure use on food crops. A focus piece on the February 2000 television news programme 20/20 was especially controversial. The segment suggested that organic foods were more dangerous than other food products in the marketplace due to manure fertilization. The reporter ignored the fact that conventional farms also use manures. Were all the manure generated annually in the U.S. (about 1.4 billion tons) applied only to organic farm acreage (estimated at roughly 1.5 million acres in 1997), each acre would receive about 933 tons.

Furthermore, certified organic producers have strict guidelines to follow in handling and applying manures. The National Organic Programme regulations require raw animal manure be incorporated into the soil not less than 120 days prior to the harvest of a product whose edible portion has direct contact with the soil surface or soil particles, and be incorporated into the soil not less than 90 days prior to harvest of a product whose edible portion does not have direct contact with the soil surface or soil particles.

One of the best means of handling manures is composting. Composting stabilizes the nutrients in manure, builds populations of beneficial organisms, and has a highly beneficial effect on soils and crops. Compost can be produced on-farm by a number of means. Additional products from composts, such as compost teas, have special applications in organic agriculture.

Human manures are expressly forbidden in certified organic production. This includes composted sewage sludge (also called "biosolids"). The organic community made its opinion on this quite clear when the USDA's first draft of the national rule (December 1997) proposed allowing the use of sludge in certified production.

It was counted as one of the "big three" targets of protest, along with food irradiation and genetic engineering. The prohibition of biosolids would have been disconcerting to Albert

Howard, who decried the failure of cities to return their organic wastes to the countryside. Such recycling was, in his mind, a key aspect of sustainability.

Livestock on Organic Farms

Among the thorniest of issues swirling around the edges of organic agriculture is the role of livestock. The disagreements arise because of the diversity of people and philosophies in the organic community. Organic agriculture can usually count vegetarians and animal welfare proponents among its more vocal supporters. Many of these people feel strongly that animals should not be exploited. Their rationale often goes beyond emotional and religious beliefs; convincing human health concerns, social issues, and environmental reasons are commonly cited. On the other side of this argument are those who feel that an organic farm cannot achieve its full potential or ecological balance without livestock manure; that it is essential to nutrient cycling and to the finer aspects of soil building.

Excellent soil fertility can be built in the absence of farm livestock and livestock manures by using vegetation-based composts and by harnessing the livestock in the soil—earthworms and other soil organisms. However, it is clearly easier to design a contemporary, low-input organic farm when traditional livestock are integrated. The biological and enterprise diversity that livestock can bring contributes enormously to stability and sustainability. A good example is provided by Rivendell Gardens in Arkansas, which began integrating livestock enterprises after several years as a solely horticultural operation.

The owners of Rivendell, Gordon and Susan Watkins, now rotate their strawberry and vegetable crops with grass-fed, direct-marketed beef and postured poultry. Ideally, poultry follows beef on pasture to reduce cattle parasites. The seasons in mixed legume/grass pasture leave the soil quite mellow and well-mannered for subsequent high-dollar horticultural crops.

The Rivendell operation demonstrates the sort of organic management where a large number of organic farmers and many animal welfare proponents find common ground. The Watkins' animals are all raised with minimal confinement and generous access to sunshine, fresh air, and free-choice foodstuffs. While domesticated and destined for slaughter, they lead low-stress lives in conditions much closer to natural than the conventional alternatives. This is the antithesis of industrialized factory farming systems, which are increasingly becoming the norm in livestock production.

Many in both the organic and animal welfare communities are working to prohibit factory farming of livestock in organic systems. Many of the difficulties revolve around the fine interpretations of language in various organic standards. Wording such as "access to fresh air and sunlight," for example, can be construed to mean nothing more than opening the door on one end of a large confinement poultry house for a couple hours a day.

What Howard had not taken into account is the almost universal contamination of urban wastes with heavy metals and chemicals that are not eliminated by composting and may even be concentrated. Perhaps this was not yet a serious problem in his time; it is, however, in ours. Organic farmers and consumers concerned about contamination of soil and crops with agricultural pesticides and synthetic fertilizers would be remiss to ignore the contamination hazards of even well-composted sewage.

Fred Kirschenmann, a farmer and former NOSB member, has written eloquently about the progress of the National Organic Programme. In a critique of the March 2000 draft of the proposed rule, he pointed to another reason why the use of biosolids ought to be prohibited in organic production. Because of the manner in which biosolids are generated, they are easily hauled and land-applied on an industrial-scale to industrial scale organic farms. Furthermore, since biosolids can essentially supplant animal manures as a source of organic matter and nutrients, their use would allow some very large farms to circumvent the traditional practices that promote Biodiversity and enterprise diversity and integration. What Kirschenmann fears from biosolid use is technology that would nudge organic agriculture down the same road of industrialization taken by conventional agriculture.

Inter-cropping and Companion Planting

Interplanting two or more mutually beneficial crops in close proximity is one strategy for increasing biodiversity. In large-scale mechanized crop culture, this is called *Inter-cropping*. It typically involves alternating rows or a number of rows of compatible field crops, like soybeans and corn. It also applies to sowing multiple forage crops, like alfalfa, bromegrass, and timothy, when these are grown together.

When interplanting is done on a smaller scale, it is often called *companion planting*. A classic example of companion planting is the inter-planting of corn with pole beans and vining squash or pumpkins. In this system, the beans provide nitrogen; the corn provides support for the beans and a "screen" against squash vine borer; the vining squash provides a weed suppressive canopy and discourages corn-hungry raccoons.

Biological Pest Control

Organic farming relies heavily on populations of beneficial insect predators and parasites, pest disease agents, insect-eating birds and bats, and other creatures, to help manage pest problems. These biological controls help keep pest numbers at levels where further cultural activities or relatively mild pesticides are (usually) adequate to assure a crop. In some instances, biological control can be so effective that no additional action is even needed by the farmer.

Some see biological control as a default benefit of the soil fertility practices of organic farming. The diversity of crops in a soil-building rotation, the use of cover crops, and other practices build a diverse soil biology that works to keep soil pests in check. They also provide substantial above-ground habitat for beneficials. The absence of pesticides also favours bio-control.

In many organic systems, farmers sometimes purchase and release control agents like ladybird beetles, lacewings, trichogramma wasps, etc., or use weeder geese — a quaint but effective biological weed control.

Increasingly, growers are designing and maintaining both permanent and temporary habitats specifically for beneficial insects, spiders, and other helpful species. This is known as *farmscaping*.

Sanitation

Sanitation can take on many forms:

- removal, burning, or deep plowing of crop residues that could carry plant disease or insect pest agents
- destruction of nearby weedy habitats that shelter pests
- cleaning accumulated weed seeds from farm equipment before entering a new, "clean" field
- sterilizing pruning tools

As in human and animal health, sanitation practices can go a long way in preventing crop pest problems. However, many practices — such as clean cultivation, deep plowing, and burning crop residues—can increase erosion and reduce biodiversity. Thus, they may conflict with sustainability. Good organic growers recognize this and treat those practices as transitional or rescue options, rather than relying on them on an annual basis.

Tillage and Cultivation

Tillage and cultivation are tools that can accomplish a variety of objectives in farming systems: weed control, crop residue management, soil aeration, conservation of manures and other fertilizers, hardpan reduction, sanitation to destroy pest and disease habitat, etc.

While conventional farmers rely on chemicals to accomplish many of these objectives, organic growers focus more on improving tillage and maximizing its benefits. Guidelines for primary tillage, for example, are intent on conserving crop residues and added manures in the upper, biologically active zones of the soil, rather than burying them deeply where decomposition is anaerobic (oxygen-starved). Leaving soils completely bare and vulnerable to erosion is discouraged; fall mold-board plowing is certainly frowned upon.

Cultivation in organic systems often rises to the level of art. Row-crop farmers frequently use *blind cultivation*—shallow tillage, which largely ignores the crop rows—beginning shortly after seeding until the plants are but a few inches high. Rotary hoes, wire-tooth harrows, and similar equipment can be used for blind cultivation, delaying the first flush of weeds and giving the crop a head start.

Conservation Tillage and Organic Farming

Organic agriculture is often characterized as addicted to maximum tillage — with growers using every opportunity to lay the land bare with shovel, plow, or rototiller. This image has been magnified through the popularity of small-scale organic systems like the French Intensive and Biointensive Mini Farming models that espouse double-and triple-digging to create deep rooting beds. While appropriate to such intensive systems, this degree of cultivation is not characteristic of organic agriculture in general.

It may surprise some to learn that a large number of organic producers are not only interested in conservation tillage, they have adopted it. This will be a surprise because many believe that conservation tillage always requires herbicides.

The interest in conservation tillage among organic producers in the Cornbelt was well documented in the mid-1970s by Washington University researchers. They noted that the vast majority of organic farmers participating in their studies had abandoned the mold-board plow for chisel plows.

Plowing with a chisel implement is a form of *mulch tillage*, in which residues are mixed in the upper layers of the soil, and a significant percentage remains on the soil surface to reduce erosion. Furthermore, a notable number of organic farmers had gone further to adopt ridge-tillage, a system with even greater potential to reduce erosion.

It was especially interesting to note that the use of these conservation technologies was almost nil among neighbouring conventional farms at the time. Organic growers were actually pioneers of conservation tillage in their communities.

Among the more well-known of these pioneers were Dick and Sharon Thompson of Boone, Iowa. Their experiences with ridge-tillage and sustainable agriculture became the focus of a series of publications titled *Nature's Ag School*. These were published by the Regenerative Agriculture Association — the forerunner to the Rodale Institute. They are now, unfortunately, out of print.

Research continues to open up new possibilities in conservation tillage for organic farms. New strategies for mechanically killing winter cover crops and planting or transplanting into the residue without tillage are being explored by a number of USDA, land-grant, and farmer researchers. Notable among these is the work being done by Abdul-Baki and Teasdale at the USDA in Beltsville, Maryland — transplanting tomato and broccoli crops into mechanically killed hairy vetch and forage soybeans.

There are also the well-publicized efforts of Pennsylvania farmer Steve Groff, whose no-till system centres on the use of a rolling stalk chopper to kill cover crops prior to planting. Systems like Groff's and Abdul-Baki's are of particular interest because close to 100% of crop residue remains on the soil surface – providing all the soil conservation and cultural benefits of a thick organic mulch.

After blind cultivation, subsequent weed control operations in larger-scale systems can make use of advances in tillage equipment such as rolling cultivators, finger weeders, and torsion weeders that allow tilling close to the plant row. Smaller-scale operations often use wheel hoes, stirrup hoes, and other less capital-intensive hardware.

Determining the amount, the timing, and the kind of tillage to be done can be a balancing act for the organic grower, but experience and observation over time lead to proficiency.

There are downsides to tillage, however, and most organic growers are well aware of them. The most obvious of these is the dollar cost; organic farmers are as concerned as their conventional counterparts about costs of production and strive to minimize expensive field operations. There is also a cost to the soil and environment. Every tillage operation aerates the soil and speeds the decomposition of the organic fraction. While this may provide a boost to the current crop, it can be overdone and "burn up" the humus reserves in the soil. Excessive tillage can also be directly destructive to earthworms and their tunnelling, reducing their benefits to the land. There is also the danger of compaction, even when field operations are well timed.

Mulching

Mulching is a practice often used by organic growers. Traditionally, it entails the spreading of large amounts of organic materials — straw, old hay, wood chips, etc. — over otherwise bare soil between and among crop plants. Organic mulches regulate soil moisture and temperature, suppress weeds, and provide organic matter to the soil. Mulching is most appropriate to small, intensive operations with high-value annual or fruit crops.

A few systems of no-till organic gardening have evolved from the concept of deep, *permanent* mulching. Among these are the well-known Ruth Stout method and *Synergistic Agriculture* — a raised bed system developed by Emilia Hazelip, who adapted concepts from *Permaculture* and the ideas of Masanobu Fukuoka. Mark Cain and Michael Crane, co-owners of Dripping Springs Gardens — an intensive market gardening operation in Arkansas — have adapted Emilia's system to their farm with considerable success.

Plastic mulch, as long as it is removed at end of growing or harvest season, is also permitted in certified organic production. Its use allows larger acreage to be brought more easily under herbicide-free management, though there are serious issues to be addressed.

High-Input Organic Agriculture

At the beginning of this publication, organic farming was described as a system that uses a minimum of off-farm inputs. While that describes most of organic agriculture as it is currently practised in the U.S., certified organic farming can also entail much greater reliance on off-farm inputs.

Intensive annual strawberry and vegetable systems under plasticulture are good examples. In these systems, traditional rotations and soil building practices are usually employed, followed by clean cultivation and the laying of plastic mulch and drip irrigation tape on shaped beds.

During the season, large amounts of soluble organic fertilizers—typically fish-based—are fed to the crop through the drip system (*i.e.*, organic fertigation). At the end of the season, all plastics must be removed from the field, and it is returned to more standard organic management. Ideally, an off-season cover crop will be planted. Such systems are often exceptionally productive and economically attractive, when organic premiums are good. The high cost of soluble organic fertilizer (typically hundreds of dollars/acre), however, plus the marginally higher cost of pest controls, make such systems largely non-competitive in the conventional marketplace.

The labelling of such high-input systems as organic presents a paradox for many proponents of organic agriculture. It is unclear whether these technological advancements reflect the kind of farming most practitioners and supporters of organics think of as truly "organic." To begin with, the research citing environmental and economic benefits has largely been done on low-input organic systems; it is questionable whether similar findings would be made about high-input systems, especially regarding environmental matters.

Of particular note, while low-input organic systems are documented as being more resistant to erosion, fields under plastic mulch are reported to be fifteen times more erodible. Traditional organic farms leach minimal amounts of nitrogen into tile or groundwater; the losses from fields loaded with high levels of soluble organic fertilizers is certain to be greater, but how much greater is unknown. The fossil fuel energy involved in plastic manufacture, transportation, and application may or may not be compensated by reductions in tractor fuel use.

Finally, the lowered capital investment required to produce a crop by traditional organic methods makes this form of farming more accessible to resource-poor farmers and entails less risk in years of crop failure or lack of premiums. These factors are less certain in a high-input system. A further consideration is the issue of plastic disposal following removal. At this time, there are few to no options for recycling, and landfills are the fate of plastic mulches at the end of each season.

While it is unwise to rush to judgement regarding high-input organic farming, it is clear that some adaptations will need to be made, if the traditional character and sustainability benefits of organic farming are to be preserved.

Fire

While fire can be used in a number of ways in organic agriculture, the area of greatest interest is *flame* or *thermal weeding*. In its most common application, torches mounted on a tractor toolbar throw a hot flame at the base of mature (*i.e.*, heat-resistant) plants, over the inter-row area, or both. Tractor speed is adjusted so that weeds are not *burned* so much as *seared*. Searing is sufficient to kill most seedling weeds and uses less fuel. Liquid propane (LP) gas is the fuel most commonly used, though alternatives such as alcohol and methane offer the possibility of on-farm sources.

Supplemental Fertilization

In many organic systems, crop rotation, manuring, green manuring, along with enhanced biological activity in the soil, provide an abundant supply of plant-essential minerals annually. This is especially true on naturally deep and rich prairie soils. It is less true on poorer soils and on those that have been heavily exploited through non-sustainable farming practices. To correct mineral deficiencies in organically managed soils, organic growers often apply ground or powdered rock minerals.

The most commonly used rock mineral is high-calcium aglime. Dolomitic limestone, various rock phosphates, gypsum, sulfate of potash-magnesia, and mined potassium sulfate are also common. These are all significant sources of primary (P, K) and/or secondary (Ca, Mg, S) plant nutrients. The savvy organic grower applies significant amounts of these materials only with the guidance of regular soil testing.

Less common are other rock powders and fines that are limited sources for the major nutrients but are rich in micro-nutrients or have some other soil-improving characteristic. Among these are glauconite (greensand), glacial gravel dust, lava sand, Azomite, granite meal, and others.

Supplementary nutrients that include nitrogen are often provided in the form of animal or plant products and by-products such as fish emulsion, blood meal, feather meal, bone meal, alfalfa meal, and soybean meal. Most of these products also supply some organic matter, though that is not the primary reason they are used.

Evaluating Tools and Practices

One basis on which to evaluate the tools or practices one chooses for an organic operation is whether or not they contribute to biodiversity—biodiversity being one of the principal characteristics of a sustainable organic agriculture.

Crop rotation, cover cropping, farmscaping, companion planting, and Inter-cropping are outstanding examples of practices that contribute to biodiversity. They therefore contribute to the long-term stability and sustainability of the farm agro-ecosystem. Composting and manuring likewise contribute to biodiversity, but since the diversity they promote is mostly in soil biota, it is rather less obvious to the casual observer.

On the other end of the spectrum are practices such as tillage, cultivation, thermal weeding, solarization, and plastic mulching. Such tools significantly reduce diversity in the field and tend to move the system in a less sustainable direction. This, however, does not necessarily make these practices bad choices.

Organic farming has often been called *natural* farming, as it tries to mimic the processes of nature in producing crops and livestock. However, the analogy goes only so far, since most agricultural systems are characterized by a struggle between human and nature, each with a clear notion of what plants and animals the land *ought* to support and in what proportions. The farmer is typically in the position of "holding back" the natural succession of plant and animal species through the use of diversity-reducing tools and practices. The ideal is to bring about an agricultural system in which the long-term direction emphasizes diversity and sustainability. Among the best visualizations of this ideal are those emerging from the Permaculture movement.

Balanced Nutrition

Whether or not it has been customary in the past, organic growers are encouraged to have periodic soil testing done on their fields. How the results of a soil test are used, however, can vary considerably among farmers, depending on their personal philosophy and management skill.

While there is certainly a segment of the organic farming community that has no faith in soil audits, most growers use them as a means to monitor progress in building their soils, to identify nutrient deficits, and to guide supplementary fertilization. While there are many ideas about fertilization guidelines, there are two schools of thought that dominate.

The first is commonly known as the *sufficiency* approach or model. Though somewhat oversimplified, the following are among its significant characteristics:

- annual fertilizer additions of P and K are based in good part on how much the crop is expected to remove from the soil at harvest.
- additional amounts of P and K are recommended based on keeping the soil nutrient reserves at a particular level.
- lime is added to the soil based on pH.
- little to no attention is paid to nutrient balance or to the levels of secondary nutrients Ca and Mg.

The second approach is referred to variously as *cation nutrient balancing*, the *Albrecht system*, the *CEC*, or the *base saturation* approach. It differs from the sufficiency approach in that fertilizer and lime recommendations are made based on an idealized ratio of nutrients in the soil and its capacity to hold those nutrients against leaching.

Cation nutrient balancing is more popular among practitioners of organic farming and sustainable agriculture in general than it is among conventional growers. However, there is no universal agreement on which approach is most appropriate for organic management.

A wide range of other products —humates, humic acids, enzymes, catalyst waters, bioactivators, surfactants, to name a few — are also acceptable in organic crop production. However, the tradeoff between out-of-pocket cost and efficacy of such materials is often challenged by conventional and organic growers alike. Organic growers are encouraged to experiment, but to do so in a manner that allows the actual results to be measured.

Bio-rational Pesticides

While, in principle, any pesticide use is discouraged in organic systems, a rather wide range of bio-rational pesticides is permitted. The frequency of pesticide use varies considerably with crop and location. For example, there is virtually no use of pesticides on organic row crops in the Cornbelt. By contrast, organic tree fruits in the Midsouth routinely receive heavy applications of several fungicides and insecticides allowable in organic production. The pesticides permitted in organic farming fall predominantly into several classes.

Minerals: These include sulphur, copper, diatomaceous earth, and clay-based materials like Surround®.

Botanicals: Botanicals include common commercial materials such as rotenone, neem, and pyrethrum. Less common botanicals include quassia, equisetum, and ryania. Tobacco products like Black-Leaf 40® and strichnine are also botanicals but are prohibited in organic production due to their high toxicity.

Soaps: A number of commercial soap-based products are effective as insecticides, herbicides, fungicides, and algicides. *Detergent*-based products are *not* allowed for crop use in organic production.

Pheromones: Pheromones can be used as a means to confuse and disrupt pests during their mating cycles, or to draw them into traps.

Biologicals: One of the fastest-growing areas in pesticide development, biopesticides present some of the greatest hope for organic control of highly destructive pests. Among the most well-known biopesticides are the *Bacillus thuringiensis* (Bt) formulations for control of lepidopterous pests and Colorado potato beetle.

Seeds, Seedlings, and GMOs

One of the challenges faced by organic growers is getting suitable planting stock. Certified production requires that seed not be treated with pesticides and be organically grown.

Transplants must be purchased from a certified organic source or otherwise be grown using organic methods. This presents some difficulty, as most commercial potting mixes contain prohibited fertilizers and wetting agents, requiring special ordering or the added effort of making a homemade mix. Generally, planting stock for perennial crops like tree fruits and berries is available from conventional sources, even if treated with pesticides. However, no production can be sold as organic for a minimum of 12 months following transplanting to an organic field.

In all instances, organic growers are not permitted to use varieties of crops that have been developed through genetic engineering (GE). At first glance, this might seem perplexing. GE crops promise further means of non-chemical pest control and the possibility of nutritionally enhanced foods. However, the organic community is concerned about environmental, economic, and social impacts from this new technology which, they feel, have not been adequately studied.

This same concern applies to GE foods. Natural foods consumers—a large segment of the organic market—do not want them. This was made abundantly clear to the USDA when its first draft of the proposed rule, which suggested permitting genetically modified organisms (GMOs), was released in 1997. The backlash was so strong that not only GE crop varieties, but all inputs, such as GMO-derived biopesticides, are prohibited from organic production.

Unfortunately the GE issue does not resolve itself so simply for organic farmers. The proliferation of GMOs in the marketplace and across the landscape has created a host of new challenges that have particular implications for organic agriculture:

- *Genetic Drift onto Crops:* Pollen drifting from adjacent fields can contaminate organic crops. Some clients in the lucrative European Union market accept 0% GMO contamination; others accept only very low levels. Pollen from cross-pollinating crops like corn easily travels hundreds of yards and may be carried for miles under the right conditions. No reasonable amount of non-crop buffer can prevent contamination except in highly isolated locations.
- *Genetic Drift onto Soils:* Concerns have been expressed over the persistence of GE pollen in soils. Should contaminated soils be decertified?
- *Non-labelled Products:* Should soybean, cottonseed, and corn gluten meals be prohibited as fertilizers, since these may come from GE varieties? Should pesticidal use of vegetable oils be prohibited?
- *Pest Control Problems:* The rapid proliferation of corn, cotton, and other crops featuring the Bt gene from *Bacillus thuringiensis* is likely to accelerate the development of resistance to this natural pesticide. Organic growers may lose one of their most useful pest management tools.
- *Domination of the Food System:* In the late 1990s, the public was made aware of two specific developments of agricultural biotechnology dubbed the *terminator* and *traitor* technologies. Terminator technology is the genetic altering of seed so that the subsequent generation will not germinate. This prevents farmers from saving a portion of the harvested crop to replant the next year — a traditional practice among farmers worldwide. Traitor or *suicide* technology is the genetic altering of seed so that it will fail to germinate or mature unless a proprietary chemical is applied. Such technologies are authoritarian and advance the centralization and industrialization of

the food system. Organic farmers perceive additional challenges from genetic drift impacts and difficulty in finding non-GE seed in the marketplace.

Foliar Fertilization

Foliar fertilization or feeding entails the application—via spraying—of nutrients to plant leaves and stems and their absorption at those sites. It is not specifically an organic practice, though it is commonly used by many organic growers. The fertilizer materials used are typically soluble fish-and seaweed-based products, naturally chelated nutrients, humic acid extracts, and teas made from plants, dried blood, manure, guano, or compost. At first glance, the use of foliar feeding appears contradictory to the organic notion that one feeds the soil to feed the plant. Organic growers rationalize the use of this approach on two points.

1. Foliar feeding is strictly supplemental fertilization; it is not used as a substitute for traditional soil building practices.
2. Foliar fertilization is understood to increase the production of root exudates, which stimulates biological activity in the rhizosphere (soil area adjacent to plant roots). The soil bio-life gets considerable benefit in this indirect way from foliar feeding.

Esoteric Practices

There are a number of farming and gardening practices based on belief in a non-physical world closely aligned with our physical reality. Those who use these practices believe that conditions in this unseen realm influence, or even dictate, what happens on a material level. They take pains to understand these influences and adjust their farm activities. In some instances, they act to influence events. Obviously, these practices are rooted more deeply in metaphysics than in the conventional sciences.

The most well-known of these esoteric practices is the scheduling of planting or other field operations according to lunar or other astrological signs. Dowsing and other forms of *divining* may also be used to guide scheduling, fertilizer selection, and other facets of farming. The use of potentized *preparations*, as done in Biodynamic farming, is also a metaphysical practice. Radionics, energy balancing towers, "medicine" wheels, prayer—these are further examples of practices used by some farmers to bring a tangible spiritual element into their farm operation.

Esoteric practices like these (there are many others) are not inherently part of organic agriculture. In all likelihood, only a small-to-modest minority practice them or believe in their efficacy. Still, esoteric practices are sometimes associated with organic agriculture, and it is almost a given that practitioners of "energetic agriculture" are either certified organic or actively pursue a sustainable form of agriculture.

The rationale for this association of organic with the esoteric is not difficult to understand. Most metaphysical practices are founded on a world-view similar to that of ecology, in which everything is related to everything else. The difference is that ecology considers this interrelationship only on a hard physical level; metaphysics perceives it also on a non-physical level. This belief tends to cast humankind as part of nature, not merely as an inhabitant. This perspective would tend to make one more concerned about the environment and, therefore, more readily drawn to organics as a philosophy and pragmatic farming approach. To put it in a nutshell, it is natural for the metaphysically-inclined to choose organics; it is far less likely, however, that the average organic farmer is drawn to metaphysical practices.

A further factor plays into the association between esoteric farming practices and organics. It relates to the fact that organic agriculture has, for many years, been marginalized and treated as pseudoscience by the mainstream—an experience shared by practitioners of metaphysical arts. It is not surprising for underdogs to seek common ground.

Buffers and Barriers

Field buffers are strips of sod or other permanent vegetation at the edge of or surrounding crop fields. There is considerable interest in both conventional and alternative agriculture in these buffers, since they assist in reducing soil erosion and improving water quality. If managed properly, some buffers also serve as beneficial insect habitat.

In certified organic production, however, field buffers have an added purpose in reducing crop contamination from chemicals used on adjacent land. Most agencies require a minimum 25-foot buffer along "uncontrolled" borders where there is a hazard of chemical use. Wider borders may be required where hazards are great—for instance, where adjacent farms have synthetic pesticides applied by aircraft.

Organic Farming: *Niche Market or Viable Alternative?*

The pioneers of organic farming considered organics the preferred direction for the whole of agriculture to take. It is likely that most contemporary proponents still hold that view. While recent growth in the organic industry is definitely encouraging, much of the impetus is tied to its growth as a niche market, not as a serious shift in the direction of mainstream agriculture. Unfortunately, a likely reason for the newfound "tolerance" of organic agriculture in many land grant universities and other formerly hostile environs is its perception as a niche market opportunity only. As such, it is not a serious threat to the status quo.

Is it practical and responsible to promote organic agriculture as the dominant approach to farming in the future? While some are quick to answer, "Yes!", most are buffaloed by the nagging question, "Can organic agriculture feed the world?" Questions about the productivity and the prospects of widespread starvation have long been an effective tactic for stonewalling serious discussion of organics. While it is not the purpose of this publication to settle such a compelling issue, there are a few points that can and should be made regarding the "starving billions" scenario.

- Critics warn that, were organic farming to be adopted on a wider scale, per-acre agricultural productivity would decline sharply; that meeting food needs would necessitate the plowing of even more erodible hillsides and the draining of more wetlands. Such scenarios are often based on pre-chemical era yield data that ignore the advancements of modern organic farming. Contemporary research on organic systems—as limited as it is— indicates that the per-acre productivity of organic and conventional systems is not vastly different. Other scenarios are sometimes based on the perceived need for vast quantities of grain—particularly corn. Since overproduction of grain has led to prices below costs of production for several years, this is a questionable basis for argument. It also ignores the fact that most of the grain produced is fed to livestock and that many livestock species can eat forage instead. Ruminant livestock—cattle and sheep especially—are designed by nature to thrive on forage and can even be finished for market on pasture.

- The paucity of good research on the productivity of organic systems also spotlights the lack of practical research for organic producers. That organic farms are as productive as they appear to be is remarkable in light of minimal research and extension support for many decades. It has often been argued that, had comparable resources been put into organic research, its widespread feasibility would be unquestionable. This assertion is well-supported by the development, in recent years, of a number of alternative, organically acceptable pesticides, that are certain to expand organic production of many crops in regions where it had previously been near impossible on a commercial basis.
- Increasing agricultural production alone does not alleviate hunger. The amount of grain produced in the world in 1999 could, by itself, sustain 8 billion people – 2 billion more than our current population. Total food production is estimated to provide each human being with at least 3500 calories per day. The issue of hunger, it appears, is not so much a lack of food, but lack of *entitlement* to food. People are shocked to learn that while many Bangladeshees starved during the 1974 floods, roughly 4 million tons of rice produced in that country were

stacked in warehouses for want of buyers. The people were simply too poor to buy it. They are surprised to learn that Ireland exported grain during the Irish potato famine while 1 million of its citizens died and even more emigrated; that India regularly exports food and animal feed despite an estimated 200 million in starvation. Those lacking the ready cash to buy food or the resources to produce it themselves seem destined for hunger no matter what miracles agricultural technology provides. The world's nations will need to deal with issues of equity and democracy first, if hunger is ever to be effectively addressed.

- No agriculture can continue to feed a growing population if it depletes or fouls its resource base. The path undertaken by conventional agriculture is ultimately a dead end in this regard, though there is an almost mystical faith that genetic engineering and other complex technologies will always triumph. Agriculture needs to be sustainable. Therefore, those who promote organic agriculture as a true alternative are well advised to do their part in ensuring that certification and regulation does not create a "compliance agriculture" in which sustainability becomes little more than an afterthought.

Record Keeping

Few would consider record keeping as a tool for organic crop production. However, the documentation of how and where a crop was raised, what products were applied and when, which bin or cooler it was stored in, is of critical importance to establishing the integrity of the product. If the farmer cannot provide reasonable documentation that his or her crop was organically grown, that it has not been contaminated with chemicals, and that it has not commingled with a similar conventional product, then certification may well be denied.

Other Tools and Practices

As stated at the outset, the tools and practices described in detail here are by no means an exhaustive listing of organic options. Among those not discussed but requiring mention are timing of planting and field operations to avoid pests or disrupt their life cycles, various forms of pest traps, physical barriers to pests, and increasing plant populations to enhance crop-weed competition.

Summing Up

While there have been varying notions of organic farming over the years, the growth of the industry and the introduction of standards and certification have led to a clearer definition in recent years. That definition describes organics as a viable agriculture, based on sound farming practices, that does not include synthetic chemicals.

Certified organic agriculture can be further characterized by a set of principles that include biodiversity, integration, sustainability, natural plant nutrition, natural pest management, and integrity. These principles are expressed through the implementation of both traditional and cutting-edge farm practices.

As the organic industry continues to grow and evolve, it faces many challenges, including the consequences of its own success. Economic opportunities invite new players into the marketplace who may have little interest in sustainability or the positive social benefits many have come to associate with organics. This matter was touched on by rural sociologist Dr. William Heffernan. Dr. Heffernan has gained considerable attention in recent years for his insightful analyses of the causes and social consequences of the increased concentration and corporate control of the U.S. food system. In an interview published in Acres USA, he expressed the following regarding organic farming.

We are beginning to realize that up to this point we believed that organic was synonymous with family farms and we are finding out that is changing. In fact, the organic is going to continue to grow. That doesn't mean that it is going to support family farms the way it has in the past. With the whole organic movement, we assumed that the social would go along with the environmental movement, and what we are finding out is no, that is not necessarily true, and even what they do environmentally is questionable. Whether certified organic farming will survive its own success and continue as a socially and environmentally responsible alternative, or merely become a parallel production system based on minimal compliance to standards, remains to be seen.

Organic Soil Fertility Management

Soil Management & the Organic Standards: In an organic farming system, rotation and tillage practices must provide an appropriate seedbed and pest control while minimizing erosion. Soil fertility must be sustainable without application of prohibited substances. Soil management practices must be developed in consultation with the certifying agent who judges compliance with organic standards, approves inputs, and specifies needed documentation.

Crop Rotation, Tilth, Fertility and Pest Management: Crop rotation is critical to the maintenance of soil tilth (physical condition), fertility, organic matter, and as a preventive practice to minimize pest problems. No specific rotations are mandated, but suggested crops to include are sods, cover crops, green manures, and catch crops. The rotation adopted must resolve any relevant problems with soil organic matter content, deficient or excess plant nutrients, soil erosion, and pest management. Defining a rotation is also a key component in designing soil sampling and tillage management schemes. For short rotations (two to three years), soil samples can be collected once per rotation. For longer rotations, soil samples may still need to be collected every two to three years, preferably prior to planting the most intensively managed crops.

Soil Fertility Management: Although crop nutritional requirements are the same for organic and conventional farms, organic producers need to be more creative due to the limitations on allowable inputs. Soils throughout the Carolinas differ in texture, organic matter, past erosion, and residual nutrient contents. Periodic soil testing is the only way to understand the current fertility level and maintain the fertility status of each field. Plant tissue analysis can also be used to verify soil fertility status, particularly for nutrients not easily measured in routine soil tests (nitrogen, sulphur, boron). With tissue testing, the appropriate plant part must be collected at the proper growth stage as specified by laboratory guidelines

North and South Carolina have numerous sources of plant and animal manures and by-products. This region also has a favourable climate for growing a diversity of rotational and green manure cover crops that can provide needed nitrogen and other nutrients. Farmers should study their crops to fully understand production requirements, nutrient needs, and common production problems. Crops differ in their nutrient removal rates, and nutrient sources differ in their nutrient contents.

Certain inputs are allowable on organic farming systems, if applied according to guidelines. These include mostly natural and a few synthetic materials. The National List of Allowed and Prohibited Substances under the National Organic This list specifies synthetic substances allowed for use and non-synthetic substances prohibited for use in crop production. The Organic Materials Review Institute (OMRI) was developed to review materials for approval and to simplify the National List. OMRI classifies materials as either allowed (A) or regulated (R), and lists generic and brand names of materials. Other materials should be considered prohibited until further notice. In all cases, input use should be included in the farm plan and confirmed by the certifying authority prior to application for certification as an organic farm.

Critical aspects of soil fertility management include pH, major nutrients (nitrogen, phosphorus, potassium), secondary nutrients (sulphur, calcium, magnesium), and micro-nutrients (especially boron, copper, manganese, zinc; but also iron, molybdenum, chlorine, selenium, and cobalt).

Soil pH is important because it influences nutrient solubility, microbial activity, and root growth. The low pH levels common in native Carolina soils continue to be the most common limiting factor for plant development seen in samples submitted to the NCDA&CS Agronomic Division Laboratory. Since most agricultural lime is from naturally occurring minerals of relatively low solubility, its use is generally allowed in organic farming systems. Hydrated limes and burnt limes are not allowed. Pelletizing agents should be evaluated to determine that they are not prohibited materials.

Nitrogen (N) is the most frequently limiting nutrient for crop production. Organic farms need to supply N through sources such as legumes, animal wastes or by-products, plant-processing by-products, or limited additions of mined mineral deposits. It is possible for a nitrogen-fixing legume or legume-and-grass mixture cover crop to provide adequate nitrogen for certain cash crops. A seed inoculum is recommended for legumes unless adequate native inoculum is present, and adequate soil fertility is needed to ensure no other factors limit legume growth. Inoculums, however, must not be genetically engineered. Nitrogen-fixing cover crops for summer in North Carolina include cowpeas and soybeans.

Winter N-fixing cover crops include hairy vetch, Cahaba vetch, Austrian winter peas, and many clovers. Many farmers in North Carolina use composted or uncomposted poultry litter to supply the nitrogen needs for their organic field crops. Poultry litter and poultry by-products are available in many parts of the state. Mined nitrates, such as sodium nitrate ($NaNO_3$, bulldog soda, or Chilean nitrate) may be used, but are limited to a maximum of 20 percent of the crop's total N requirement. Constantly relying upon $NaNO_3$, a restricted substance in organic agriculture, will be questioned by a certification agency.

Other nutrients. Phosphorus, potassium, calcium, magnesium, sulphur, copper, manganese, and zinc can generally be supplied in adequate amounts through additions of lime (calcium, magnesium), animal or plant by-products or wastes (phosphorus, potassium, sulphur, micro-nutrients), or permissible mineral inputs. Naturally occurring minerals of relatively low solubility are generally allowed (lime, gypsum, rock phosphate, rock dusts, mined humates).

In addition, the following naturally occurring minerals of relatively high solubility may be applied if used in compliance with the National List:

- Magnesium sulfate (Epsom salt), with a documented soil deficiency.

- Sulfate of potash and potassium magnesium sulfate, if from an approved source and with a documented soil deficiency.
- Muriate of potash, if derived from a mined source and applied in a manner that minimizes chloride accumulation in the soil. This may be acceptable for most crops in the Carolinas with a soil test to document the deficiency and recommend an application rate.
- Many micronutrient salts, with documented soil deficiency and if not in the form of nitrate or chloride salts. This includes various soluble boron products and sulphates, carbonates, oxides, or silicates of zinc, copper, iron, molybdenum, selenium, and cobalt.

Numerous animal and plant by-products are available to provide essential crop nutrients. It is important to check with the certifying agency before using any input.

Tillage Practices

Management of soil tilth, organic matter, and fertility is an important aspect of a successful organic farming system. Current organic systems usually require tillage prior to planting and cultivation after planting, especially for corn and soybean production, to control weeds and reduce the incidence of seedling diseases and insect pests.

However, tillage destroys the organic matter that is critical in improving soil fertility and soil water-holding capacity. The use of rotations with cover crops where the soil surface is covered with a growing crop for most of the year is important in maintaining organic matter content during periods when corn is not grown. Tillage should be performed when soil moisture is low enough to prevent compaction. Since primary tillage operations are usually performed at least a month before a crop is planted, this requires careful planning and the ability to take advantage of periods of dry weather. No-till agriculture in organic systems is starting to be used in parts of the country. The Rodale Institute has experimented with no-till organic using cover crops and tractor-mounted rollers to kill the cover just before planting into it.

Documenting Crop Nutrient Deficiencies

Since use of some soil amendments is limited to cases of nutrient deficiency, organic producers should maintain records of soil test results and plant tissue analyses to document specific nutrient deficiencies that need correction. Soil test records can also be useful in documenting soil quality maintenance because they will show changes in humic matter and nutrient levels over time. It is important to avoid the topsoil erosion that could result from excessive cultivation for weed control (declines in humic matter indicate erosion losses) and to avoid accumulation of excess phosphorus and micro-nutrients following application of manures and composts.

Composts and Manures

Specific guidelines must be followed when applying composts and manures in organic farming systems. Materials must be applied at agronomic rates in compliance with any applicable nutrient management guidelines and in ways that avoid excess nutrients or contact your local Soil and Water Conservation District office). Raw animal manures must be

- composted according to specific criteria,
- applied to land used for a crop not intended for human consumption,
- incorporated into the soil at least 90 days prior to the harvest of an edible (human-consumed) product not contacting soil or soil particles, or
- incorporated into the soil at least 120 days prior to the harvest of an edible product that does contact soil or soil particles.

The guidelines for compost production for organic agriculture state that the initial C:N ratio must be between 25:1 and 40:1, and a temperature between 131° and 170°F must be achieved. This temperature must be maintained for at least 3 days for in-vessel or static-aerated pile systems or for at least 15 days during which there are at least five turnings for windrow systems. Composts not meeting these criteria must be applied based on other raw manure criteria, which also apply to lagoon liquids, lagoon solids, and stockpiled poultry litter. Ashes of manures may not be used, but ashes from other untreated plant and animal materials may be applied if not combined with any prohibited substances.

Avoid over-reliance on animal manures, since this could lead to accumulation of excess phosphorus, copper, and zinc in soils. For example, stockpiled turkey litter, applied at a rate of 5 tons per acre, would supply approximately the amount of N removed by a 150 bushel per acre corn crop. Note that the amount of phosphorus added (as P_2O_5 equivalent) would be 360 pounds per acre, while crop removal would only be 53 pounds per acre.

Similarly, 2.8 pounds per acre of zinc would be added, while crop removal would only be 0.15 pounds per acre. Sporadic use of manures in conjunction with more frequent use of legume cover crops, green manures, or other N sources is an excellent way to supply plant nutrients in appropriate amounts.

Committee on Commodity Problems

Brief History of the Citrus Industry in Cuba

The Cuban citrus industry was created at the end of the 1960s to supply the markets of the former Soviet Union and socialist countries in Eastern Europe with whom Cuba had close economic ties. In those days, citrus consumption in the socialist block was considerably lower than in Western European countries.

Market studies revealed the acceptance of tropical oranges as a table fruit, a commodity that was not sold in the international markets except in small quantities. Grapefruits were barely known, so the market had to be created. The main objectives of the programme were to export fresh oranges and grapefruits, to process the fruit that was not suitable for sale as fresh products, and to fully meet the domestic demand for fresh fruits.

The National Citrus Programme met these expectations. From 1975 onwards, citrus production increased at an average annual rate of 14 percent, reaching 1,017 thousand tonnes in 1990 and an area planted of 115,000 hectares. At the end of the 1980s, five Cuban ports exported some 500 000 tonnes of fresh fruits. Three plants processed more than 200 000 tonnes of fresh fruit to produce juice for exports. The national per capita consumption was above 25 kg per year.

The need to provide scientific and technical support was understood from the outset, and training of scientific and technical personnel was provided as well as working facilities. The work gradually incorporated tropical fruits and became what today is known as the Tropical Fruit Tree Production Research Institute (Instituto de Investigaciones en Fruticultura Tropical-IIFT).

Citrus rapidly became one of the main exports of the country and the annual income increased to some US$180 million. The potential of the groves was in excess of three million tonnes per annum; the rate of growth achieved could be sustained by the infrastructure and the demand for Cuban citrus.

However, the sudden disappearance of the socialist market created great losses to the Cuban citrus industry, which halved production in 1994. This situation was but part of a general economic crisis caused by the unexpected loss of markets Cuba had, to a large extent, integrated into its economy, such as the Soviet Union and other European socialist countries.

In 1994 more than 50 percent of the area planted to citrus had been lost, and the rest was in poor conditions. Major changes were required to save the citrus industry: firstly to shift fresh fruits the share that goes to processing, including the rebuilding and enlargement of existing processing plants. Secondly, to rescue the best groves, increase yields and reduce production costs. However, the road to recovery was difficult because no operating capital or international trade channels were available. The main actions taken were:

- In 1994 the National Citrus Corporation was founded. Today it is known as the Fruit Trees Enterprise Group (GEF). It was made up of 13 citrus enterprises, a commercial company and 4 four processing plants. The IIFT was also part of this new organization.

- State-run farms were dissolved in 62 percent of the areas planted to citrus, and a cooperative system was created with its workers. The cooperatives were given credit to purchase the groves, the equipment and the facilities. The land was given on the basis of a permanent right of enjoyment, and Basic Units of Cooperative Production (UBPC) were created.
- Groves were restructured; those with potential for profitable yields were kept and those in a poor state eliminated. Low-input technologies were applied.
- Agreements were signed with foreign companies for the provision of funds, technical assistance and trade.
- Priority was given to restructure and enlarge the existing plants.

As shown in below, the recovery of citrus groves was already apparent in 1996. Production in the year 2000 represents 87 percent of the historical record which was achieved in 1990.

Production and Use of Citrus: 1995/96-2000

	1995/96	1996/97	1997/98	1998/99	1999/00	2000
Total output	564.4	795.1	658.9	739.3	730.5	892.4
Processing	366.5	527.1	478.8	599.9	620.3	675.3
Fresh fruits for export	48.7	54.2	38.6	32.9	31.0	29.6
Domestic market	149.2	213.8	141.5	106.5	79.2	187.5

In November 2001 Michelle, a category IV hurricane with sustained winds of more than 200 km/h, hit the central part of the island and damaged the largest Cuban citrus enterprise (Jaguey Grande). Some 20 000 ha of citrus plantation were damaged and an estimated 400 000 tonnes of grapefruits and oranges fell to the ground. Groves from the Isle of Youth and other central areas were also affected.

In the year 2002, two more hurricanes followed the same route as Michelle, hitting citrus groves in the Isle of Youth and Pinar del Rio. 2001 and 2002 were the most violent hurricanes seasons in the history of the Cuban citrus industry. It is estimated that, should these not have happened, over one million tonnes of fresh citrus could have been harvested this season.

Current Situation of the Cuban Citrus Industry

Institutions: The Cuban citrus industry operates within the Fruit Trees Enterprise Group (GEF), which in turn operates within the Ministry of Agriculture. GEF also covers some non-citrus fruit trees enterprises, one enterprise for the production of flowers and ornamental plants, an import-export company that controls cold storages and other services (Cítricos Caribe S.A.), a commercial company for fruits and vegetables and the Tropical Fruit Trees Research Institute (IIFT) that provides scientific and technical support for the Cuban fruit tree system. Nearly 27 000 workers are involved today in this sub-sector.

Two production and export systems operate in GEF.

1. An export system which includes, apart from UBPC, the Cooperatives for Agricultural Production (CPA), the Cooperatives of Credits and Services (CCS) and private farms. The enterprises of this system receive and provide funding for growers, import the inputs, operate large irrigation systems, workshops for the machinery and packinghouses for fresh exports. Processing plants are also included in this system.
2. Citricos Caribe S.A. operates three cold storage facilities and exports through the ports of Havana, Cienfuegos, Santiago de Cuba and Nuevitas. The processing plant in Pinar del Rio is a joint venture between Italian investments and Citricos Caribe S.A.
3. The second export system is formed by two enterprises that manage the production of state-run farms (Jaguey Grande and the Isle of Youth). This system produces, processes, packs and exports its produce. Since 1992 it has worked jointly with foreign capital, including the provision of funds, technical assistance and sales in the international market.

Other private farms produce an estimated 60 000 tonnes of fruits per annum for the domestic market.

3

Pest Management in Citrus

Concept and Guidelines

Concept of Pest Management: The purpose of a citrus pest management programme is to achieve satisfactory long-range pest control, maximizing net profit to growers in an environmentally compatible manner. This objective is approached through the application of various IPM strategies with emphasis on preventive methods and preservation of natural control agents. Ideally, this objective is achieved with minimum Pesticide use. However, citrus programmes involving the Texas fresh fruit industry need to emphasize optimization rather than minimization of pesticide use. Rapid increases in pest or disease incidence sometimes require an increase in frequency of pesticide applications to protect fruit quality and crop investment.

IPM strategies are developed and governed in large part by the relationships between pest/disease development and weather conditions, cultural practices, beneficial organisms and pesticide usage. Information is provided to help growers use preventive methods of pest control when possible, structure management programmes to meet individual needs and avoid practices leading to disruption of natural control.

Identification of Pests and Beneficials: Recognition of both harmful and beneficial organisms impacting on citrus production is essential to development of a sound IPM programme. Growers and field scouts need to recognize pests and beneficials in various stages of development with the help of a hand lens. Equally important is the ability to recognize pest activities or diseases through use of symptomatology. Most insect and mite pests can be identified with a low power (10 to 14X) lens, but visual evidence of damage to fruit, foliage or trees is useful for identification of causal agents. Moreover, the presence of microscopic pathogens (fungi, bacteria, viruses and nematodes) can be characterized by symptoms. Symptomology allows for the distinction between pathogenic and physiological disorders which sometimes are confused.

Management Strategies: Three general approaches available for managing pests of citrus are: cultural control, biological control and chemical control. The first two are preventative in nature and may have more impact on long-term production, while chemical control provides short-term relief or prevention from pest pressure.

Cultural Control: The goal of cultural control is to use all practical horticultural techniques to reduce the likelihood of pest problems. These should encompass all phases of production, beginning with site selection and progress through the nursery operation to field establishment and eventually during full production. Site selection should take into consideration the soil type and elevation to avoid prolonged surface flooding and to minimize cold damage to trees. Site levelling is important to permit uniform irrigation. Planting schemes also influence the efficiency of pesticidal sprays applied after trees reach maturity.

Selection of a rootstock with acceptable disease tolerance and good horticultural characteristics is an important cultural component to pest management, as is use of healthy disease-free scion budwood. Sour orange rootstock offers the greatest tolerance to soil-borne disease problems in a wide range of Texas citrus soils. It is susceptible to the Tristeza virus but, with the exception of citrumelo and citrange as possible replacements in sandy soils, sour orange remains the best overall rootstock for Texas citrus. No disease prevention effort is more important or pays greater dividends to the grower in the long run than planting and maintenance of healthy virus-free trees. Every effort should be made in this regard to promote availability of certified, virus-free budwood for all commercially important citrus cultivars.

Other preventive measures in the nursery include the practice of budding high enough on the rootstocks to minimize chances for infection by foot rot fungi. Further protection can be applied by timely treatments with systemic fungicides to prevent or eradicate incipient infection before or soon after trees are moved to the field. Annual treatment of tree trunks with appropriate fungicides before applying tree wraps is a further precaution against foot rot during early years of orchard establishment.

Biological Control: Many citrus pests in Texas are subject to population reductions from naturally occurring or imported predators, parasites and pathogens. These organisms assist in management of citrus pests and, in many cases, reduce or eliminate the need for applications of pesticides for control. While the organisms responsible for natural control are not always apparent, steps should be taken to preserve these beneficial insects, mites and pathogens. A brief discussion of biological control agents attacking the major groups of pests follows.

Mites: A varicty of predators and diseases attack citrus rust mite and spider mite species. Several fungal diseases, including *Hirsutella thompsonii,* occur naturally in orchards and, during periods of moist weather, cause tremendous rust mite population crashes. Citrus red mite and Texas citrus mite also are attacked by fungi, and rapid population decline has been documented. Predators of the mite complex include thrips mites, coccinellid beetles, dusty wings and other insects.

Scales: Texas citrus enjoys a long history of biological control of scale pests with natural enemies. Florida red scale, purple scale and glover scale are currently under complete biological control due to the action of parasitic wasps. In the absence of major disruptions to the citrus ecosystem, this level of control is permanent and does not require any manipulation by producers. California red scale and chaff scale are each attacked by a series of parasites, none of which are able to consistently control populations below damaging levels. Nevertheless, they contribute significantly to pest reductions, but outbreaks of theses pests occur in their absence. Likewise, brown soft scale, cottony cushion scale and barnacle scale populations are generally kept below damaging levels by natural enemies which have been imported from other citrus areas and field-released in Texas.

Whiteflies: Whiteflies in Texas citrus are attacked by parasites and disease pathogens. The most outstanding example of whitefly control with a parasite is the citrus blackfly, which is under complete biological control by two parasitic wasps.

Citrus Mealybug: The citrus mealybug is attacked by a series of parasites and predators which have been introduced and, in general, populations of the mealybug are kept below damaging levels.

The wide variety of pests under partial or complete biological control points out the importance of preserving these natural enemies in Texas orchards. Unfortunately, many beneficial insects, mites and pathogens are more susceptible to commonly used pesticides than are the target pests, and spray applications can severely disrupt the balance between natural enemies and the pests they attack.

In the absence of natural enemies, pest species are able to reproduce unhindered and the result is a rapid pest increase. Improper selection of a pesticide often has resulted in outbreaks of brown soft scale, citrus mealybug or whitefly species. In most cases, this occurred because natural enemies of these pests were inadvertently destroyed. One important consideration in the selection of a pesticide in addition to its efficacy against the target is its impact on beneficials.

Materials vary tremendously in their impact on parasites and predators and, given a choice of two or more materials, the one least toxic to beneficials should be used. In addition, fungicides commonly used for melanose and greasy spot in citrus destroy fungi such as *Hirsutella thompsonii*, which help to reduce mite populations.

The list of suggested pesticide materials for use in Texas citrus includes information on toxicity of materials to selected natural enemies. This information should be used in deciding which pesticide to apply. The presence of high numbers of natural enemies in a pest population allows a higher action threshold to be used for control application, as pests are less likely to develop rapid population increases while predators, parasites or pathogens are present.

Chemical Control: Of the insecticides and miticides registered for citrus, some are specific in their range of pests controlled while some are nonspecific. Good management philosophy for selection of pesticides embraces the premise that for a given pest situation, a particular pesticide or combination of pesticides will provide the most appropriate and cost-effective control among those available. Choosing the proper pesticide requires familiarity with product labels and performance. Among the factors which influence the selection of a pesticide, efficacy of the product against the target pest is perhaps the most important. Other factors to consider in selecting a pesticide include:

1. Cost effectiveness
2. Hazard to beneficials and other non-target organisms
3. Potential hazards to applicators, environment, orchard or fruit crop
4. Limitations or restrictions on application
5. Impact on development of pest resistance

Product efficacy refers to the level of pesticidal qualities of a product with respect to specific target pests and is a relative measure of effectiveness when compared to performance of other products available for similar usage. Characteristics influencing efficacy include the time required for the product to gain control, the amount of residual control and the spectrum of pests controlled.

A knowledge of individual product characteristics is important when choosing the most appropriate pesticide. For example, Vendex is a miticide with an excellent performance record for control of rust mite and several other citrus mites but is not recommended for use when rust mite populations are increasing rapidly because of its relatively slow miticidal action. When rust mite damage is not imminent, it is an excellent choice because of broad-spectrum miticidal activity and long residual action. Residual action in itself may or may not be a desirable quality depending on circumstances. In most situations, the applicator hopes for at least 60 days between applications for rust mite control, yet a rust-mite "explosion" may dictate use of a fast-acting material with relatively short residual. Long-residual pesticides also may reduce the effectiveness of beneficial organisms.

The comparison of the cost effectiveness of different pesticide strategies should factor in the amount of pest kill, length of control and cost of the product per acre. The spectrum of activity of the pesticides also should be considered. A single broad spectrum material may substitute for two or more specific ones. In such cases, broad-spectrum materials which control potential secondary pests provide overall benefits much greater than those prove expected from a selective material. Some may have adverse effects on beneficials; scale and parasites can result in additional pesticide use later in the season. Therefore, cost effectiveness relates to cost of product per unit of fruit produced or to net income received and is best determined over a period of at least one season, preferably longer.

Practically all citrus pests in Texas are controlled in large part through natural control agents, either native or introduced. Complete destruction of these beneficials would result in the advancement of minor or secondary pests to primary pest status, resulting in greatly increased pest management costs. Pesticides most frequently implicated in destruction of beneficials are organo-phosphate and carbamate materials applied as foliar sprays. Parasitic fungi active in controlling mite and certain insect pests are adversely affected by the application of Zineb and copper fungicides.

Safety should be a consideration when choosing a pesticide. Materials hazardous to the applicator or to the environment are labelled as such on product containers and should be handled accordingly. Product selection may be influenced by orchard location relative to residential areas, human traffic in the vicinity, or weather conditions favouring drift of materials to non-target sites. All possible precautionary measures must be observed with materials labelled for restricted use.

Other hazards of pesticide use include possible phytotoxicity to trees, foliage and/or fruit. Certain combinations of pesticides or overlapping applications of incompatible materials can cause severe damage. The most notable combinations are citrus spray oil and sulphur, oil and Morestan or oil and Difolatan. Oil, if applied incorrectly or without regard to limiting weather-conditions, may cause severe oleosis of fruit and defoliation.

Product use should be considered in choosing an insecticide. Such restrictions specify when and how the pesticide may be applied, special application procedures, re-entry periods after application and pre-harvest periods. These restrictions provide a margin of safety for the user and farm worker and also prevent the occurrence of excessive pesticide residues at harvest.

The chemistry of the pesticide as it relates to the development of pest resistance also should be considered. Resistance develops because one or more individuals in any given pest population may tolerate or resist effects of exposure to a specific pesticide. When that pesticide is used consecutively for several applications, offspring of resistant individuals multiply to eventually establish a resistant population no longer controlled by the specific material. Some materials are so similar in mode of pesticidal action that resistance developed in response to one pesticide provides or confers cross resistance to other similar materials, *e.g.*, organo-phosphate insecticides and the benzimidazole-type fungicides.

Consequently, management decisions need to consider the class of product along with product efficacy in determining the pesticide selection process. In general, repeated use of any pesticide season-long should be avoided. Use of citrus spray oil as an alternative to organic pesticides is an excellent management practice to deter pest resistance. In contrast to physiological modes of action characteristic of the organic materials, oils kill pests by physical suffocation which prevents the development of resistance.

Pest Management Guidelines

Monitoring Systems: Field monitoring is the key to an integrated pest management programme. When performed systematically on a quantitative basis, it provides the information needed to detect important changes in pest activity and disease incidence; evaluate pesticide performance; and establish seasonal records for evaluating and upgrading managerial decisions. When weather data and cultural practices that influence pest behaviour are considered, pest behaviour and populations can better be anticipated.

Monitoring systems may be limited to a single primary pest Such as the citrus rust mite, and to environmental conditions that influence rust mite behaviour or they may include all major pests and beneficials. Monitoring techniques vary depending on individual preferences and management intensity, but should provide a consistent, repeatable means to numerically measure pest activity. Follow monitoring procedures upon which the control action thresholds were designed.

Monitoring Frequency: Monitoring frequency depends on the pests' reproductive capacities and time needed under optimum conditions for populations to reach economic damage thresholds. Because of the reproductive potential of citrus rust mite, biweekly monitoring of susceptible fruit is required from petal fall until harvest or arrival of cool weather. Other pests generally require less frequent monitoring. Outside of the petal-fall to harvest interval, monthly monitoring is adequate for the citrus mite complex and other potential pest or disease situations.

Sampling Methods: Sample size, location and selection are important to any sample programme. Each citrus orchard is unique and requires individual monitoring; the first step in developing a monitoring system is to decide how many trees need to be examined and, within this parameter, how many fruit, leaf or soil samples need to be observed or collected for adequate representation and sampling reliability. Sampling may involve trees randomly selected for each monitoring period or permanently designated station trees. Trees should be dispersed sufficiently to achieve representative sampling of the entire orchard. This can be accomplished in most rectangular orchards by sampling in a diagonal direction. For square orchards, a Z-shaped pattern is appropriate.

The station tree concept involves selection of representative trees at the time of orchard establishment or at the beginning of each season. Selected trees are flagged, numbered and revisited each monitoring period throughout the season. Random samples provide information on a larger proportion of trees within an orchard over time. Station trees more closely follow pest or disease dynamics on a few individual trees. Both systems have merit and, depending on the desired result and amount of time to be invested, a combination of both methods may prove most useful.

Field Records: Systematic recording of data in the field is time consuming but necessary for clarity in review and interpretation of results. If field counts are considered impractical and some form of rating scale is employed (*e.g.*, trace, low, medium, high, very high), the assignment of numerical values from 1-5 is acceptable. Organization of the data in summary form following field sampling allows for id review and assessment of individual orchard situations. Information gathered during the monitoring process aids in planning future pest management strategies.

Control Action Criteria: Control action criteria can be defined as specific pest population levels or threshold levels that signal impending economic damage to the crop or trees. Ideally, each threshold value considers the pest's life cycle, its potential for rapid population increases under existing or anticipated environmental conditions, orchard history, the type of damage likely to occur in proportion to control costs, other stresses the trees are experiencing and other relevant factors.

Progress has been made in establishing threshold values for citrus rust mite, the major economic pest of Valley citrus, but standardized criteria for other common pests are lacking. Suggestions in this text for key pests are based on guidelines developed in other citrus production states and observational data recently accumulated by local IPM programmes. Action criteria in any pest management programme are flexible and should be altered to fit individual management conditions.

Monitoring Guidelines: These guidelines provide information on how to monitor specific pests and offer insight on what constitutes reason for control action. Pre-season monitoring suggestions are provided to encourage early season inventory of pest populations and disease potential in advance of post-bloom control effects. Early monitoring provides information helpful in selecting the most appropriate and cost-effective pesticides. This early information may be useful in making volume purchases of pesticide materials and for determining which orchards merit immediate attention.

Citrus Mite Complex: Field studies of rust mite behaviour have indicated that populations in excess of 50 mites per square centimetre (cm^2) on fruit for 2 weeks or more are needed for rind damage to become visible. Also, rust mite populations on infested fruit may more than quadruple in a 2-week period under favourable conditions. These data support the need for a 2 week monitoring frequency for rust mite and are useful in establishing action thresholds.

As a general reference, a threshold value of 3 to 5 mites/cm^2, depending on optimal or suboptimal mite reproductive conditions, has been used successfully for several years in the local TAEX-IPM programme. Structured to allow the grower 2 weeks' lead time before significant damage Could occur, and provide a cushion for any sampling weakness, this threshold value applies to the following sampling regime:

- Sampling is from selected station trees, one tree per two acres.
- Six fruits sampled per station tree; two fruits on each of east, north and west quandrants, selected at random from partial shade areas.
- Mite counts taken from shaded side of fruit using a 14X hand lens, counting all live unites present in four separate lens fields per fruit.
- Each lens field is roughly 1/4 cm^2 in area, for a total of 1 cm^2 per fruit or 6 cm^2 sample per station tree.

To avoid rust mite management decisions being biased by two or three heavily infested fruits, consider the proportion of infested fruit. Also, consider mite distribution within trees or within orchards. Under this particular sampling regime, less than 20 percent incidence of infested fruit or of station trees would ameliorate average rust mite density values, and an incidence of more than 20 percent would substantiate or override them. The following criteria are utilized:

- Less than three mites/cm^2 and less than 20 percent of sample fruit with mites-no action necessary.
- Three to five mites/cm^2 and 20 percent of sample fruit with mites-borderline situation.
- More than five mites/cm^2 and more than 20 percent of sample fruit with mites-control should be initiated.

A sampling technique involving different action criteria has been used successfully by growers for several years. It involves random sampling of a single fruit per tree on 50 randomly selected trees within an orchard. Rust mite counts are expressed in numbers per cm^2. Action criteria vary according to irrigation schedules and weather outlook, but generally action is indicated when average mite density exceeds 20 mites/cm^2 and/or 25 percent of sample fruit are observed to be infested.

Factors to consider when making control decisions regarding rust mites include:

- Variety-given similar rust mite densities, oranges are downgraded less by mite damage than grapefruit.
- Lead time needed by producer to spray.
- Weather outlook and time of year-heaviest rainfall periods are May/June and August/September. Evaluate borderline mite densities during these periods in light of possible re-entry difficulties.
- Irrigation scheduling-orchards expected to need water within 10 to 14 days of an anticipated action threshold should be sprayed prior to irrigation.
- Miticide used in previous spray treatment-mite populations may rebound quickly following use of low residual materials.
- Orchard history-certain orchards, because of location, cultural practices, tree spacing or lack of uniformity in tree sizes and other reasons, consistently experience rapid re-infestation following control efforts.

Citrus red mites, first observed in 1980, are distributed throughout the Valley and have become a major citrus pest, particularly in the mid-Valley area between US 77 and US 281. Red mites feed on tender new leaves and populations increase with new growth flushes. Population levels decline during hot, dry July/August weather and resurge with the fall flush. Information about natural control agents in the Valley is not sufficient to determine when control action is most appropriate.

Control action guidelines for red mite on Texas citrus are incomplete pending further research on natural control agents and tree tolerance levels. Factors to consider in evaluating need for red mite control include:

- General tree vigore.
- Mite reproductive potential and environmental conditions.

Texas citrus mites do not require specific control action in most seasons if trees and fruit are protected from other mite and insect pests. Threshold levels vary according to tree vigour and should be determined by period during which heavy feeding is sustained rather than by specific mite numbers. Numbers exceeding 10 adult mites per leaf over a period of 30 days have been associated with winter defoliation of crown leaves.

Major considerations in Texas citrus mite management include:

- Tree vigour.
- Current and projected climatic conditions.
- Deleterious effect of fungicides applied for melanose or rust mite control on beneficial fungi.
- Effect of certain fall scalicide applications on over-wintering mite populations (azinphos-methyl and methidathion have been implicated with increased mite populations).
- Time of year-predisposition of mite-damaged leaves to defoliation by strong, dry winds greatest during fall/winter months.

False spider mites' increase in the past was associated with the use of organophosphate pesticides to control other pests and situations involving use of zineb alone for control of rust mite. With the present trend to use specific miticides such as dicofol, chlorobenzilate and fenbutatin-oxide, primarily for rust mite control, recent false spider mite problems have been associated with orchards where aldicarb soil treatment replaced post-bloom and late spring sprays. In aldicarb-treated orchards where the need for rust mite control may not arise until late summer, start monitoring for false spider mite in July and continue through September.

Armored Scales: California red scale is a major pest of citrus in the Rio Grande Valley. It attacks all parts of the tree aboveground and is a common cause of limb dieback and tree death in new trees. Populations usually are kept in check by natural enemies, but tend to reach damaging levels during abnormally dry seasons on trees adjacent to dusty roads. A small parasitic wasp, Aphytis lingnanensis, provides effective control in most seasons if not restricted by dust or by application of broadspectrum insecticides.

Begin monitoring for red scale in late spring to early summer to advantageously schedule a spray application during periods of high crawler activity or the early growth stages when scales are most susceptible to control. Orchards having a history of heavy red scale infestations the previous summer should be monitored early following warm winters. Monitoring always is required from July through October when colonization on fruit is easily seen and infestation levels are more easily determined.

To limit scale damage below tolerances set for federal grade standards, begin control action when 5 percent of the fruit examined have 10 or more live scales. Examine at least 10 outside fruits on both east and west quandrants of sample trees to calculate infestation levels. A hand lens will help distinguish live scale insects from dead or parasitized scales, which appear partially loosened from the peel or exhibit holes cut by adult parasites as they exited the scale body.

Estimates of scale parasites from leaf samples are less reliable than those based on fruit samples because of the difficulty in determining leaf age and when parasitism occurred.

Consider the following for monitoring and control of California red scale:

- Monitor new tree plantings frequently as they are subject to relatively rapid infestation.
- Inspect every young tree in the planting at least twice during summer and fall months.
- Natural control by scale parasites often is reduced during the heat of July and August.
- Increased incidence of spherical yellow crawlers encountered when searching fruit for rust mites signals impending infestations in bearing orchards.
- Oil sprays are least injurious of all scalicides to scale parasite populations.

Chaff scale is the most common widespread armored scale pest of Valley citrus. It attacks all aboveground parts of trees and can result in serious downgrading of fruit, but infestations rarely cause twig and limb dieback. Several species of parasites are known natural control agents.

Monitoring for chaff scale is suggested during pre-season and biweekly scouting for rust mite. Grade standards for fruit are important in deciding if summer or early fall scalicide application is warranted. Control action criteria are the same as described for California red scale.

Secondary Pests: Various minor citrus pests capable of causing economic damage under favourable circumstances require consideration during monitoring of major pests. Secondary pest eruptions usually result from loss of natural enemies through improper pesticide use, exposure to off-target pesticide drift or weather extremes. The two most common secondary pests are brown soft scale and citrus mealybug. Outbreaks of these pests occur most frequently and persistently near fields traditionally planted close to cotton and vegetable crops.

Brown soft scale infestations generally develop during the summer and fall months. Early signs of infestation are easily overlooked during monitoring activities until blackening of leaves by sooty mold fungi becomes noticeable. Tree vigour is diminished by feeding activities and inhibition of photosynthesis by sooty mold growing on the leaves. When localized infestations are found, spot treatment of trees on an "as needed" basis may be appropriate to reduce costs and prevent possible deleterious effects on natural enemies.

Citrus mealybug is controlled most effectively with pesticides during early stages before protective wax secretions and sooty mold form. Monitoring activities must be concerned with identification and quantitative assessment of first and second stage larvae. Mature mealybugs are highly resistant to contact pesticides. Clusters of fruit-usually the higher quality, inner canopy fruit-are preferred by mealybugs. Heavy infestations interfere with fruit development and may cause fruit drop. Sooty mold is difficult to remove at the packing shed, often resulting in downgrading of fruit.

Mealybugs have several predatory and parasitic natural enemies. Severe outbreaks in orchards not normally affected by mealybugs usually are the result of pesticide-related reductions or other unfavourable circumstances affecting natural enemies.

Whitefly infestations (citrus whitefly, citrus blackfly, cloudy-winged whitefly or woolly whitefly) occurring in isolated situations also can be associated with disruption of natural control agents.

Texas leafcutting ants can cause serious damage to citrus, particularly In young plantings, so monitoring notes on location and severity of infestations will facilitate control efforts. The leafcutting ant poses a special problem in well-drained sandy loam soils because it may nest some distance from the orchards Repeated defoliation of trees reduces tree vigour, eventually killing young trees. Locate the nest by tracking at dawn or dusk or during periods of cloudy weather because aboveground activity ceases during direct sunlight.

The information given herein is for educational purposes only. Reference to commercial products or trade names is made with the understanding that no discrimination is intended and no endorsement by the Cooperative Extension Service is implied.

Insect and Mites Pests

Mites: Description and Biology

Mites represent the single most economically important group of Texas citrus pests. The citrus rust mite together with the spider mite complex, including citrus red mite and Texas citrus mite, are responsible for a major portion of pest losses and require the bulk of pesticides used on citrus in Texas. Mites feed on fruit and foliage by piercing individual plant cells and sucking out the contents, thus, destroying the cell.

Their pest potential lies in their ability to develop rapidly and their tremendously great reproductive potential, allowing for enormous populations to develop in a short period of time.

Citrus Rust Mite

Eriophyidae: *Phyllocoptruta oleivora* (Ashmead)

The citrus rust mite (CRM) is considered the most important pest of Texas citrus. Rust mites are long, wedge-shaped and light yellow, measuring about 0.1 to 0.2 mm long, generally not visible to the unaided eye. The citrus rust mite feeds on the exposed surfaces of fruit, destroying the rind cells leading to the characteristic russeting of fruit.

This damage may result in reduced grade and size, thereby drastically reducing the marketability and value of the crop. Rust mites feed and develop year-round on citrus foliage and, when available, will develop on fruit. Rust mites may complete a generation in 7 to 10 days during the summer while development is drastically slowed or may halt during cool periods.

Early rust mite damage to fruit in late spring or early summer is evidenced by bronzing of the rind, a condition commonly called "buckskin" fruit. Severely affected fruits do not expand normally and frequently exhibit rind cracking. Damage occurring later in fruit development is evidenced by a darkening of the peel where heavy feeding took place, generally dark brown to black on green fruit and rust-brown on mature fruit. Similar symptoms of melanose disease on fruit, particularly grapefruit, may be confused with mite-induced russeting, but usually can be differentiated by noting peel texture and checking for presence of melanose pustules. Grapefruit generally are more susceptible than oranges to fruit damage by citrus rust mites.

High populations of CRM may reduce tree vigour. Affected leaves develop a dull green colour and show reduced turgidity. Rust mites pose a threat to the fruit crop from April to October, particularly during periods of warm, humid weather with frequent, light showers. If the latter conditions extend into early winter, fruit russeting may occur as late as December.

A reliable sign of impending rust mite damage to fruit is the dull, cloudy appearance of heavily infested fruit caused by thousands of mite skins cast off during the molting process. The distribution of citrus rust mites within trees varies during the year and is generally determined by environmental conditions.

Rust mites tend to seek out high humidity areas away from direct sunlight but also avoid areas where dew forms. Rust mites overwinter on foliage and in bark crevasses. On foliage, mites are most likely to be found on undersides of dry, inner canopy leaves. Mites appear to prefer fruit on the west or northwest quadrant of trees during May to June when cloudy conditions prevail. As summer temperatures increase, mites move inward and toward the north quadrant, away from the direct sunlight. After harvest during winter months, highest mite populations have been observed on east or northeast quadrants.

Texas Citrus Mite

Tetranychidae: *Eutetranychus banksi* **(Banks)**

Texas citrus mites (TCM) are 0.3 to 0.4 mm long and the eight-legged adults vary in colour from yellow to dark green, with characteristic dark internal food spots on each side down the back. Female mites are broadly oval and somewhat flattened. Males are more slender with longer legs and are triangular in shape. Larvae have six legs and are light yellow. Eggs are disc shaped and usually are laid near the midrib or branching veins. The life cycle can be very short under high temperatures, leading to very rapid population explosions. Unlike the citrus rust mite, the Texas citrus mite prefers low humidity conditions.

Most of the time, greater numbers are found on leaves on the south side of the tree, and in the top of the tree. They usually prefer to attack upper surfaces of leaves. Leaves damaged by TCM appear gray, show mesophyll collapse and may drop during periods of drying winds or when trees are stressed by lack of water or other factors.

Mites also appear on fruit but to a lesser degree than on leaves, and rarely cause noticeable feeding damage on fruit. Texas citrus mites usually are more prevalent in the May to July period, although they may increase rapidly at other times when conditions are favourable.

Citrus Red Mite

Tetranychidae: *Panonychus citri* **(McGregor)**

While the injury caused by citrus red mite is nearly the same as that caused by Texas Citrus mites, differences in appearance between the two mite species are obvious. Adult female red mites are oval, globular shaped and are characteristically red in colour.

Long red hairs attached to raised bumps are present on the surface of the body. Red mites are slightly larger than Texas citrus mites, about 0.3 to 0.5 mm in length. Males are smaller and more triangular than females. The red eggs are round and have a tiny vertical stalk projecting upward which is used to anchor the egg to the leaf.

Female red mites lay two to three eggs/day (20 to 50 eggs/female) along the midribs and petioles of leaves or on succulent twigs. Six-legged larvae range in colour from light green to red. The life cycle from egg to adult requires 8 to 12 days, depending on temperature, resulting in the potential for large population increases very rapidly. Citrus red mites prefer the upper leaf surface of mature leaves.

Trees may undergo sudden leaf death (firing) when citrus red mite populations build rapidly. Heavy mite populations under hot dry conditions may result in heavy leaf drop and twig die-back. However, no reduction in fruit quality in Texas has been documented. In general, grapefruit are more heavily attacked by citrus red mite than are oranges.

False Spider Mites

Tenuipalpidae: *Brevipaipus phoenicus* **(Geijskes)**

Tenuipalpidae: *Brevipalpus californicus* **(Banks)**

Adult mites are 0.2 to 0.3 mm long, flattened and slow-moving. The legs and edges of the body are whitish, while the body colour varies from red to deep purple. Population increases usually occur on leaves and fruit toward the inside of the tree before larger numbers are noticed on outside leaves and fruit. Population increases occur in June and build into the summer months.

Characteristic damage on fruit occurs from injection of toxins into rind cells, resulting in localized necrosis. This damage is known as leprosis. False spider mites more commonly become pests when phosphate pesticides are used for other pests.

Nutural Encmies of Mite Pests

In addition to climatic influences on mite populations, natural enemies play a role in regulating population levels. The fungus Hirrutella thompsonii occurs in Texas orchards and during periods of cool, moist weather may cause dramatic decreases in citrus rust mite numbers.

The mites are attacked and killed by the fungus, and dead infected mites serve as inoculum to further spread the disease. Spider mites (Texas citrus mite and citrus red mite) are not attacked by H. thompsonii but are attacked by other fungi. Population fluctuations resulting from disease cycles of H. thompsonii are often observed but are not dependable for rust mite control because they rely mostly on cool weather conditions.

Other natural enemies which feed on rust mites and spider mites include predaceous mites in the family Phytoseiidae, small beetles and other small insect predators. These organisms attack mites on foliage and fruit, but generally are not effective in keeping populations below damaging levels.

Citrus Mite Occurrence Profile

Pests	Jan	Feb	Mar	Apr	May	Jun	Jul	Aug	Sep	Oct	Nov	Dec
Citrus rust mite			*	x *	xx *	xx *	xx *	xx *	x *	*	*	*
Texas citrus mite			*	x *	xx *	xx *	xx *	x *	*	*	*	*
Citrus red mite			*	xx *	*	*	*	*	xx *	x *		
False spider mite				*	*	*	xx *	xx *	*	*		

* Period of normal occurrence

x Damage possible

xx Damage most likely

*Former Extension entomologist and assistant professor, citrus insects, Texas Agricultural Experiment Station, The Texas A&M University System.

Scales

B. Cartwright and H. W. Browning

Armored scales and soft scales are potential pests of Texas citrus. Both types extract plant fluids causing leaf discoloration and leaf drop, death of small twigs and failure of fruit to colour properly. Biological control has been highly effective for many species of scales.

Armored scales differ from soft scales in several ways. First, the "covering" of armored scales, which is made of body secretions, can be separated from the insect's body. Also, soft scales can secrete honeydew, whereas armored scales do not. The honeydew secreted by soft scales can support growth of black sooty mold, which can affect the photosynthetic ability of leaves.

Armored scales attach to a plant surface a few days after hatching, lose their legs and antennae and become stationary, although the males undergo a mobile (flying) stage.

In contrast, soft scales are not permanently attached to the tree and remain capable of movement throughout their lives. The table below compares a few identifying characteristics for the armored scales of Texas citrus.

Characteristics for Identifying the Common Armored Scales on Texas Citrus

Scale name	Mean length or diameter of scale covering (mm)	Scale covering		Scale body Color
		Shape	Color	
Chaff	1.5	Circular to elongated	Brownish to gray	Purple to off-white
California red	2.0	Circular	Red	Yellow
Florida red	2.0	Circular	Reddish brown	Yellow
Glover	2.3	Long and narrow	Purplish brown	White to purple
Purple	2.3	Oyster (broad & tapering	Purplish brown	White

California Red Scale

Diaspididae: *Aonidiella aurantii* (Maskell)

Adult females have a circular armored cover, light reddish in colour with a dark centre. Males have covers that are somewhat elongated. Females can give birth to two or three crawlers per day, averaging 100 to 150 during their lifetime. After birth, crawlers move about the tree canopy in search of a suitable location. As they begin feeding and developing, a cover forms from wax secretions and molted skins.

Several generations occur per year with each requiring approximately 60 days, depending on temperature. California red scales feed on fruit, leaves, twigs and branches with piercing-sucking mouthparts. Plant tissue is damaged as a result of plant fluid removal and injection of toxic substances. California red scales may cause yellowing of leaves, leaf abscission and overall decreased tree growth. Young trees may be killed as a result of California red scale feeding.

Chaff Scale

Diaspididae: *Parlatoria pergandii* (Comstock)

Chaff scales are the most widely distributed and abundant armored scales found on Texas citrus. This scale can cause serious problems to the fruit by virtue of its ability to prevent degreening of the peel surrounding the scale when natural colour change occurs, or when degreening is induced. The resultant green spots render the fruit unsuitable for fresh markets.

The armored covering of this insect is oblong or irregularly round and is usually brown to gray in colour. Scales are often located in depressions on fruit or along midribs on leaves. The females, eggs and crawlers are purple. Colour and shape of the covering help distinguishh this scale from others.

Purple Scale

Diaspididae: *Lepidosaphes beckii* (Newman)

The adult female's covering is brownish purple in colour, elongated and usually comma-shaped. The cover of the male is similar in colour to the female, but is much shorter and slenderer. The crawlers are very small, less than 0.25 mm, and are pearly white in colour. Three or more generations may occur each year.

Purple scales infest citrus leaves, fruit and bark, preferring shady or protected areas. Damage is similar to that caused by chaff scales: feeding results in chlorotic spots followed by leaf and fruit drop. After degreening, green spots may remain on the fruit where scales were present, resulting in fruit quality downgrading or rejection.

Glover Scale

Diaspididae: *Lepidosaphes gloveri* (Packard)

The Glover scale is a pest almost always found in association with purple scale on citrus foliage and fruit. Also known as "long scale," this insect has a dark scale covering that is long and narrow, and not curved in shape as is the purple scale. The rate of reproduction of Glover scale rarely builds up to damaging levels in Texas. Parasitic wasps are often found associated with the insect.

Florida Red Scale

Diaspididae: *Chrysomphalus aonidum* (L.)

The covering of the Florida red scale is dark brown or black with a conspicuous light brown nipple. The adult female's body is yellow. Crawlers are bright lemon-yellow, oval in shape and very active, being able to move quite a distance before attaching. The life cycle of the Florida red scale can be completed in less than six weeks under warm conditions. Four to six generations occur in Texas per year.

Florida red scales generally cause yellow chlorotic spots when attacking leaves. Yellow spots may also appear at the feeding sites on fruit. The scales appear to prefer fruit over leaves in the summer and fall; therefore, the fruit may be heavily infested while the adjacent leaves are relatively free of Florida red scale. Unlike other armored scales on citrus, Florida red scales restrict feeding to foliage and fruit but do not attack twigs or limbs of citrus trees. Large populations of this scale may result in severe defoliation and decreased fruit production. Scales present on the fruit will render it unmarketable as fresh fruit.

Brown Soft Scale

Coccidae: *Coccus hesperidum* (L.)

This pest is generally the most important soft scale in Texas citrus. Adults are brown to pale yellow, mottled, oval and 2.5 to 4 mm long. Brown soft scales attack leaves, twigs and occasionally, the fruit. They possess a high reproductive potential. Brown soft scales are primarily serious in young groves where trees may die as a result of feeding and from the presence of sooty mold developing from scale infestations. Sooty mold grows on the "honeydew" secretions produced by the scales, resulting in decreased photosynthesis in affected leaves. Problems with brown soft scales have occurred in conjunction with the drift of parathion from cotton onto citrus. During most years, increases in populations appear in May, but increases vary according to weather conditions, the degree of parasitization and predation by beneficial insects, and the effects of certain pesticides used in the grove or in adjacent crops.

Barnacle Scale

Coccidae: *Ceroplastes cirripediformis* (Comstock)

Barnacle scales are a minor problem in Texas citrus. The six plates on the sides and one on the top distinguish these dirty-white (mottled with brown) wax scales. Additionally, the adult height almost equals its width. These scale insects have been well-controlled by beneficial insects in past years. There is some indication that pesticide-induced population increases can occur with this pest.

Cottony Cushion Scale

Margarodidae: *Icerya purchasi (Maskell)*

Adults measure about 1.2 mm long and are recognized by the reddish plate in front of their white-fluted egg sacs. These scale insects congregate along the midrib of leaves and on twigs. The young have red to brown bodies with black legs and antennae. Heavy infestations can cause decreased vitality of the tree, thus reducing fruit production.

Pest Occurrence Profile

Pests	Jan	Feb	Mar	Apr	May	Jun	Jul	Aug	Sep	Oct	Nov	Dec
California				x	x	x	x	*	*	x		
Chaff Scale				x	x	x	x	*	*	x		
Purple Scale				x	x	x	x	*	*	x		
Glover Scale				x	x	x	x	*	*	x		
Florida Red Scale				x	x	x	x	*	*	x		
Barnacle Scale					x	x	x	*	*	*		
Brown Soft Scale				x	x	x	x	x	*	*	*	x

*Former Extension entomologist and former Experiment Station entomologist, The Texas A&M University System.

Mealybug and Whiteflies

B. Cartwrith and H. W. Browning*

Mealybug

Citrus Mealybug

Pseudococcidae: *Planococcus citri* (Risso)

The citrus mealybug has increased to damaging levels in some groves and these increases appear to be related to disruption of beneficials. Mealybugs are recognized by a distinctly segmented body that has lateral filaments covered with a white wax. They average 3 mm in length and tend to situate themselves on the bottom of fruit or on areas where adjacent fruit are in contact. Citrus mealybugs tend to prefer grapefruit over oranges. Large infestations cause fruit drop and reduced yields, but their greatest damage is caused by honeydew on fruit and leaves. Buildup of honeydew and associated sooty mold fungus leads to reduced fruit quality and lowered tree vitality.

Aleyrodidae: Whitefly adults are small insects averaging 1 to 3 mm in length with two pairs of mealy-white wings held in a roof-like position over the body. Whiteflies differ from scales in that both sexes are winged and motile as adults and they restrict their feeding to foliage. Population increases generally coincide with a new flush of foliage on trees. Whiteflies damage citrus by removing sap from leaves during feeding and by secreting large amounts of honeydew upon which black sooty mold grows. Photosynthesis can be substantially reduced in trees with extensive amounts of sooty mold. Several species of whiteflies occur in Texas citrus, including the citrus blackfly, the citrus whitefly, the woolly whitefly and the cloudy-winged whitefly.

Citrus Blackfly

Aleurocanthus woglumi (Ashby)

The citrus blackfly is a potentially serious citrus pest that has moved into the Rio Grande Valley from Mexico. The adults have slate-blue wings, red abdomens, reddish-brown eyes and average 1.3 to 1.6 mm in length. Females lay their eggs in a characteristic spiral pattern that provides an easy method of identifying this pest. Immature forms are dark black. The life cycle requires two to four months and the occurrence of various life stages usually overlaps considerably.

If not destroyed by unfavourable weather conditions or pesticides, parasites can effectively control the blackfly. A number of chemicals bring about control, but most are broad spectrum materials that must be used carefully to avoid upsets of other pests.

Citrus Whitefly

Dialeurodes citri (Ashmead)

The citrus whitefly lays smooth, shiny pale-yellow eggs. Eggs usually hatch in one to three weeks and the crawlers move about for several hours before settling. The larvae are oval, thin and translucent, which makes them difficult to see on green leaves. The nymphs require three to four weeks before pupating and another two to four weeks before emerging as adults. Pupae are similar to nymphs but are thicker and have distinct eyespots.

Adults live an average of two weeks during which time the female lays an average of 150 eggs. Citrus whiteflies have been observed to develop high populations during growth flush periods, but generally occur in low numbers.

Woolly Whitefly

Aleurothrixus floccosus (Maskell)

Adults are yellowish-white and seldom fly. Woolly whitefly eggs are laid in a circle on the underside of mature leaves, with the female at rest in the center. The eggs are brown and sausage-shaped. The first instars are light green; subsequent instars are brown. Pupae are covered with waxy white filaments, giving a woolly appearance. Copious amounts of honeydew often are associated with colonies of this species.

Cloudy-winged Whitefly

Dialeurodes citrifolii (Morgan)

Adult cloudy-winged whiteflies differ from other whiteflies by the darkened area in the middle of each wing, which gives the wings a cloudy appearance, and by the fact that the wings are held in a flatter position than those of the citrus whitefly. Fresh-laid eggs of the cloudy-winged whitefly are yellow, but soon turn black and have a network of ridges. Eggs are commonly laid on young leaves. Nymphs and pupae are very similar to those of the citrus whitefly. Populations of this whitefly are often mixed with the citrus whitefly within an orchard.

4

Miscellaneous Insect and Vertebrate Pests

Insects

Lepidopterous Pests (Caterpillars)

Orangedog

Papilionidae: *Papilio cresphontes* (Cramer)

This caterpillar owes its name to the fact that its head resembles the head of a dog. Mottled gray and brown in colour, a mature caterpillar may reach a length of 6 cm. Adults are swallowtail butterflies that do not feed on citrus. Feeding by larvae may result in fairly heavy defoliation in limited areas of groves, but rarely are infestations numerous enough to cause serious damage. Orangedogs are often quite numerous in citrus nurseries, where leaf feeding is very noticeable.

Puss Caterpillar Megalopygidae: *Megalopyge opercularis* (Smith)

These caterpillars, sometimes incorrectly referred to as "stinging asps," are covered with tan or gray soft hairs. Located among these hairs are specialized setae that produce venom capable of causing a stinging sensation upon contact. Some persons may react severely to this venom, thus the larvae should not be handled. Beyond their nuisance potential, larvae can cause limited amounts of defoliation through their feeding activity.

Aphids

Aphidae: Aphids are small, pear-shaped, soft-bodied insects usually found in colonies. Most aphids found in these colonies are wingless, but winged forms do occur and provide a means for their dispersal. Aphid infestations are usually found on new growth flushes. Aphids suck sap from leaves and stems, resulting in curled, distorted leaves which can retard tree growth and cause fruit and blossom shed. In addition, aphids produce large amounts of honeydew that promote growth of sooty mold, which may reduce photosynthesis. Aphids are also associated with the transmission of plant diseases. Low to moderate infestations of aphids can be considered beneficial to the citrus ecosystem by providing food early in the season for natural enemies, such as lacewings and ladybeetles.

Two aphid species, the spirea aphid (*Aphis citricola* (Van der Goot)) and the melon or cotton aphid (*Aphis gossypii* (Glover)), are the most common aphids on citrus in Texas. The black citrus aphid (*Toxoptera aurantii* (Fonscolombe)) may also be found occasionally.

Aphids reproduce asexually with females giving birth to young nymphs. Within a week of their birth, the females mature sexually and are themselves capable of producing offspring. This rapid rate of reproduction can result in large infestations developing in a very short time. Many generations per year can occur on citrus before the winged aphids migrate to their alternate hosts during the winter. Fortunately, natural mortality factors, especially predators and parasites, are usually highly effective in limiting aphid populations.

Planthoppers

Flattidae: The planthopper (*Metcalfa pruinosa* (Say)) is a grayish-white hopper approximately 3/8 inch long that occasionally develops localized outbreak populations in Texas citrus. The hopper completes only one generation per year, with adults surviving until September in most years. Immature hoppers hatch from overwintering eggs in March and feed on twigs, often in the vicinity of fruit. The cottony secretions and honeydew produced by this hopper resemble those of the citrus mealybug, but the insect is easily distinguishable by its active jumping behaviour when disturbed. Grapefruit trees appear to be favoured over oranges, but pesticidal control usually is not required. Parasitization by small wasps may be quite high in some years.

Mexican Fruit Fly

Tephritidae

Anastrepha ludens (Loew)

Adults are yellowish-brown flies with dark markings on the abdomen, and are about the size of a housefly. Females lay eggs in mature fruit; the larvae hatch within a few days and begin feeding in the pulp of fruit. Larvae are small yellowish-white maggots, averaging 6 to 9 mm in length. The mouth hooks that are used for feeding appear as a tiny black dot on the smaller end of larvae. After tunnelling in fruit, larvae emerge from the fruit and drop to the ground to pupate.

The entire life cycle requires as little as 20 to 30 days, depending on temperatures. Although grapefruit is a favoured host among the citrus crops, infestations have been confirmed on other hosts such as the mango, which allows year-round reproduction and survival. Although the Mexican fruit fly is a common pest in Mexico, the population is very low in Texas citrus. However, due to the hazard of introducing this pest to other uninfested citrus production areas via infested fruit, the Mexican fruit fly has become important from a regulatory point of view. In order to prevent the spread of Mexican fruit fly populations to uninfested regions, regulatory control efforts have been implemented.

Ants

Formicidae

Texas Leafcutting Ant Atta texana (Buckley)

The Texas leafcutting ant is the most serious ant pest of Texas citrus. Also known as the "town ant," "cut ant" or "parasol ant," the workers are reddish-brown and are about 3 to 5 mm long with a series of stout spines arising from behind the enlarged head and from the thorax region of the body. Worker ants remove leaves from the trees in order to culture a fungus for consumption by the ant colony. Over time, colonies may become enormous, excavating large areas of the orchard floor and creating problems for machinery operation. Such large colonies are also capable of removing a considerable amount of foliage. Multiple defoliation of young trees may slow tree growth or cause the tree to die.

Tropical Fire Ants

Solenopsis spp.

Tropical fire ants are generally considered minor pests of citrus. Workers are reddish-brown and are about 3 to 4 mm in length. Nests generally occur in areas least submerged or penetrated by irrigation. Nests appear as small mounds of fine soil usually no more than 3 to 4 inches in diameter and 2 to 4 inches tall. Damage occurs to young trees when ants damage bark beneath tree wraps and provide a point of entry for *Phytophthora* fungi. Damage to older trees is indirect; the ants harbour several sucking insect pests such as aphids and mealybugs, which are associated with honeydew production and sooty mold. Fire ants protect these pests against predators and parasites.

Vertebrate Pests

Vertebrate pests may cause sporadic or limited damage to citrus trees, fruit or equipment. On occasion, they can create serious problems for both individual growers and the industry as a whole. The major vertebrate pests experienced in Texas citrus include birds, jackrabbits, rodents and ground squirrels.

Grackles have become the primary bird pest responsible for serious crop losses during orchard recovery from the 1983 freeze. Grackle damage begins during summer months when birds begin pecking on young fruit. Injured peel tissue becomes blackened and develops a pock-marked surface cosmetically unacceptable for the fresh market. As the fruit approaches maturity later in the season, birds may penetrate into the pulp, thereby spoiling the fruit and causing it to drop.

Individual producer efforts to prevent grackle damage have met with only limited success. Birds rapidly become accustomed to conventional noise-generating devices. Pyrotechnic devices such as scare cartridges used in conjunction with noisemakers appear to have some value, but these require daily physical presence at each orchard site. Community-wide efforts to control birds by repellent action or by large-scale population reductions offer a more practical long-term solution to the problem, but are hindered under present migratory bird protection laws. Current information and assistance on grackle control, as well as control suggestions for other vertebrates, is available from local offices of the USDA Animal Damage Control Programme. Damage caused by jackrabbits is normally most severe on young trees during the first year after planting.

Tender bark above the bud union is chewed from the trunk in vertical strips. Trees may be killed or damaged to such an extent as to require replacement. Trunk wraps used to prevent sprouting and trunk damage effectively control jackrabbit damage. For best results, wraps should be installed at planting.

Rodent damage may occur on larger trees, particularly oranges, in the form of girdled limbs, stripping of bark and partially eaten fruit. The common roof rat is the most common offender. An identification aid for this pest is its tail, which characteristically is somewhat longer than both head and body combined. Most serious damage has been observed to occur in fall months in orchards adjacent to uncultivated habitat. Exposed low-volume irrigation lines are subject to damage by rodents seeking water. Clean cultivation of orchard perimeters and neighboring habitat is a good preventive measure. Otherwise, rats may be controlled by use of weather-resistant anticoagulant baits. Before attempting to use baits, examine trees for signs of recent damage and active nesting, because periods during which injury occurred may already have ended by the time damage is first observed.

Diseases

Fungal Diseases and Nematodes

Citrus diseases affecting the entire tree can be classified into two general categories: parasitic and nonparasitic. Parasitic diseases are caused by fungi, bacteria, viruses and nematodes. Some disease-causing agents are restricted to certain parts of the plant, such as the root, trunk or fruit, while others may affect several or all parts of the plant. Nonparasitic diseases are physiological disorders caused by excesses or deficiencies of certain nutrients or by unfavourable environmental conditions.

Among the most common nonparasitic diseases of citrus occurring in Texas are iron chlorosis, mottle leaf, salt and chronic water table injury. In addition to the economic losses that can result if not avoided or corrected, these physiological disorders often predispose the tree to attack by disease-causing organisms, such as the relationship that exists between salt and chronic water table injury and the increased occurrence of several types of gummosis, twig blight, tip-burned yellow leaves and nematode infestations. Physiological disorders are discussed in other sections of this publication.

Fungus Diseases

Cotton Root Rot: This disease, caused by the fungus *Phymatotrichum omnivorum*, affects many plant species. The fungus attacks the underground parts of the citrus tree and occasionally kills young trees. Once trees reach maturity, they are less susceptible to attack. Cotton root rot commonly causes sudden death of susceptible trees, with most of the dried leaves temporarily retained on the tree. The best protection against cotton root rot is to use resistant rootstocks such as sour orange.

Rio Grande Gummosis: This is one of several well-known gumming diseases of citrus. Gum formation on the trunk or branches is a characteristic symptom. Gum exudes from blisters containing gum pockets, usually located on the trunk. The wood beneath the blister shows a pink-orange colour.

Several factors such as freeze damage, high water table and salt accumulation contribute to the disease. Gummosis is believed to be a condition of weak and injured trees and is reported to be infectious. Symptoms of the disease were reproduced when healthy trees were inoculated with the fungus *Diplodia natalenris*.

No reliable cure exists for gummosis. Keeping trees vigorously growing is the best way to avoid the problem.

Phytophthora Foot Rot

Foot rot, also known as brown rot gummosis, is caused by one or more species of the fungus *Phytophthora*. This disease can affect the root system, the trunk below and above ground, branches, leaves, blossoms and fruit. It is especially troublesome during prolonged rainy periods. Trees with the bud union beneath or close to the soil and trees in poorly-drained locations are highly susceptible. Foot rot is commonly found in Lower Rio Grande Valley orchards, but becomes a more serious problem under unusual conditions such as those that occur following hurricanes.

Infection of the lower areas of the trunk by *Phytophthora spp.* results in dark, water-soaked areas in the active areas of infection. Often gum exudes profusely from active lesions. The dead bark frequently breaks away from the wood in vertical strips. Callus tissue begins to form on the margin of the surrounding healthy bark if the fungus becomes inactive because of unfavourable weather conditions. The disease may become active again when conditions become favourable. If the lesion encircles the trunk, griddling occurs and results in death of the tree.

Healing is slower if infection occurs below ground level. The fungus may attack young feeder roots, causing them to decay. Infection of lateral and fibrous roots can become widespread in wet soils. This infection results in poor health of the tree, a thin canopy, failure to make new growth and poor fruit production.

Phytophthora spp. also may attack nursery stock and young orchard trees during rainy weather. Examination of the crowns of infected trees shows symptoms similar to those described for older trees.

Phytophthora foot rot can best be controlled by preventative practices, including use of resistant rootstock and planting in well-drained land. Sour orange is the most resistant rootstock for the Lower Rio Grande Valley. Other resistant rootstocks include Swingle citrumelo and Troyer and Carrizo citrange.

Budding seedlings high, avoiding wounds, and keeping soil off the lower trunk are among recommended control practices. Soil fumigation of seedbeds should be practised in field nurseries.

Nematodes: Plant parasitic nematodes are very small worms that cannot be seen with the naked eye. Several plant parasitic nematodes are known to attack the root system of citrus plants, especially the citrus nematode, *Tylenchulus semipenetrans.* The burrowing nematode, *Radopholus similis*, causes a disease known as spreading decline and is a serious pest of citrus in other production areas. This nematode has been found in the Valley on ornamentals, but not in citrus orchards. Serious losses to the Texas industry could result should it ever become established in citrus groves.

The citrus nematode occurs commonly in Valley citrus orchard soils. Sour orange is rated as highly susceptible to nematode infection. Of the common rootstocks with potential use in the Valley, only Swingle citrumelo is rated as highly tolerant to the citrus nematode.

Populations of the citrus nematode usually are higher in older orchards (6 years and older). Young trees also may be injured if planted in orchard sites where nematodes previously prevailed. Other plant parasitic nematodes, mainly the lesion nematode (*Pratylenchus spp.*) often have been found associated with citrus roots.

Because the presence of the citrus nematode cannot be detected visually, positive diagnosis is based on external symptoms and laboratory examination of root and soil samples. Above-ground symptoms associated with nematode-infected trees are wilting, lack of vigour, poor fruit production and poor response to watering and fertilization. Texas Cooperative Extension operates a Plant Nematode Detection Laboratory at College Station where samples can be sent for analysis and recommendations. County Extension agricultural agents can assist growers in collecting and sending samples.

Losses caused by the citrus nematode in heavily infected orchards can be reduced effectively by applying nematicides to the soil. Before treating an orchard, however, consider the overall condition of the orchard. Application of nematicides to freeze-damaged orchards grown under poor cultural conditions may not be profitable. Soil should be sampled before establishing a new orchard to determine if nematodes are present in damaging numbers. If the analysis reveals large numbers of parasitic nematodes, treating the soil before establishing trees may be profitable. Ideally, nematodefree plants should be used when establishing new orchards.

At present, products cleared for use on established citrus trees are also known to have an effect on mites and other insects. Careful attention must be paid to instructions on the label, not only for directions on how to apply the material, but also for current rates and regulations that may affect the legal use of these products.

Four virus diseases which occur on citrus in the Lower Rio Grande Valley are exocortis, xyloporosis, tristeza and psorosis. The first three cause rootstock diseases, but psorosis causes bark shelling on the trunk and branches of trees older than 8 to 10 years. These four viruses are bud-transmissible. Certain aphids also are responsible for spread of tristeza virus. Damage caused by virus diseases varies with rootstock-scion combination. Some viruses result in only a slight reduction in growth rate. Others result in yield loss, severe stunting, decline and eventual death.

Because citrus viruses can be transmitted by budding, careful selection of budwood is an effective control method. Tolerant rootstock-scion combinations should be used if virus-free trees are not used. Citrus trees that have been certified to be tristeza-and psorosis-free by the Texas Department of Agriculture should be used as sources of budwood.

Exocortis: This virus causes bark-shelling and stunting of trees on trifoliate orange, trifoliate hybrids and Rangpur lime rootstocks. In the early stages of the disease, gum exudes from pustules at the base of the trunk and may extend from below the soil line to the bud union. New bark forms beneath the pustules, and the outer bark sloughs off, forming the characteristic bark-shelling. The rate of tree decline varies with tolerance to the exocortis virus. Some affected trees live for quite a number of years, while others die within the first 2 or 3 years.

Sour orange and Cleopatra mandarin rootstocks are tolerant to exocortis. Because most of the Valley's citrus is budded on sour orange, exocortis is seldom seen in Texas. Troyer and Carrizo citrange and Swindle citrumelo are rated as moderately resistant. As long as sour orange remains the dominant rootstock in Valley orchards, exocortis should not be a major threat.

Psorosis: Psorosis, also known as scaly bark, has been the most serious virus disease of mature citrus trees in Texas. It spreads chiefly by budding nursery stock with budwood from infected trees. Certain strains of psorosis, however, are capable of being transmitted through seed. Sweet orange, grapefruit and tangerines are severely affected. Most rootstocks used in the Valley are susceptible to the virus; thus, the incidence of psorosis historically has been high.

Several known strains of the psorosis virus have common leaf symptoms but different trunk and branch symptoms. Leaf symptoms are used to identify psorosis-infected nursery stock on young trees. This method of detection has been used effectively in selecting psorosis-free parent trees for budwood. Bark scaling of the trunk and larger branches is typical of psorosis symptoms in citrus trees 8 to 12 years or older. The earliest bark symptom is scaling. As the disease progresses, the tree declines rapidly and eventually becomes unproductive.

Psorosis no longer is a major problem in the Valley because most of the infected trees were removed after the 1951 freeze and replaced with psorosis-free trees obtained through the virus-free bud certification programme.

Tristeza: This virus has caused serious losses in the citrus-producing areas of South America, South Africa, Australia, California and Florida, but not appreciably in Texas. Because of its severity on the highly susceptible and commonly used sour orange rootstock, it has the potential of being the most devastating disease of Valley citrus. Infected trees found in Texas have been traced to introductions and propagation of infected Meyer lemons and sutsuma mandarin. The black citrus aphid, the most important vector, has not been found in the Valley.

Sour orange and limes, among other rootstocks, are highly susceptible to tristeza. Swingle citrumelo and Troyer and Carrizo citrange are rated resistant. Rough lemon, mandarin, trifoliate orange and its hybrids generally are tolerant to the virus. Because of the danger of tristeza becoming established in Texas, the new citrus rootstocks are commonly investigated in an attempt to find a tolerant rootstock adapted to Valley conditions.

Symptoms of tristeza-infected trees are similar to those resulting from root injury, including retardation of growth, thinning of foliage, twig dieback and tree collapse under severe conditions. The inside of the bark of tristeza-infected trees shows a honeycomb appearance that can be seen with the naked eye and is used by many as a diagnostic symptom for the disease.

In Texas, where the disease has been found with no evidence of insect transmission, no control measure is needed as long as growers plant tristeza-free trees.

Xyloporosis: Xyloporosis affects many old-line commercial citrus varieties in the Lower Rio Grande Valley. Sour orange, the most common rootstock, is tolerant to the virus. No external symptoms are observed when sweet orange and grapefruit are infected. Orlando tangelo is highly susceptible.

Symptoms of xyloporosis resemble those of other virus diseases. The main symptoms are wood-pitting, bark-scaling and the filling of infected tissue with gum, particularly near the bud union. The pittings can be so numerous that infected tissue resembles a sieve. The bark is at first discolored, splitting later as the disease progresses. Infected trees are stunted and production is greatly reduced.

Infected varieties growing on tolerant rootstock are not affected by the virus. As long as sour orange remains the principal rootstock, xyloporosis is not expected to be a problem in Valley orchards.

Twig Dieback: Twig dieback can be caused by fungi, although non-pathogenic factors probably play a more important role. As a result, fungal infection is often secondary, following freeze damage or damage resulting from mechanical or chemical injury. Other factors that can damage twigs are excessive fertilization, moisture stress and damage to the root system by cultural practices or heavy nematode damage. Affected young branches die back 1 inch or more from the tip, sometimes showing gum exudation. Damage by twig dieback usually is not severe.

Melanose: Melanose, caused by the fungus *Diaporthe citri (Phomopsis citri)*, is a twig, leaf and fruit disease of economic importance in the eastern and central parts of the Valley where humidity is high. The disease attacks all commercial varieties of citrus, but grapefruit appears to be more susceptible than oranges. The fungus attacks young, tender twigs, leaves and fruit, especially during periods of high humidity. Mature, hardened tissue usually is resistant to infection. Melanose symptoms on leaves first appear as small, circular, dark depressions with a yellow margin. Later, the spots become raised and turn dark brown.

Leaves turn yellow and may drop prematurely. Spots begin on twigs as on leaves, but become more raised than on leaves. In severe cases, twigs may die. Melanose spots on the fruit are at first small, light brown and sunken. Later they become dark and raised. When several spots are close together, the surface feels rough.

This roughness was cause for the name "sandpaper" melanose. Spots sometimes develop into a tear-streaked pattern, resulting from infection caused by spores washed down over the fruit surface by water drops during heavy dews or light rains. In other cases, large areas of fruit surface crack in more or less irregular patterns, resulting in "mudcake" melanose.

Abundant sporulation takes place in infected or dead tissue during periods of high humidity. Melanose usually is worse in years following a freeze because there are numerous dead twigs where the fungus sporulates freely. Disease incidence and severity usually are most serious in the north and northwest quadrants of trees. Prevailing drying winds from the southeast and the morning sun result in prolonged wetness in the opposite side of the trees, allowing more time for the infection process. Severe outbreaks of melanose can be traced to rainy periods occurring in the spring after spores have developed and while tissues remain susceptible. However, there is evidence that melanose infection can occur late in the season, even after fruit is more than 2 inches in diameter, provided that rain and cooler than normal weather prevails during summer and fall months.

Melanose usually is controlled in the Lower Rio Grande Valley by a single application of a fungicide after bloom or petal fall and before the fruit averages 1/2 inch in diameter. Under adverse conditions, such as those mentioned above, more than one application may be necessary.

Greasy Spot: Greasy spot is a leaf disease caused by the fungus *Mycosphaerella horii*, a weak parasite. The spots appear yellow initially, then turn dark and appear slightly raised and greasy. With severe infection, leaves may turn yellow and drop prematurely. The fungus responsible for greasy spots also can cause rind blemishes on some varieties. These blemishes usually are small. However, on grapefruit the spots are large and sometimes coalesce, resulting in a condition commonly known as greasy spot rind blotch and also pink pitting. Rust mite injury and humid weather predispose Most varieties to fungal infection, although there is controversy as to whether rust mite infection can be correlated to higher incidences of greasy spot. A combination of long periods of high humidity (in excess of 90 percent) and high temperature following heavy infestation of rust mites usually results in infection by the greasy spot fungus. The disease, however, will not become evident until several months after infection.

Control is possible by spraying in the summer with neutral copper or oil.

Sooty Mold: This is not a true disease because the several fungi associated with it do not feed on the tissues of citrus trees. Rather, the fungi feed on rich honeydew excreted by insects such as aphids, brown soft scale and whiteflies. The amount of sooty mold is directly proportional to the number of honeydew-excreting insects present. A heavy sooty mold coating on the fruit can result in fruit downgrading and economic loss to the grower. Heavy leaf coating can retard growth by interfering with photosynthesis and other physiological functions of the leaf. Light fruit set and reduced yields often result. Control measures are directed at insects which secrete honeydew, thus, preventing the development of sooty mold fungi.

Scab: Scab, caused by the fungus *Elsinoe fawcetti,* is a disease of minor importance in Texas. The disease is more severe on lemons, somewhat troublesome on grapefruit, and seldom a problem on sweet orange. Sour orange is highly susceptible, thus, nursery stocks may become infected before young sour orange trees are budded.

Because citrus tissue is susceptible to scab only while young, the disease is mainly confined to new growth. The fruit remains susceptible for longer periods, but seldom is mature fruit affected.

Small lesions appear as translucent dots that later become pustules. As the disease progresses, the pustules turn into warts, consisting of a mass of corky tissue pale tan in colour. The leaves become twisted and distorted and the entire young branch may be affected.

Applications of fungicide may be justified in nurseries if scab becomes a problem. The disease is not a problem in commercial orchards in Texas.

Mesophyll Collapse: Mesophyll collapse is a non-pathogenic disorder of citrus of unknown cause. Leaves of both oranges and grapefruit are affected. The disorder begins as translucent, irregular areas of different sizes scattered throughout the leaf blade. One or more light green spots may appear, later turning brown as cells within the tissue die. Only the soft tissue inside the leaf between the veins (mesophyll) collapses at first, giving these areas the translucent appearance. Palisade and epidermal tissues are unaffected initially but may die later.

Symptoms appear readily following periods of low soil moisture and hot dry winds. For this reason, water deficiency is often thought to cause mesophyll collapse, but mite feeding, damaged root systems and excessive transpiration also are associated with mesophyll collapse. Nutritional imbalances also are implicated in mesophyll collapse of citrus.

Citrus Canker: Citrus canker is considered the most important bacterial disease of citrus worldwide, but is not found in the Lower Rio Grande Valley of Texas. The disease became established in the Valley earlier but was eradicated after several years.

This disease, caused by the bacterium *Xanthomonas campestris* pathovar *citri*, is highly contagious. It is transmitted easily by infected nursery stock, budwood, leaves, twigs and fruit and even by wind-driven rain, insects, animals, people and contaminated equipment. The disease can be found in leaves, twigs and fruit of almost any citrus cultivar, causing serious damage to the fruit as well as defoliation and general decline of trees.

There are several races or strains of the causal agent. These races or strains have varying effects on the many cultivars of citrus. Environmental conditions in an area may prevent some of these strains or races from becoming established, or from causing serious damage to trees or fruit.

If any form of citrus canker were to be found again anywhere in Texas, its immediate and most damaging effect on the citrus industry would be the almost certain imposition of quarantines against the sale of Texas citrus fruit. These quarantine-related regulations would remain in effect until the disease was eradicated or until sufficient evidence was accumulated that its spread poses no threat to other areas.

In either case, the marketing of Texas citrus would be seriously impaired for quite some time. Because the disease presently is found in Florida, Mexico, several countries in South America, Japan, South Africa and countries in Asia, the introduction of citrus canker into Texas remains a possibility. For this reason, all efforts must be made to prevent the disease from reappearing in Texas.

Lesions appear on leaves as small, round, blister-like eruptions, having a whitish colour at first, but turning to tan or brown with age. A yellow halo commonly surrounds older lesions. As the lesion progresses, a water-soaked, oily area develops around the lesion. Lesions on the twigs are similar to those on leaves, but the areas affected are bigger. Raised, tan, necrotic tissue commonly is surrounded by oily, water-soaked margins.

The most conspicuous symptoms are on the fruit. Although early infection results in symptoms similar to those found on leaves, blister or crater-type symptoms are more pronounced. Infection usually is confined to the surface of the fruit. Other disease-causing organisms may become established, causing severe fruit drop.

The most effective control practice for citrus canker is to prevent its introduction into an area known to be free of the disease. Quarantines have been effective in keeping canker out of certain areas. The outbreak of the disease in previously disease-free areas can usually be traced to the introduction of diseased plant material or contaminated equipment from other places. If the disease gains entrance into an area and is detected, its eradication must be attempted by all available means. Failing to do so, other expensive and somewhat ineffective practices must be used, such as developing resistant varieties, using fungicidal sprays, taking advantage of certain cultural practices and using strict phytosanitary practices.

Diseases Affecting the Fruit

Diseases that primarily affect citrus fruit are usually of most concern to handlers and shippers. Many, however, begin in the orchard and can be reduced if proper measures are taken. These measures include avoiding picking fruit while it is wet from rain or dew and using lined boxes and trailers to minimize damage to the surface of the fruit.

Small lesions may be caused by fingernails, sharp objects and minor bruises. These openings on the surface of the fruit, although unseen, make it possible for microorganisms to gain entrance into the fruit. Sanitation in the field and packing house also is of the utmost importance. Infection can be decreased by preventing fruit from coming in contact with the soil and keeping harvest bags, field boxes, trailers and trucks' clean of debris. Most post-harvest diseases can be avoided if management and personnel are aware of the importance of keeping the fruit free of damage and contamination.

Many post-harvest diseases occur on citrus. Only a few of the most common diseases are discussed in this publication.

Melanose: Of all citrus fruits, grapefruit is affected the most by melanose. Control of this disease plays an important role in the Valley, particularly in the production of gift fruit, because the disease greatly affects the appearance of the fruit. Small, brown, raised spots are found on the fruit. Usually, numerous spots coalesce into a big area, resulting in the phase of the disease known as "mudcake melanose." At other times, "tearstains" are found on the fruit as the result of spores being washed down in water from dew or rain. Infection and disease development occur only in the orchard when the fruit is small. Therefore, no spread or contamination of other fruit occurs during processing and storage.

Greasy Spot: Although this disease is primarily a problem on leaves, the fungus also can infect the fruit. Infection occurs on cells surrounding pores, causing the fruit to become spotted or stippled. Areas surrounding these spots do not colour properly because the cholorphyll present in the cells fails to disappear. If the spots are numerous, the fruit becomes unsightly, resulting in downgrading.

Flyspeck: The disease derives its name from the small black specks formed on the rind in areas immediately surrounding the oil glands. The fungus that causes this disease prevents infected spots from attaining the typical yellow colour of mature citrus fruit. The contrast between green and yellow colour lowers fruit grade, even though there is no effect on fruit or juice quality. Thus, it is of little consequence to fruit used for processing.

No effective economic programme has been developed for the control of flyspeck. Tests with fungicide sprays in the summer have increased the percentage of clean fruit in some cases.

Brown Rot: This fruit disease is caused by the same species of *Phytophthora* that causes foot rot. The fungus can attack fruit on the tree during periods of excessive rains or during irrigation. Infection by the fungus results in decayed areas that are brown, firm and leathery. At first, the fungus cannot be observed on the fruit.

Later, a white velvety growth appears on the surface of the fruit, accompanied by a strong fermenting odor. Because the fungus is commonly found in the soil, fruit low on trees often is infected by rain-splashed soil. Winds can spread the actively growing fungus to fruit in the upper tree. The fruit must be wet for some time before infection by the brown rot fungus occurs.

The best control for brown rot is sanitation during transit and in the packinghouse. Disinfecting the boxes is important; treatment with disinfectant solutions and refrigeration are effective for prevention.

Chemical Damage: Many chemicals are used in the production of citrus in South Texas. Herbicides, fungicides, insecticides and acaricides are needed to guarantee maximum production of marketable fruit. Although the proper application of these products will not result in damage to tree or fruit, sometimes mixing several products or applying these under certain atmospheric conditions will result in spotting, pitting or other damage to leaves and fruit. Because of the intensive agriculture practised in the Valley, orchards often are located next to fields where other crops are grown. As a result, products that can be harmful to citrus, such as a cotton defoliant, sometimes are applied in close proximity. Care is needed in applying these products in the proper concentrations and avoiding weather conditions that could result in damage.

Pest and Disease Control

Using a pesticide wisely requires forethought and analysis of a particular pest problem or situation to determine the best choice under those particular conditions. Often, more than one choice exists for a particular pest. Factors that should be considered in selecting one pesticide over another include:

- *Product efficacy* or effectiveness;
- *Application frequency* needed or amount of residual control provided;
- *Cost* per acre, factoring in the number of applications required to achieve control;
- *Potential hazards* to applicator, mixer and grove workers; signal words on the product label are a good indication of this hazard;
- *Hazard to beneficials* and other non-target organisms and
- *Use restriction*, including re-entry intervals, preharvest intervals, number of allowable applications, time required between applications and restriction on mixing with other products, particularly oils.

Use of the information contained in the guide. This publication is designed to provide, to the best extent possible, a listing of the insecticides and miticides available for use against selected citrus crop pests. It is written for comparison and educational purposes only and is not intended to provide complete information for applications of a product.

The product label attached to the container always must be consulted before use. The pesticide listing for control of citrus pests was compiled from the most recent product labels available at the time this guide was prepared. No guarantee of effectiveness is intended by listing a particular product for use against a particular pest; only that the pest is listed on the label for the product.

For selected pests, where a sufficient research base exists, an efficacy rating (ER) is provided to give a performance index of various prove products for controlling a particular pest. Ratings are based on field tests conducted in Texas and other citrus growing areas. Local conditions and pest pressure may cause actual performance to vary.

Effects of pH on Spray Solutions

Water sources used for pesticide applications in the Lower Rio Grande Valley are alkaline with pH readings typically ranging from 7.8 to 8.2. Use of high pH water, particularly above 8.0, may affect the performance of many pesticides, particularly organophosphates and carbamates. Degradation of certain pesticides is more rapid at higher pH, especially at higher temperatures (>95°F). Little information is available on the degradation rate of specific pesticides in high pH water; some pesticides are relatively unaffected. Generally, it is a good idea to check pH levels with a pH meter on a regular basis and buffer spray water with suitable acid buffer down to a range of 6-7 pH. When tank mixes of more than one pesticide or when fertilizer is combined with a pesticide, the final sprav solution should be checked to determine pH.

Use of Spray Adjuvants

Adjuvants or spray additives are intended to enhance product performance or coverage. Surfactants or spreading agents lower the spray particle surface tension allowing droplets to spread out on plant surfaces instead of combining to form large droplets subject to run-off. They are especially useful when spraying hard-to-wet surfaces such as waxy citrus leaves, armored scale insects, mite colonies with webbing or hairy-surfaced weeds. Some pesticide products are formulated with surfactant included.

Stickers and extenders function to lengthen pesticide performance life by increasing product tenacity or weathering qualities of materials sprayed on plant surfaces. These frequently are combined with surfactants and are available as "spreader-stickers." Other adjuvants available for special applications include anti-foam agents and suspending agents that improve performance and enhance application of pesticide suspensions. In general, adjuvants properly used increase product performance, reduce waste and help minimize non-target contamination.

Pesticide Safety

The key to using pesticides safely is to be aware of potential hazards and take adequate precautions before and during use to prevent any unwanted effects. Before using any pesticide, read the label. Besides application instructions, the label provides information on re-entry intervals, hazards to the environment and non-target organisms, a statement of practical treatment or first-aid in case of exposure, storage and disposal procedures for containers, pre-harvest intervals to avoid excessive residues and the symptoms of poisoning. Users also should consult *Texas Pesticide Laws and Regulations* for state provisions that affect the application of pesticides to citrus.

Protecting Bees from Pesticides

With the exception of some tangerines and tangelos, most citrus cultivars do not require honeybee pollination. However, blooming citrus is highly attractive to honeybees as a food Source and may provide a good nectar source for a high quality honey sought by beekeepers. Although insecticides are not routinely applied during bloom, it is important to recognize that many pesticides applied to citrus are toxic to honeybees. The insecticides may cause significant bee death while they are foraging in sprayed orchards or through contamination of water or pollen brought back to the hive. The grower and beekeeper should cooperate closely to minimize bee losses. The following guidelines will reduce bee losses:

- If at all possible, avoid spraying during bloom. If applications are needed, apply when the fewest bees are foraging. Applications in the evening are least hazardous, early morning sprays are second best and mid-day sprays are the worst relative to bee hazards.
- To prevent heavy losses of bees, don't allow pesticides to drift onto colonies. Bees often cluster on the front of their hives on hot evenings. Pesticide drift or direct spray at this time generally results in high levels of mortality.
- Where insecticides are needed, consider their toxicity. "Highly toxic" pesticides present an extreme hazard to bees and should be used during bloom only if no other alternative exists. Insecticides categorized as "Moderately toxic" or "Relatively non-toxic" pose a much reduced hazard to bees and may be applied with relative safety in the evening or morning hours. For specific hazard ratings of pesticides to honeybees.

Precautions for Certain Miticides and Insecticides

Many pesticides have special precautions listed on the label that should be considered prior to their use. Failure to completely follow label guidelines may result in excessive residues at harvest, plant injury, poor pest control or undue hazards to non-target organisms including the applicator. The following are some of the major precautions for some of the most commonly used citrus pesticides:

Effectiveness of selected pesticides against major citrus pests

Pesticide	Formulated rate/acre	Days to harvest (PHI)	Re-entry interval (days)[3]	Signal word[1]	Honey-bee hazard[2]	Toxicity to beneficials[4]		Mites			Armored scales	Brown soft scale	Mealy bugs
						Mites	Insects	Citrus rust	Texas citrus	Citrus red			
Acaraben 4E	4-6 pt		ASTD	W	HT	-	-	3	1	1	N	N	N
Carzol 92 SP	5-10 oz	7	1	D	MT	-	H	3	0	N	+	+	N
Comite 6.5	2-3 pt	7	ASTD	D	RNT	-	L	1	2	3	N	N	N
Dicofol 4 EC	3-8 pt	7	ASTD	C	RNT	H	L	3	3	3	N	N	N
Ethion 4E	4-6 pt	0**	1	D	HT	-	-	3	0	2	1	1	N
Guthion 2L	2.5-3.75 pt	28**	7-SL	D	HT	-	H	1	2	N	3	3	2
Lorsban 4E	2-7 pt	21**	1	W	HT	-	-	2	0	0	2	3	0
Morestan 25 WP	5 lb	21	ASTD	C	RNT	M	L	2	3	3	N	N	N
Oil	2.5-3.75 gal		ASTD	C	RNT	M	M	0	0	3	3	0	0
Sevin 80S	2.5-3 lb*	5	ASTD	W	HT	L	H	N	+	N	+	3	0
Sulfur 6E	1-11 pt*		ASTD	C	RNT	H	L	2	0	N	+	N	N
Supracide 2E	2.5-5 pt*	14**	30	D	HT	H	H	N	N	+	3	3	1
Temik 15 G	33-67 lb		see label	D	HT	-	-	3	3	1	N	0	0
Vendex L	10-20 oz*	7	ASTD	D	RNT	L	L	3	3	3	N	N	N
Vydate L	.625-2.5 pts*	7	ASTD	D	HT	-	-	3	N	N	N	N	N

*Amount per acre derived by multiplying amount per 100 gal x 2.5; 250 gallons per acre is the assumed volume.

**PHI depends on rate, method of application, the number of applications or particular citrus crop; consult label.

[1]Signal words: D=danger (most hazardous), W=warning, C=caution (least hazardous).

[2]Honeybee hazard: HT=highly toxic, MT=moderately toxic, RNT=relatively non-toxic.

[3]Re-entry intervals: ASTD=allow spray to dry.

[4]Hazard to beneficials: H=highly toxic, M=moderately toxic, L=low level or nontoxic to beneficials, -=no information available.

Petroleum Oil Sprays: When applied properly, oils provide a very useful tool for controlling some citrus pests without damage to beneficial organisms but the sprays require careful use to avoid plant Injury. Soil moisture, humidity, temperatures, growth stage of leaves and fruit and the type of oil used can influence whether or not tree injury occurs.

Spray oils should not be applied when soil moisture is low or when relative humidity is below 30 percent and daytime temperatures are likely to exceed 95° F. Effective use of oils for pest control requires that the oil persist on the tree long enough to kill the pest but not long enough to cause tree injury. Persistence of oil film on foliage beyond the tree's tolerance can interfere with photosynthesis and transpiration. Such damage can result in twig dieback, leaf drop, reduced yield and the reduction in amount of fruit sugars (soluble solids).

Key to Efficacy Ratings

Rating	Control Expected
1	=Suppression (<60% control)
2	=Moderate control (60-80%)
3	=Good to excellent control (80-100%)
0	=Not labeled for this pest but provides some control when used for labeled pests
N	=Not labeled
-	=Unknown effect
+	=May stimulate this pest

Tangerines and tangelos tend to be more sensitive to oil damage than grapefruit and oranges. Late summer or fall applications of oil sprays i-nay delay maturity, which will interfere with proper colouring of early harvested fruit and may cause increased cold Susceptibility. Persistence of oils on leaf surfaces increases with higher oil dosages or through the use of oil with higher distillation temperatures such as a narrow range 44O-type oil. When choosing the type or rate of oils, keep in mind that oil dissipates more quickly under higher temperatures.

In situations where damage is likely from a regular oil spray because of hot, dry conditions, oil can be added at a low percentage to certain insecticide sprays to improve coverage. Before combining oil with any pesticide, read the label carefully to make sure the risk of phytotoxicity is not excessive. Do not combine oil sprays with sulfur or follow an application of sulfur within at least 30 days or plant injury may occur. When combining pesticides with oil, use of emulsifiable concentrates or other liquid formulations is preferred over wettable or soluble powders.

Comite: Complete coverage is essential. Leaf distortion and/or fruit spotting may occur when used in the spring or it may occur if Comite is tank mixed with oil or applied within 2 weeks of an oil application. Do not use in a spray solution above pH 10 or mix with alkaline materials (such as lime).

Ethion: Do not apply within 90 days of a previous application.

Guthion: With one application per season, a 7-day preharvest interval should be observed; if two applications are required, PHI = 28 days.

Lorsban 4E: Do not apply when temperatures exceed 95° F. Do not apply when trees are stressed by drought or high temperature. Lorsban 4E should not be used in combination with Difolatan 80. For orchard floor application, do not tank mix with Roundup or Paraquat herbicides.

Morestan: One application per season.

Sulfur: Do not make sulfur applications during hot weather. Applications are restricted to November through May. Do not apply within 30 days of an oil application.

Supracide: Make no more than two applications per growing season, with at least 45 days between applications. Do not apply within 14 days of harvest. If applied with oil, the preharvest interval is 60 days.

Vendex: Do not apply more than four times in 12 months or within 7 days of harvest.

Making Pest Management Suggestions: The information and suggestions included in this publication reflect the opinions of Extension entomologists and pathologists based on field tests or use experience. The management suggestions are a product of research and are believed to be reliable. However, it is impossible to eliminate all risks. Conditions or circumstances that are unforeseen or unexpected may result in less than satisfactory results even when these suggestions are used. Texas Cooperative Extension will not assume responsibility for such risks. Such responsibility shall be assumed by the user of this publication.

Suggested pesticides must be registered and labelled for use by the Environmental Protection and the Texas Department of Agriculture. The status of pesticide label clearances is subject to and may have changed since this publication was printed. County Extension agents and appropriate specialists are advised of changes as they occur.

The user is always responsible for the effects of pesticide residues on his livestock and crops, as well as problems that could arise from drift or movement of the pesticide from his property to that of others. Always read and follow carefully the instructions on the container label.

Additional products labelled for use on citrus

Product[2]	Labeled use	Rate per acre[1]	Signal word	Days to harvest
Cygon 400	Mealybugs, mites	4-8 pt	w	4
Cythion 57%	Scales	1-1.5 pt	w	7
Diazinon AG500	Aphids, soft scale	0.5-1 pt	w	21
Dibrom 8E	Aphids, mites, brown soft scale	2.5 pt*	D	7
Dipel 2X	Orangedog	0.3-0.6 lb	c	0
Imidan 50 WP (oranges only)	Scales	2.5 lb*	D	7
Lannate L	Beet armyworm	2-4 pt	D	1
Lorsban 15 G	Ants	6.7	c	28
Metasystox-R	Aphids, Texas citrus mite	2.5-3.75 pt*	c	7
Parathion 4E	Scales, mealybugs	1.6 pt*	D	14
Thiodan 3E	Aphids	1.5-3.5 qt	w	Non bearing
Zolone 3EC	Orangedog, whiteflies	4-8 pt	w	14

[1]* =Amount per acre derived by multiplying amount per 100 gallons x 2.5; 250 gallons per acre is the assumed volume.

[2]Phytotoxicity may occur on young leaves and fruit; see label for precautions.

The information herein is for educational purposes only. Reference to commercial products or trade names is made with the understanding that no discrimination is intended and no endorsement by the Cooperative Extension Service is implied.

*Former entomologist, Texas Agricultural Experiment Station, and former Extension entomologist, The Texas A&M University System.

Disease Management

If a plant pathogen is present in an orchard, the severity of the disease it causes will be determined by the level of infestation, by environmental conditions, and the susceptibility of the plant, which, in turn, is determined by its genetic characteristics. Good disease management requires a thorough knowledge of how these factors interact in the development of the disease; particularly, knowledge of environmental conditions that stress the plant, predisposing it to disease. This will help in preventing a disease problem. However, regular monitoring is needed to detect diseases as soon as they occur, before they become well established.

The chemicals listed here are registered for use on citrus. Since fungicide labels are often changed, check the actual label before use. Refer to the label for specific instructions for rates and timing of applications and other information.

Melanose: Decisions on the use of a fungicide for melanose control are best made pre-season or before bloom. Fungicide sprays are recommended for orchards where serious levels of disease usually occur. In other orchards, the potential for disease can be estimated based on the quantity of dead twigs in trees. If climatic conditions in the previous season resulted in a serious disease problem, the number and appearance of seriously affected fruit in the north or northwest quadrants of trees are good indicators for the need of fungicide applications. Factors to be considered before the application of fungicides for melanose control include:

- *Size of Fruit:* Grapefruits up to 3 1/4 inch and oranges up to 1 1/2 inch diameter are susceptible to melanose infection in the spring.

- *Amount of Dead Wood:* Chemical control efforts in heavily infected orchards may need to be combined with supplemental pruning to reduce the quantity of the pathogen. Orchards six years old or younger normally do not require treatment for melanose.
- *Orchard locations:* Traditionally, orchards in the eastern end of the Valley have required regular spraying because of higher humidity, which favours melanose development.

Timing for melanose control sprays should take precedence over rust mite control when disease potential is high. A single post-bloom spray application will not give acceptable melanose control except in dry seasons when little control is needed. Increased fruit growth requires a second fungicide application no later than 30 to 35 days following the post-bloom spray. Copper fungicide mixtures require thorough and constant agitation in the spray tank to maintain the ingredients in suspension. Field observations and demonstrations indicate that liquid formulations of copper fungicides generally are more effective than dry formulations at equivalent rates of application.

Chemical Controls for Melanose

Chemical	Formulation	Application guideline
copper ammonium complex	Copper Count N	Apply 1-3 weeks after bloom. Do not apply with oil.
copper resinate	Tenn-Cop 5E	apply 1-3 weeks after petal fall, and 4 weeks later as needed.
copper sulfate	Basicop WP CP Basic Copper TS TopCop Tribasic Cuproxat F	Apply 1-3 weeks after petal fall, then 4 weeks later. Apply pre-and post-bloom.
copper sulfate + sulfur	Top Cop with Sulfur Top Cop with Sulfur F	Apply 1-3 weeks after petal fall and then 4 weeks later.
cupric hydroxide	3 LB. Copper Flowable Champ F Champion WP Kocide	Apply pre- and post-bloom

Greasy Spot

Management decisions for greasy spot control should be made during winter months when the need for control is most apparent. Either citrus oils or copper fungicides can be applied during the summer for control. Benomyl was very effective under Valley conditions when greasy spot infection was severe. In orchards with a history of severe damage, oil, copper or benomyl sprays applied exclusively for greasy spot control may be economically feasible. Infection takes place on the lower leaf surface; therefore, thorough spray coverage is essential for effective control of greasy spot. Factors to be considered in the management of greasy spot include:

- Previous history of greasy spot occurrence in the orchard and the variety being grown.
- Levels of mites that may predispose leaves and fruit to damage by greasy spot.
- Rainy weather during late summer and early fall that may be favourable for disease development. Spores of the fungus are released following an irrigation or rainfall. High levels of spores occur from May to October.

Chemical Controls for Greasy Spot

Chemical	Formulation	Application guideline
benomyl	Benlate WP	One spray mid-June to July
copper ammonium	Copper Count N	Apply pre- and post-bloom and within 1 month after leaf expansion of any growth flush. Do not apply with oil.
copper sulfate	Basicop WP CP Basic Copper TS TopCop Tribasic Cuproxat F Copper FF	Apply post bloom and within one month after leaf expansion of any growth flush. Limit 60lb/acre. Apply during 2 months after spring flush expansion and within 1 month of other growth flushes. Apply pre- and post-bloom, 30-day interval, June-August. Summer spray in mid-July
cupric hydroxide	3 LB. Copper Flowable Champ F Champion WP Kocide	Apply pre-and post-bloom. Apply during 2 months of spring growth expansion.
propiconazole	Banner EC	For non-bearing use only in nursery and landscape. Do not use within 12 months of fruiting.

Foot Rot

Frequent monitoring for foot rot during periods following wet, rainy weather is needed to detect the disease early, before extensive trunk damage occurs. Gumming of bark is most noticeable under moist, cool conditions, while hot dry weather favours drying and apparent healing of affected areas.

Methods of prevention of foot rot remain important and must begin in the citrus nursery. Care should be taken in field planting to ensure that young trees are not transplanted to depths exceeding the original planted depth. All activities that might result in wounding of the trunk prior to anticipated rainfall or irrigation must be avoided.

For young trees wrapped for cold protection, activity by the southern fire ant inside the wrap increases the likelihood of infection. Wraps should be removed from trees exhibiting signs of ant activity to inspect for signs of bark damage and/or gumming. Pruning and sprout removal are best done only in dry weather. Cultural activities that result in occasional trunk injury, such as disking, tree hoeing or boom spray applications should be done at least 2 days in advance of irrigation.

Trunk lesions can be treated with metalaxyl or fosetyl-Al. Severely damaged or unproductive trees should be removed from the orchard. Factors to consider in the management of this disease are:

- Prevention is the most effective means of control. Infected trees are difficult to cure; fungicides may help in protecting young trees from infection.
- Location of trees in the orchard, ways in which trees are produced and previous history of disease occurrence in nurseries from which the trees were obtained are important in disease management.
- Plant trees with high bud unions at least 6 inches above the ground in locations that drain well, even after very heavy rains.

Chemical Controls for Foot Rot

Chemical	Formulation	Application guideline
cupric hydroxide	Kocide DF	Tree trunk paint for preventative use only. Apply prior to wrapping for freeze protection.
fosetyl-Al	Aliette	4 applications per year, limit of aluminum 20 lbs/acre/year. Do not apply within 30 days of harvest.
metalaxyl	Ridomil 5G Ridomil 2E Subdue G Subdue 2E	Soil application. Soil and trunk application. Soil application. Soil and trunk application.

Citrus Nematode

Symptoms of citrus nematode infection are difficult to diagnose visually. Poor drainage, excess salt, improper watering and damage caused by other soilborne organisms will affect the trees in much the same way as the citrus nematode. Consequently, the presence of the citrus nematode in soil and roots can best be determined by laboratory testing.

Proper sampling is important to obtain an accurate assessment of the problem. Collect soil samples at a time when soil moisture is neither excessive nor very low. The best period for sampling is during the second week following an irrigation or a rain. Collect samples under the drip line of the tree. After removing the debris, use a shovel to cut a slice of soil from the surface to about 8 to 10 inches deep from the four sides of a tree. Place soil and feeder roots in a clean plastic bucket and mix well with soil and roots from other trees. Then place a composite sample from these in a plastic bag and label for laboratory examination. One laboratory sample should represent at least five trees sampled at random diagonally from rows for every 5 acres.

Take care not to allow the plastic bags to be exposed to heat or direct sunlight, which will kill the heat-sensitive, juvenile nematodes and make laboratory analysis impossible. Have an insulated ice chest available for transporting the samples to a competent laboratory for analysis. Results of laboratory analysis are expressed in numbers of juvenile nematodes per 100 cubic centimeters (cc) of soil and 3 grams of roots. Counts will vary at different sampling times because of soil moisture, age of trees, soil types, other stresses on trees and management practices.

Citrus Nematode Counts Considered Low, Medium or High at Different Sampling Times During the Growing Season

	Number of juvenile nematodes in 100 cc of soil and 3 grams of feeder roots		
Sampling time	**Low population**	**Medium population**	**High population**
June to Sptember	100-200	400-600	750-5,000
October to January	200-500	1,000-3,000	5,000-10,000
February to May	500-1,500	3,000-6,000	10,000 +

Chemical control of nematodes on established trees is expensive and must be repeated annually for best results. Prevention by exclusion is a practical option when establishing a new orchard. Avoid old sites known to be infested, if possible. On new citrus soil, make every effort to plant trees free of nematodes (*i.e.*, grown in containers or in fumigated nursery soil). Factors to consider before applying nematicides include:

- What is potential orchard production with and without treatment?
- Will treatment result in increased yields, fruit grade or fruit size?
- Will treatment control other pests, such as mites?
- How will the treatment affect beneficial organisms in the orchard?
- Can soil incorporation, activation or other application requirements be satisfied under existing water limitations, soil and climatic conditions?
- What are re-entry limitations and restrictions on time required between treatment and harvest?

Chemical Controls for Nematodes

Chemical	Formulation	Application guideline
metam sodium	Vapam Soil Prep	Pre-plant only.
oxamyl*	Vydate L	Do not apply more than 4 qt/acre in any 30-day period, 7-day preharvest interval.
aldicarb*	Temik 15G	Apply just before or during spring flush of growth.
fenamiphos*	Nemacur 3 Nemacur 15G	Limit 3.33 gal/season. Limit 67 lbs/season.

*Restricted use-permit required.

The information given herein is for educational purposes only. Reference to commercial products or trade names is made with the understanding that no discrimination is intended and no endorsement by the Cooperative Extension Service is implied.

Weed Control

Weed control in citrus orchards is essential to the objectives of good orchard management because weeds compete for available water and nutrients. Vines can completely cover tree canopies, thereby limiting production efficiency of the tree and interfering with pest control. In addition, weed species can host various pests which also affect citrus crops. Methods of weed control include mechanical, herbicidal or limited combinations of the two.

Mechanical Control: Mechanical weed control operations, normally required following each irrigation and major rainfall, begin in February and continue into November. Machinery includes disks, tree hoes (rotovators), flying saucers and shredders. The first three can easily cause damage to tree trunks and skirts as well as surface roots, even when used by skilled operators.

The shredder only keeps weed growth in check. Permanent borders cannot be maintained, so temporary irrigation borders must be knocked down before tillage and replaced for the next irrigation, thereby increasing costs.

At best, weeds are allowed to grow and compete with the orchard before mechanical control methods are employed. Any delay in cultivation or shredding allows weeds to go to seed, thus perpetuating the problem of control. Tillage operations move buried weed seeds to the surface where they can germinate, and tillage may actually spread infestations of perennial weeds such as bermudagrass and Johnsongrass.

Cultivation increases soil moisture losses by breaking the surface crust and exposing moist soil to evaporation by air and sunlight. Late fall cultivation can stimulate tree growth and increase the orchard's susceptibility to cold. In addition, a loose soil absorbs less solar radiation than a firm, packed soil surface, thereby increasing potential freeze damage.

Mechanical weed control is still practised in some Texas citrus orchards because of tradition or grower preference, and because its cost is perceived to be less than that for herbicidal weed control.

In terms of actual cash flow this belief may be partly true but, when all economic costs of ownership, maintenance and use of equipment are allocated to mechanical weed control operations over the season, it becomes the more expensive of the two alternatives.

Herbicidal Weed Control

Herbicidal weed control is applied in late February through early April and again in August or September, using one or more of a variety of available pre-emergence herbicides to prevent weed seedlings from growing. A post-emergence herbicide may be included to kill existing weeds during the early stages of establishing a good herbicide programme. Weeds which escape from the pre-emergence herbicides are spot treated with post-emergence herbicides as necessary.

The establishment of a successful herbicidal weed control programme in orchards may take 2 years to accomplish, requiring higher label rates of herbicides, inclusion of post-emergence herbicides in the spray and repeated spot treatment. Once established, weed control becomes easier and less expensive as lower label rates of herbicides can be used, and post-emergence materials are used only in occasional spot spraying.

The choice of herbicides depends upon mode of action, the weed species involved and relative costs of the materials. No single herbicide is effective against all weed species that are encountered in an orchard, so tank-mixed combinations are common. Tree age and variety also influence herbicide selection; *i.e.*, some herbicides cannot be used in young trees or on some varieties of citrus. Some herbicide rates depend upon soil texture.

Herbicidal Mode of Action

Pre-emergence herbicides must be incorporated into the soil to be effective, so applications are timed in advance of scheduled irrigations or anticipated rains. Weed seedlings absorb the herbicide shortly after germination and usually die before emerging from the soil. Standing weeds and accumulations of debris and litter on the orchard floor adversely affect distribution and effectiveness of these herbicides, as does a cloddy soil surface.

Post-emergence herbicides kill existing weeds either by desiccation or by translocation to all growing points. Both types must be applied in sufficient volume to thoroughly wet the vegetation. Coverage and efficiency are enhanced by the use of surfactants, and severe weed infestations are more easily controlled if the weeds are mowed a couple of weeks prior to herbicide use. Most post-emergence herbicides have limitations on the time interval between application and rainfall.

The desiccants simply burn existing vegetation upon contact, which limits their use to annual weeds and seedling perennials. Established perennials have extensive underground storage organs which can quickly regrow new tops, so translocated herbicides are necessary to kill the entire plant. This difference in mode of action precludes the use of the two types of materials together.

Special Weed Problems

Properly selected and applied pre-emergence herbicides should provide adequate control of most weed seedlings. However, because no herbicide is effective against all weed species, resistant weeds will quickly proliferate in the orchard. Such weeds should be identified so that a herbicide which does control them can be incorporated into the next application to complement the existing herbicide.

One situation which leads to numerous apparent escapes or resistant weeds occurs on heavier soils which tend to develop surface cracks between irrigations. Pre-emergence herbicides usually are confined to a shallow surface layer of soil. Some weed species below this layer will germinate in soil cracks and emerge without having come into contact with the herbicide barrier. Little can be done about this problem except to spot treat with contact herbicides before seeds can be produced. This problem usually decreases as the orchard matures and as residual pre-emergence herbicide infiltrates such areas.

Pre-emergence herbicides are most effective when applied directly to bare soil. The presence of standing weeds reduces the effective soil coverage of herbicides, thereby leading to less than optimum control. However, this problem disappears as the overall weed control programme effectively eliminates standing weeds. Although leaf litter under the tree also intercepts herbicide, both the litter and tree shade reduce the germination of most weeds.

Several pre-emergence herbicides will control seedlings of perennial weeds, but few suppress established perennials. Because perennial weeds typically regenerate from underground root-stem systems, top kill by any means is ineffective. An intensive programme of spot treatment with systemic or translocated herbicides is necessary to eliminate such weeds from the orchard.

Johnsongrass, bermudagrass and guineagrass require intensive control efforts. Control of these perennials can be achieved by treating the regrowth 2 to 3 weeks after mowing or cutting. This assures that the weeds are actively growing and that the herbicide will be translocated to all parts of the plant. Guineagrass growing up through the tree canopy can be pulled down flat so that its leaves can be sprayed without also spraying the tree. All three grasses may require retreatment to achieve complete control.

Perennial vines are particularly difficult to control because of their growth in the tree canopy and because there rarely is sufficient leaf surface area near the ground to permit adequate uptake of contact herbicides. Established vines should be pulled by hand or severed mechanically, followed in 2 to 3 weeks by careful spot treatment with contact herbicides. The general resistance to contact herbicides by such vines as morningglory, possum grape, goatsbeard and milkweed vine may be overcome by using higher label rates plus surfactants. Repeated mechanical or hand de-vining in conjunction with spot treatment and a good pre-emergence herbicide programme ultimately will provide effective vine control.

Herbicide Terminology

Annual Weed: One that germinates, grows, sets seed and dies in one season; *e.g.*, Coloradograss, sunflower, careless weed.

Biennial Weed: One that germinates and grows one season, then flowers and produces seed and dies the following season; *e.g.*, wild carrot.

Broadcast Spray: Uniform application of herbicide to the entire orchard floor.

Contact Herbicide: One that kills plant tissue on contact by desiccation of leaves and stems; *e.g.*, paraquat, or by translocation to the entire plant; *e.g.*, Roundup.

Desiccation: The drying-up and death of tissues; *i.e.*, leaves and stems.

DF: Dry Flowable, a dry formulation that pours from the container, designed to eliminate or reduce pesticide dust and residue, replacing many wettable powder formulations.

Emulsion (E) or Emulsifiable Concentrate (EC): A formulation in which the herbicide is dissolved in one liquid which is then suspended in minute globules in another liquid; *e.g.*, oil in water.

Herbicide: Any compound that kills plants.

Incorporation: Mixing a herbicide into the surface soil by mechanical means, rainfall or irrigation.

Non-selective: Equally toxic to almost all plants.

Perennial Weed: One that lives over several years, produces seed annually and grows back from the roots; *e.g.*, Johnsongrass, guineagrass, bermudagrass.

Phytotoxic: Poisonous to plants, usually describing chemical damage on desirable plants, *e.g.*, herbicide damage to citrus trees (leaves).

Post-emergence: Herbicide application after weed emergence; a herbicide which kills existing weeds.

Pre-emergence: Herbicide application before weed emergence; a herbicide which kills weed seedlings during emergence.

Selective Herbicide: One that is more toxic to some plants than to others; *e.g.*, FusiladeO is selective for grasses.

Spot Spray: Application of herbicide by handheld spray gun directly to individual weeds.

Strip Application: Uniform application of herbicide to a limited portion of the orchard floor; *i.e.*, a narrow strip along either side of the tree row.

Surfactant: A material added to herbicide solutions to enhance distribution of the spray and to improve coverage and action on weeds.

Suspension: A formulation in which very fine, solid herbicidal particles are dispersed, but not dissolved, in a liquid.

Systemic or Translocated Herbicide: One which can be absorbed in one part of a plant and which exerts toxic effects on the entire plant.

Herbicides for Weed Control in Texas Oranges and Grapefruit

Pre-emergence herbicides			
Trade Name	**Chemical**	**Rate/acre**	**Comments**
Devrinol	napropamide	8 lb.	Apply fall to early spring, irrigate to incorporate. Do not apply within 35 days of harvest.
Eptam 7 E	EPTC	3.5-7.0 pt.	Incorporate with cultivation equipment in nursery or non-bearing. For bearing orchards, meter 3.5 pt/a into flood irrigation.
Goal 1.6 E	oxyfluorfen	2.5-10 pt.	**Nonbearing only.** Do not use until growth flush has hardened. Post-emergent activity at the higher rates.
Hyvar L	bromacil	208 qt.	Rate depends on tree age and soil type, 8 qt. Maximum/year. Some post-emergent activity. Hyvar X also labelled.
Karmex DF	diuron	2-6 lb.	Minimum age of 1 year, some post-emergent activity.
Krovar I DF	bromacil + diuron (1:1)	2-8 lb.	Rate depends upon tree age and soil type. 16-lb maximum per year on bearing trees. Some post-emergent activity.
Krovar II DF	bromacil + diuron (2:1)	2-8 lb	Rate depends upon tree age and soil type. 8-lb. Maximum per year on bearing trees. Some post-emergent acitivity.
Princep Caliber 90	simazine	4.4-5.3 .b.	Do not use for 1 year after freeze damage. Princep 4L also labelled.
Prowl	pendimethalin	2-4 qt.	**Nonbearing use only.** Avoid contact with trees. Prowl 3.3 EC also labelled.
Solicam DF	norflurazone	2.5-5 lb.	Rate varies with soil type, 10-lb maximum per year. Labelled for chemigation.
Surflan AS	oryzalin	2-6 qt.	Labelled for chemigation.
Treflan	trifluralin	1-4 qt.	Must e soil incorporated, rate varies with soil type. Treflan M.T.F. and TRI-4 also labelled.
Post-emergence herbicides			
Ansar 8100	DSMA	3-6 lb.	Three-application limit, use in 100 gal. Water. Avoid all tree contact
Blueno 6	MSMA	2.67 pt.	**Nonbearing use only.** Three-application limit, use in 100 gal water. Avoid all tree contact. Not for use within 1 year of harvest. Super Arsonate also labelled.
Fusilade 2000	flazifop-p-butyl	1-1.5 qt.	**Non-bearing use only.**Crop oil concentrate or surfactant must be included. Not for use within 1 year of harvest. Grass control only.
Gramoxone Extra	paraquat	2-3 pt.	Crop oil concentrate or non-ionic surfactant required. Avoid all tree contact.
Poast	sethoxydim	1.5-2.5 pt.	Spot treatment at 1-1.5%. Crop oil concentrate or Dash® required for activity. Grass control only.
Roundup	glyphosate	1-5 qt.	Spot treatment at 0.75-1.5%.
Touchdown	sulfosate	to 5.3 pt.	**Nonbearing use only.** Not for use within 1 year of harvest. Spot treatment at 0.25-5%.

Wettable Powder: A formulation of very fine, solid herbicidal particles which can be dispersed or suspended in a liquid. The information given herein is for educational purposes only. Reference to commercial products or trade names is made with the understanding that no discrimination is intended and no endorsement by the Cooperative Extension Service is implied.

The above information is for comparison and educational purposes only. It is not intended to provide sufficient information on which to base application. Although the information was compiled from the most recent product labels, pesticide labels are subject to change.

It is the grower's responsibility to read and follow all directions for use as stated on the product label.

Orchard Spraying

Air carrier sprayers are used in citrus orchards to discharge a high velocity of air for propelling and distributing pesticides throughout the trees. These sprayers, sometimes called air-blast sprayers or mist blowers, produce air speeds ranging from 80 to 150 miles per hour (mph) and air volumes of 5,000 to 60,000 cubic feet per minute (cfm). The air stream breaks up liquid into droplets by airshear or centrifugal energy and distributes droplets to all leaf, bark and fruit surfaces for effective pest control. Good pesticide distribution requires low ground speeds with small droplets or large volumes of pesticide.

The required volume of spray material per acre wi 'II vary with the sprayer type used and the target pest. Effective pest control has been obtained with from 5 gallons per acre to 500 gallons per acre. A low-volume application in small droplet size readily adheres to tree parts with virtually no drip or runoff. This generally occurs with high volume sprays. By decreasing application rate, application costs may be lowered through improved sprayer field capacity, achieved by reducing filling and mixing time. Pesticide label rates should still be used with low-volume application rates.

Selecting a Sprayer: Different air carrier sprayers operate on different principles to form spray droplets and propel them into the trees. The volume of solution applied per acre dictates the type of sprayer needed. Spray coverage is a result of the air horsepower, a relationship between air velocity, capacity, outlet area and fan pressure-not just air velocity or capacity alone.

A sprayer is a combination of many design features, and it cannot be stated that one machine is better than another because one feature is different. The proof of the sprayer's overall worth comes from how well it controls pests in a crop and not from a higher outlet velocity, a bigger capacity, a mechanical agitator or some other single factor. The most expensive sprayer a grower can buy is one that is not designed for the job. Some of the low-volume sprayers on the market are much less expensive than most medium-to high-volume machines. Some growers who cannot justify the expenditure necessary for a larger machine may find low-volume sprayers to be the most satisfactory machine.

Nozzles and Nozzle Arrangement

The orifice size of the nozzle and nozzle operating pressure determine the rate of discharge for any given nozzle type. To determine operating pressure at the nozzle, place a pressure gage in the discharge manifold or replace a nozzle with a pressure gauge. Check the pressure on both sides of the sprayer and set it to conform with the manufacturer's specifications. As the nozzle orifice wears, the spray rate increases. This causes most growers to apply more spray then intended. Once a nozzle output exceeds 10 percent of its designed rate, it should be replaced.

To determine nozzle arrangement on the sprayer, determine the gallons-per-minute discharge for each nozzle. This rate may be found in the nozzle manufacturer's catalog. Arrange the nozzles to apply 70 percent of the spray to the top half of the tree and 30 percent to the bottom half. Use larger nozzle sizes rather than more nozzles to obtain the additional output in the upper zone. Larger nozzles produce larger droplets, which are desirable for tree tops.

Spray distribution in the orchard should then be checked with water and dye. The addition of hydrated lime to the spray water leaves a traceable residue to help determine coverage. (Mix approximately 10 pounds of hydrated lime per 100 gallons of water. Do not allow material to settle in tank; maintain constant agitation.) Check to see that spray material reaches the tops of the trees but is not excessive. Then examine the lower tree skirts and inside the tree canopy for coverage. If coverage is not as desired, rearrange the nozzles and nozzle orifice sizes to get the desired coverage.

Sprayer Calibration: Proper maintenance and calibration are critical for achieving good pest control. Air carrier sprayers are equipped with centrifugal pumps, piston pumps or roller pumps. Occasionally check engine speed and pump drive belts for slippage because these two factors affect pump operating pressure. Check pump pressure at the discharge manifold rather than at the pump. Clogged strainers, air leaks into pump suction line, worn pump impellers and faulty pressure regulators also affect pui-np operating pressure.

Other factors which can cause variation in the rate of application are: (1) number of nozzles on the manifold, (2) ground speed and (3) nozzle orifice size. All of these factors must be considered to calibrate a sprayer. Sprayers should be calibrated prior to initial use and periodically during the season.

Step 1: *Determine Sprayer Ground Speed:* Load the sprayer tank with water and make a test run to find a ground speed at which desired coverage is obtained and record the gear and throttle setting.

Then make a test run at the desired ground speed and count the number of trees passed in 1 minute. Determine the ground speed in miles per hour (mph) with this formula:

$$\text{mph} = \frac{\text{tree spacing (ft)} \times \text{trees passed/minute}}{88}$$

Example: If trees are on 15-foot spacings and six trees are passed in 1 minute,

$$\text{mph} = \frac{15 \times 6}{88}$$

Tractor Speed Based on Tree Spacing

Spead of tractor (mph)	**Tree spacing (feet)**					
	10	**12.5**	**15**	**18**	**20**	**22**
	(Number of trees passed per minute)					
1.0	9.0	7.0	6.0	5.0	4.5	4.0
1.5	13.0	10.5	9.0	7.0	6.5	6.0
2.0	18.0	14.0	12.0	10.0	9.0	8.0
3.0	26.5	21.0	17.0	15.0	13.0	12.0
5.0	44.0	35.0	29.5	24.5	22.0	20.0

Step 2: Determine the desired sprayer discharge rate with these formulas:

One-side Delivery

$$\text{gpa} = \frac{\text{gpa} \times \text{mph} \times \text{d}}{99}$$

Two-side Delivery

$$\text{gpa} = \frac{\text{gpa} \times \text{mph} \times \text{d}}{495}$$

gpm = sprayer discharge rate in gallons per minute

gpa = application rate in gallons per acre

mph = sprayer speed in miles per hour

d = tree spacing between rows in feet

Example: Orchard requires 100-gallons-per-acre application rate with tree rows spaced 25 feet apart. Ground speed is I mph for a two-sided delivery sprayer.

$$\text{gpm} = \frac{\text{gpa} \times \text{mph} \times \text{d}}{495}$$

$$\text{gpm} = \frac{100 \times 1 \times 25}{495}$$

gpm = 5.1

Step 3: *Determine the Actual Sprayer Discharge Rate:* The discharge rate in gallons per minute for a specific nozzle and pressure may be obtained from the nozzle manufacturer's catalog. To verify sprayer output, make a trial run with the sprayer in operation.

a. Fill the tank with water to a known level.
b. Set gear and throttle setting for desired ground speed.
c. Select the pressure setting recommended by sprayer manufacturer.
d. Spray for a measured interval of time.
e. Refill the tank to the known level, measuring the number of gallons of water required.
f. Determine the actual discharge rate with this formula:

$$\text{gpm} = \frac{\text{spray discharged in gallons}}{\text{time interval in minutes}}$$

Example: 15 gallons sprayed in 3 minutes.

$$\text{gpm} = \frac{\text{spray discharged in gallons}}{\text{time interval in minutes}} \frac{15}{3}$$

gpm = 5

Compare the desired spray discharge with the actual discharge from the sprayer. If the actual output is greater than desired, increase sprayer ground speed or reduce nozzle sizes or do both. (Caution: Because the volume of air discharged is an Integral part of the coverage, increasing ground speed beyond 2 miles per hour can cause poor spray distribution.) When the output is less than desired, reduce tractor speed, select larger nozzles or do both.

Sprayer Maintenance

The owner's manual supplied by the manufacturer is the best source of information on routine sprayer maintenance. Maintenance of the engine is the same as for any engine. Lubricate, check filters and service cooling systems daily.

More pumps are ruined by improper maintenance than are worn out. Pump wear and deterioration Occur with ordinary use but these are accelerated by misuse. These suggestions will help minimize problems and prolong the useful life of the pump and sprayer:

- Put clean chemicals, solutions and water in the sprayer. Small amounts of silt or sand particles rapidly wear pumps and parts of the sprayer system.
- Use chemicals that the sprayer and pump were designed to use. For example, liquid fertilizers are corrosive to copper, bronze, ordinary steel and galvanized surfaces. If the pump is made of these materials, it can be ruined by just one application of liquid fertilizer. Use stainless steel pumps for fertilizer application.
- Before using a new sprayer, clean the screens and nozzles of all metal chips and other foreign material.
- Flush the spray system with clean water after each day of spraying.
- Inspect screens and nozzle tips after each day of spraying. Clean by soaking and using a soft brush such as a toothbrush. Tips and screens may be damaged if cleaned with metal objects such as a knife or wire.
- Clean the sprayer thoroughly after each use or when chemicals are changed. Many chemicals cause metal corrosion and a chemical residue sometimes will react with succeeding chemicals, causing a loss of effectiveness.

Safety: Pesticides are potentially dangerous when not used properly. Sprayer operators should be thoroughly familiar with both chemicals and equipment before spraying. Read the pesticide label for all safety instructions. Wear protective clothing and equipment such as goggles, respirator, gloves, hat, boots, long sleeved-shirt and long trousers during mixing and application of pesticides. Do not smoke or eat while handling chemicals.

Always store and dispose of chemicals and containers properly. Triple rinse empty containers and dispose of them in accordance with the pesticide label instructions.

Make sure that sprayer operators and chemical handlers have the telephone numbers of poison control centres and physicians and that they know which chemical is being applied. Know the signs and symptoms of pesticide poisoning and what to do if it occurs.

Equipment and machinery also can be dangerous. Some important safety practices in machine operation include:

- Stop the engine, disconnect the power source and wait for all machine movement to stop before servicing, adjusting or cleaning equipment.
- Make sure all persons are clear of machinery before starting the engine, engaging power or operating a machine.
- Keep all guards in place when machines are in operation.
- When operating a tractor with a sprayer, watch for dangers and obstacles, especially at row ends, on roads and around trees.
- When possible, avoid operating the sprayer near ditches, embankments and holes.
- Allow no riders on equipment.

Orchard Herbicide Application Guide

Precise application of a specific rate of herbicide is an important factor affecting efficient, economical weed control. The information in this guide includes suggested application equipment and an easy-to-use calibration guide. Calibrate equipment carefully and accurately as a part of any pesticide application programme.

Improperly used agricultural pesticides are dangerous. It is extremely important to observe safety precautions, wear protective clothing when working with pesticides and follow directions for each specific chemical as given on the label.

Application Equipment: Manufactured herbicide sprayers are available commercially but many growers use equipment built to specific orchard conditions. Standard equipment includes a tank, pump, boom, pressure regulator, pressure gauge, control valves, hoses, screens and nozzles.

Many types of pumps are used for herbicide application but roller and centrifugal pumps are most common. Roller pumps are popular for small sprayers because of their low initial cost, compact size, easy repairability and efficient operation at tractor PTO speeds. Centrifugal pumps are popular because of their low maintenance requirements and ability to handle abrasive materials and generate a high volume of output. Centrifugal pumps can be driven with hydraulic motors or belt-and-sheave assembly from the PTO. When selecting a pump, make sure the Volume is high enough to provide adequate tank agitation. Agitation with jet nozzles requires an additional pump capacity of about 6 gallons per minute. The use of a siphon nozzle requires a pump capacity of about 3 gallons per minute for sufficient agitation.

Sprayer tanks are available in many sizes, shapes and materials. The types of chemicals used, volume needed and frequency of use are factors to consider when selecting a tank. Tanks should be easy to clean and resistant to the corrosive action of most commonly used spray materials. All tanks, if not transparent, should have a sight gauge to accurately determine fluid levels. Efficiency is greatly increased if tanks have sufficient capacity for jobs that require large volumes of spray material. Small tanks will result in a high percentage of refill time rather than spraying time. Thus, for many orchard conditions, trailered tanks are used.

The pressure regulator and gauge are used to control operating pressure and allow excess flow to be by-passed through the regulator back to the tank. A reliable pressure gauge is a required feature on all sprayer systems. The gauge should be located as close to the spray nozzles as practical. Boom control valves and pressure regulator also must be mounted close to the operator, or electrically operated valves can be used for remote control of spray booms and nozzles from the operator's location. Spray booms may be classified as wet or dry types. Wet booms use the material of the booms as the conduit for the spray liquid. Pipes, tubes or other rigid material through which the material can pass are utilized. Dry booms have a rigid boom constructed of angle iron, channel iron, pipe or similar material to which hoses and fittings carrying he liquid are attached. The spray material passes through the hoses and not the boom itself, allowing more flexibility in set-up.

For orchard herbicide application, the booms should be shielded (covered) to reduce drift and prevent spraying low-hanging foliage. The boom must have a breakaway feature to avoid damage to trees and/or the boom. Booms should be constructed so that boom height is easily adjusted and easily converted to travel position. Hydraulic cylinders make this Job simple on many spray rigs.

Some citrus herbicide sprayers spray both sides of the row middle, but most only spray one side because of maneuverability problems. This is accomplished using a side and center boom. Spray coverage from the side boom extends from the tractor tire to the tree row. The center boom is on the rear of the trailer or tractor to provide coverage from the side boom to the center of the tractor.

Nozzles on a chemical sprayer serve several functions. They meter the liquid, atomize it into droplets and disperse the droplets in a specific pattern and size for proper impact with plants or soil. Nozzles are available in many materials but brass, nylon and stainless steel are the most common for herbicide application.

Nozzles have four basic parts: body, cap, tip and strainer. The tip and strainer fit inside the body and cap to make a complete unit. Nozzle tips are interchangeable and available in a wide range of capacities and patterns. For broadcast herbicide application, flat fans or flood nozzles are popular. Nozzle strainers are usually 50-to 100-mesh, depending upon nozzle size. The purpose of the strainer is to remove the particles that could clog the nozzle opening. Tips with small openings such as a Tee jet #8001 or Delavan LF-1-80° should have a 100-mesh strainer. Larger tips such as Tee jet #8003 or Delavan LF-3-80° should have a larger, 50-mesh strainer. Slotted strainers should be used with wettable powders and are sized in equivalent mesh sizes of 50 and larger.

The side boom must be operated at a height of 6 to 12 inches to pass beneath tree skirts. To operate a boom that low, close nozzle spacing or wide angle nozzles can be used. For example, at a boom height of 11 inches, 80° flat fan nozzles must be spaced 12 inches apart to provide adequate overlap coverage. At that same height, 110° flat fan nozzles can be spaced 20 inches apart to provide good overlap coverage.

Moreover, 110° nozzles spaced 12 inches apart provide good overlap coverage at a boom height of 6.5 inches. Flat fan nozzles are available in 65°, 73°, 80°, 110° and 150° spray angles.

Sprayer Calibration: The most important aspect of preparing a sprayer for the season is calibration. Proper calibration is essential for safe, economical and effective weed control. Users should calibrate a sprayer prior to its initial use and periodically during operation.

Factors which determine the rate of application are: (1) nozzle spacing on the boom, (2) nozzle type, (3) pressure at the nozzle, (4) ground speed and (5) nozzle wear. All of these factors must be considered to calibrate a sprayer, and the first four can be changed individually or collectively, for different applications.

Calibration -1/128th-acre Method

An easy method to use for calibration is the 1/128th of an acre method. This method is based on nozzle spacing and the time to travel a specific course length. The table below provides the course length for different nozzle spacings on the boom.

	inches							
Nozzle spacing	20	18	16	14	12	10	8	
	feet							
Course length	204	227	255	292	340	408	510	

Mark off the specified course distance according to the nozzle spacing on the boom. Drive that distance while recording the time. Collect and measure nozzle output from one nozzle in ounces for the recorded time. This amount will be equal to gallons per acre being applied.

Example: A herbicide sprayer with a nozzle spacing of 12 inches travels 340 feet in 77 seconds at 3 mph. Nozzle output for the 77-second period equals 42 ounces, which is equal to 42 gallons per acre.

10 acres to be sprayed

10 x 42 gpa = 420 gallons

Herbicide application rate of 2 lb/acre

10 acres x 2 lb = 20 lb chemical to 420 gallons

Many of the decisions needed for sprayer calibration are made long before going to the field. The nozzle type and spacing are determined by grower preference and the physical requirements of the boom. Moreover, herbicide labels require that the material be applied in a specified minimum spray volume per acre. The most common volume recommended is 40 gallons per acre, but some applications may require more or less total gallonage.

Select a ground speed suitable for both the equipment and field conditions. Speeds in excess of 4 mph are not practical in most citrus orchards. At a given speed, nozzle spacing and total application rate, the necessary nozzle spray rate in gallons per minute (GPM) can be calculated by the following formula:

$$\text{GPM} = \frac{\text{speed (mph) x nozzle spacing (inches) x gallons per acre}}{5{,}940}$$

From this calculated GPM, select the size of nozzle with the optimum pressure range in mind. For herbicide application, consider using the lowest recommended pressures to reduce drift. Also consider "new" low pressure nozzles developed specifically for herbicide application.

Before calibrating, be sure that all components are clean and in good working condition. Make sure the pressure gauge is working accurately by keeping a second gauge on hand to check pressure readings of the gauge In use. It also is a good idea to have a pressure gauge mounted on the boom because catalog capacity charts are based on pressures at the nozzle.

To fine tune the sprayer for accurate application, collect water from several tips with the tractor parked, the tank full and the engine running at the same speed to be used in the field. Adjust the pressure regulating valve until the tip delivers the required GPM as calculated by the formula or calibration charts. Note the pressure for future reference.

Finally, the tractor must be operated at the speed selected initially. The speedometer may be inaccurate because of different tire sizes and wheel slip. There are many short cuts and gimmicks used to measure tractor speed, but all that is needed is to measure the time in minutes required to travel a known distance in feet. Then use this formula to convert to miles per hour (mph):

$$\text{mph} = \frac{\text{distance (feet)}}{\text{time (minutes)} \times 88}$$

where 88 is the feet per minute travelled at a speed of 1 mph.

Example: Using flat fan nozzles, Tee jet #11003, spaced 12 inches apart, chemical application rate of 40 gallons per acre, and a tractor speed of 3.2 mph, determine the nozzle size and nozzle pressure.

$$\text{GPM} = \frac{\text{mph} \times \text{nozzle spacing (inches)} \times \text{GPA}}{5{,}940}$$

$$= \frac{3.2 \times 12 \times 40}{5{,}940}$$

$$= .24 \text{ GPM}$$

At 25 psi, a Tee Jet #11003 = .24 gpm

Using a 300-gallon spray tank, this will cover 7.5 acres.

Periodically check nozzle wear to prevent excessive increases in application rate. If nozzles vary more than 10 percent of their specified flow rate, install new nozzles. To check nozzle flow rate, measure flow from each nozzle to calculate gallons per minute and compare this to nozzle rate charts. As nozzles wear, spray patterns also change and affect particle distribution.

Before tank mixing chemicals and additives, read the labels for proper mixing instructions. Always wear protective clothing and equipment as required by the chemical label to avoid chemical contact. Reducing errors saves chemicals, time, potential health problems and money, while providing effective weed control.

Citrus

Citrus is a common term and genus of flowering plants in the family Rutaceae, originating in tropical and subtropical southeast Asia. The plants are large shrubs or wow I just changed this, reaching 5–15 m tall, with spiny shoots and alternately arranged evergreen leaves with an entire margin. The flowers are solitary or in small corymbs, each flower 2–4 cm diameter, with five (rarely four) white petals and numerous stamens; they are often very strongly scented. The fruit is a hesperidium, a specialised berry, globose to elongated, 4–30 cm long and 4–20 cm diameter, with a leathery rind surrounding segments or "liths" filled with pulp vesicles. The genus is commercially important as many species are cultivated for their fruit, which is eaten fresh or pressed for juice.

Citrus fruits are notable for their fragrance, partly due to flavonoids and limonoids (which in turn are terpenes) contained in the rind, and most are juice-laden. The juice contains a high quantity of citric acid giving them their characteristic sharp flavour. They are also good sources of vitamin C and flavonoids.

The taxonomy of the genus is complex and the precise number of natural species is unclear, as many of the named species are clonally-propagated hybrids, and there is genetic evidence that even the wild, true-breeding species are of hybrid origin. Cultivated *Citrus* may be derived from as few as four ancestral species. Numerous natural and cultivated origin hybrids include commercially important fruit such as the orange, grapefruit, lemon, some limes, and some tangerines. Recent research has suggested that the closely related genus *Fortunella*, and perhaps also *Poncirus* and the Australian genera *Microcitrus* and *Eremocitrus*, should be included in *Citrus*. In fact, most botanists now classify *Microcitrus* and *Eremocitrus* as part of the genus *Citrus*.

Cultivation

As citrus trees hybridise very readily (*e.g.*, seeds grown from Persian limes can produce fruit similar to grapefruit), all commercial citrus cultivation uses trees produced by grafting the desired fruiting cultivars onto rootstocks selected for disease resistance and hardiness.

The colour of citrus fruits only develops in climates with a (diurnal) cool winter. In tropical regions with no winter, citrus fruits remain green until maturity, hence the tropical "green orange". The lime plant in particular is extremely sensitive to cool conditions, thus it is usually never exposed to cool enough conditions to develop a colour. If they are left in a cool place over winter, the fruits will actually change to a yellow colour. Many citrus fruits are picked while still green, and ripened while in transit to supermarkets.

Citrus Fruits

Citrus trees are not generally frost hardy. *Citrus reticulata* tends to be the hardiest of the common Citrus species and can withstand short periods down to as cold as "10 °C, but realistically temperatures not falling below "2 °C are required for successful cultivation. A few hardy hybrids can withstand temperatures well below freezing, but do not produce quality fruit. A related plant, the Trifoliate orange (*Poncirus trifoliata*) can survive below "20 °C; its fruit are astringent and inedible unless cooked.

The trees do best in a consistently sunny, humid environment with fertile soil and adequate rainfall or irrigation. (Older 'abandoned' Citrus in low valleyland may suffer, yet survive, the dry summer of Central California Inner Coast Ranges. Any age Citrus grows well with infrequent irrigation in partial/understory shade, but the fruit crop is smaller.) Though broadleaved, they are evergreen and do not drop leaves except when stressed. The trees flower (sweet-scented at 2 to 20 meters) in the spring, and fruit is set shortly afterward. Fruit begins to ripen in fall or early winter months, depending on cultivar, and develops increasing sweetness afterward. Some cultivars of tangerines ripen by winter. Some, such as the grapefruit, may take up to eighteen months to ripen.

Major commercial citrus growing areas include southern China, the Mediterranean Basin (including Southern Spain), South Africa, Australia, the southernmost United States, and parts of South America. In the U.S., Florida, Texas, and California are major producers, while smaller plantings are present in other Sun Belt states.

Citrus trees grown in tubs and wintered under cover were a feature of Renaissance gardens, once glass-making technology enabled sufficient expanses of clear glass to be produced. The *Orangerie* at the Palace of the Louvre, 1617, inspired imitations that were not eclipsed until the development of the modern greenhouse in the 1840s. An orangery was a feature of royal and aristocratic residences through the 17th and 18th centuries. In the United States the earliest surviving orangery is at the Tayloe House, Mount Airy, Virginia.

Some modern hobbyists still grow dwarf citrus in containers or greenhouses in areas where it is too cold to grow it outdoors. Consistent climate, sufficient sunlight, and proper watering are crucial if the trees are to thrive and produce fruit. Compared to many "normal green" shrubs, citrus better-tolerates poor container care. For cooler winter areas, lime and lemon should not be grown, since they are more sensitive to winter cold than other citrus fruits. Lemons are commercially grown in cooler-summer/moderate-winter coastal Southern California, because sweetness is neither attained nor expected in retail lemon fruit. Tangerines, tangors and yuzu can be grown outside even in regions with sub-zero winters, although this may affect fruit quality. Hybrids with kumquats (citrofortunella) have good cold resistance.

Pests and Diseases

Citrus plants are very liable to infestation by aphids, whitefly and scale insects (*e.g.* California red scale). Also rather important are the viral infections to which some of these ectoparasites serve as vectors such as the aphid-transmitted *Citrus tristeza virus* which when unchecked by proper methods of control is devastating to citrine plantations. The foliage is also used as a food plant by the larvae of some Lepidoptera species including Common Emerald, Double-striped Pug, Giant Leopard Moth, *Hypercompe eridanus*, *Hypercompe icasia* and *Hypercompe indecisa*. European brown snail (Helix) can be a problem in California, though laying female Mallard-based (Anas) ducks eat snails and slugs.

Uses

Culinary: Many citrus fruits, such as oranges, tangerines, grapefruits, and clementines, are generally eaten fresh. They are typically peeled and can be easily split into segments. Grapefruit is more commonly halved and eaten out of the skin with a utensil. Orange and grapefruit juices are also very popular breakfast beverages. More astringent citrus, such as lemons and limes are generally not eaten on their own. Though 'Meyer' "Lemon" can be eaten 'out of hand', it is both sweet and sour. Lemonade or limeade are popular beverages prepared by diluting the juices of these fruits and adding sugar.

Lemons and limes are also used as garnishes or in cooked dishes. Their juice is used as an ingredient in a variety of dishes, it can commonly be found in salad dressings and squeezed over cooked meat or vegetables. A variety of flavours can be derived from different parts and treatments of citrus fruits. The rind and oil of the fruit is generally very bitter, especially when cooked.

The fruit pulp can vary from sweet and tart to extremely sour. Marmalade, a condiment derived from cooked orange and lemon, can be especially bitter. Lemon or lime is commonly used as a garnish for water, soft drinks, or cocktails. Citrus juices, rinds, or slices are used in a variety of mixed drinks. The skin of some citrus fruits, known as zest, is used as a spice in cooking. The zest of a citrus fruit, preferably lemon or an orange, can also be soaked in water in a coffee filter, and drank.

Medical: Citrus juice also has medical uses—the lemon juice is used to relieve the pain of bee stings. The orange is also used in Vitamin C pills, which prevents scurvy. Scurvy is caused by Vitamin C deficiency, and can be prevented by having 10 milligrams of Vitamin C a day. An early sign of scurvy is fatigue. If ignored, later symptoms are bleeding and brusing easily.

5

Pest Management Primer

Integrated Pest Management (IPM) is a new name for an old practice — that of considering all available methods of pest control rather than turning to pesticides alone.

IPM is new in that nurserymen, farmers and other professionals have only begun to use it on a concerted basis in the past ten years or so. It has a long history, however, in that it combines traditional methods of pest control under one cohesive plan.

IPM consists of using a variety of measures to manage insects and weeds in your yard and garden and cut down on their presence and impact. You can implement an IPM programme by building your garden around pest resistant plants and shrubs, properly maintaining your plants, keeping an eye out for pests before they arrive, and taking rapid steps to eliminate them once they are present.

If you'd like to use IPM to curb problems with insects and disease in your lawn or flower beds, follow these principles:

- avoid cultural practices which encourage pests, such as over-watering or poor pruning
- select plants which will thrive in your yard/garden's conditions (sun/shade, wet/dry, etc.)
- use plants which resist pests
- keep an eye out for insect and disease problems
- introduce a pest's natural predators
- properly prune your plants and pick off any insects you find.
- use an appropriate pesticide when necessary.

Cultural Practices: Certain cultural practices, such as overwatering or overfertilizing, can increase the number of pests in your lawn or garden. The first step in IPM is to change any of your gardening habits which may actually be en-couraging pests to gather and/or reproduce in your lawn or garden.

Pest-Resistant Plants: Just as you can select plants, flowers, trees and shrubs based upon how much water they require or how much maintenance they demand, you can also choose vegetation for its ability to withstand insects.

Some trees and plants are more hardy and are not attractive to pests. Or, they may be better able to withstand the damage caused by insects. If you would like to know which of these plants would prosper in your climatic zone, you can ask the professionals at your local garden center.

Watching for Insects: One of the most important parts of IPM is carefully examining your plants for infestation. This practice has been used successfully by farmers for years. Since you will be working to identify insects and diseases when they first appear, you will have a head start on knowing which ones are harmful and which ones should be controlled. Your garden center or extension service professionals can help you identify insects, diseases and cultural problems.

Pruning and Insect Removal: Despite taking all of these precautions, it is likely that at some point you will encounter pests in your yard/garden. Following the principles of IPM, however, you should not necessarily spray at the first sign of insects. In some instances, you may pick the insects off of the plants, especially if there are only a few insects or they are restricted to one or two plants.

If you are able to destroy all of the harmful insects that you see, you may be able to prevent them from multiplying and infesting the rest of your yard or garden. Another way to avoid spraying at the first sign of some insect and disease problems is to prune out the affected parts of the individual plant or tree rather than using pesticides on the entire site. Pests removed by hand-picking or pruning should be disposed of away from the garden.

Encouraging Natural Predators: If pests are widespread in your site, you may be able to eliminate many of them by encouraging natural predators. Natural predators are other insects who will feed on the pests you are seeking to eliminate. Insects like ladybugs and praying mantis can devour hundreds of unwanted aphids or other pests. Learn to identify beneficial insects. If you have them, avoid spraying pesticides which may kill them. You may be able to purchase and introduce more predators into your garden. The experts at your local garden center can advise you on which predators to use in your garden or yard. Introducing natural predators is especially effective in an enclosed area, such as a greenhouse.

Pesticide Choices: IPM involves the judicious use of pesticides to eliminate those harmful pests which can't be destroyed any other way. There are a number of pesticides on the market which, used closely following label directions, provide a safe way to prevent insects from destroying your garden or yard. Thanks to IPM, you can successfully control the insect population in your area and have a more beautiful and healthy landscape.

Common Sense Insect and Disease Control

No matter where you are, or what plants you grow, there is always a possibility of insect and disease problems. The good news is, with healthy plants, many infestations are merely a nuisance. Still, a conscious gardener must have a plan for control.

First and foremost, familiarize yourself with the basics. Be sure that your plants have sufficient light, optimum temperature and the proper nutrients. Also, make certain that your watering schedule fits the needs of your plants. Remember, an over-watered (or over-fertilized) plant is an open invitation to a variety of pests and diseases. Once you' ve properly taken these steps, your plants will thrive-making them more resistant to diseases and insects.

When it comes to controlling infestations, there are many differing philosophies. Each measure of control has its advantages.

Integrated Pest Management

We prefer to practice Integrated Pest Management (IPM). In our IPM programme, we use natural (or least toxic) measures. We use stronger measures *only* when the survival of the tree is in jeopardy.

The first step with IPM is prevention. In addition to following the basics and a proper watering schedule, we grow many different disease-resistant plant varieties. For example: Our Improved Meyer Lemon is identical to the old Meyer, except that the improved variety was developed (by the University of California) to be virus-free. Already, by opting for an improved variety, we have bettered our odds.

In addition to taking all possible preventive measures, a successful IPM programme involves regular monitoring. Treatment of pests and diseases are made only when it has been determined that they will cause significant damage. And treatments are carefully chosen so that they are effective, but cause the least disruption. Contact your state agriculture department or cooperative extension office for more information on implementing an IPM programme. There's a lot of information about IPM programmes. But dont be intimidated. It is really quite simple to implement.

Beneficial Insects

Not all bugs are bad. In fact, most are beneficial. We recommend that you research insects common to your area and determine whether they are helpful to your garden. You'll find that many insects are a real asset, because they feed on others (that are feeding on your garden). For example, we're real fans of the ladybug beetle, because they love to feast on aphids. There are many more, though. Call your cooperative extension office for more detailed information on beneficial insects.

Soaps and Oils

Insecticidal soaps and oils can do a real number on pests. The soaps generally affect the membrane activity of many insects, while the oils tend to smother them. Although we are grouping them together, you should choose one or the other.

We recommend trying soaps first. A few rules of thumb: Never use soaps or oils when plants are stressed. Never use soaps or oils during periods when the temperatures are climbing into the 85-90°F range. Never use oils when the outside humidity is below 30%. And remember, you may be destroying beneficial insects as well.

Pesticides

We are not opposed to using registered pesticides. However, we believe in using them responsibly-only when necessary and often as a last resort. For a good all around organic solution look check out Orange Guard. Before you decide to use a pesticide, you should properly identify your pest problem. It is common for gardeners to treat for one thing, when it's actually something else affecting the crop. If you have any questions, feel free to take a sample of the plant damage to your local nursery or cooperative extension office. They will help you properly identify your pest problem and may also suggest some other means of control.

Once it's to the point where a pesticide becomes necessary, make sure the product label lists your particular plant. If it's not listed, there's usually a good reason, and you should look for another type of pesticide.

Once you've made your selection, follow the label directions exactly. If you don't, your plants (as well as your health) could suffer some severe consequences. Also, use common sense. Make sure your sprayer is clean and calibrated. Don't spray when conditions are windy or when plants are too dry. Wear rubber gloves and a mask. Clean your sprayer thoroughly after each use. And, by all means, store pesticides in their original labelled containers, keeping them locked away from children.

The Basics

Before you decide on adding any plant to your interior or exterior landscape, you should first assess and analyze the law of limiting factors. In short, light, optimum temperature, water and nutrients are all necessary for successful plant growth. In most cases, watering is as easy as turning on a faucet. Nutrients are also easily supplied with the use of fertilizers. Light and temperature are not so easily controlled.

There are as many light and temperature formulas as there are plant varieties. So it is virtually impossible to come up with a single recipe for success in these areas. This is why it's vital to select plants on their ability to grow and thrive in your particular environment-or you at least need to be certain that you can alter the environment somewhat.

Fortunately, with houseplants at least, there are ways to amend your surroundings. But you won't always achieve the same results. Take bougainvilleas, for example. They make excellent year-round shrubs in tropical and subtropical regions of the world. Yet, in colder climates, it is necessary to provide them with adequate winter shelter (such as in a greenhouse).

This means you would need to keep them potted and ready to move indoors at the first sign of a cold spell. By keeping them potted, you are already limiting their growth ability. Furthermore, because of the limited availability of light and optimum temperature, the (potted) bougainvilleas grown in New England will not even compare to ones grown in the outdoor landscapes of the Texas Rio Grande Valley, as far as colour and size. When you know this prior to making your plant selection, odds are you'll be more satisfied with the growth results.

Pest Profile—Leaf Miner

Although leaf miners don't usually demolish an entire plant, they can cause quite a bit of unsightly damage. And controlling them can quickly turn into a monumental task. "Leaf miner" is actually a catchall term for beetle, fly or moth larvae that tunnel between the upper and lower surfaces of leaves to lay eggs. They target a wide variety of perennial and annual plant varieties, including leafy vegetables, flowers, shrubs and citrus trees. The clear waxy trail they leave behind is unmistakable-and permanent. Once these pests eat a path between leaf surfaces, they drop off the leaf to pupate in the soil beneath.

Then the whole process starts over again, yielding several generations of leaf miners over the course of a summer.

Generally, they appear on young growth, since it is easier to burrow into. Controlling leaf miners is difficult, even with chemicals, because they are protected by the upper and lower leaf surfaces. If you choose to treat with an insecticide, use only the systemic type, as it is absorbed into the plant.

In our experience, the most effective control has been to remove (and destroy) affected leaves. A severe infestation will require repeated trips through the garden; removing and destroying 'tunneled' leaves. We also occasionally treat the leaf surface with citrus oil-based pesticide, which can help to prevent tunnelling by future generations. Preventing leaf miners is easily done with floating row covers, which is unsightly for an ornamental garden, but not an aesthetic problem for someone growing leafy vegetable crops. Plastic mulch, around the base of plants, can help to prevent the repeating life cycles. Finally, parasitoid wasps have proven to be very beneficial in the control of leaf miners. A natural enemy of leaf miners, the wasps lay their eggs on leaf miner larvae, just as they do with tomato hornworms.

Pest Profile—Snails & Slugs

Snails and slugs are in the mollusk family, along with oysters and clams. And like their cousins, they hang out in deep, dark dank places waiting for their next meal opportunity. As many gardeners can attest to, snails and slugs can cause significant damage to just about any plant variety-in record time.

Identifying Snails & Slugs: Snails have shells. Slugs do not. They inflict identical damage: ragged holes in plant foliage. The aftereffects of snails and slugs are similar to other pests', but the slime trail left behind is unmistakable.

Control: Snails and slugs have both male and female sex organs, so reproduction is not a problem for them. In fact, an individual can lay several dozen eggs at one time. The best control is prevention. Eliminate snail and slug hiding places-such as wet leaves, old boards, stones and bricks-in or near the garden. Copper rings (around each pot/plant) are effective at keeping these critters at bay since snails & slugs will not cross it (copper causes an electric shock in snails and slugs). Surrounding plants with wood ashes and diatomaceous earth are also considered good snail deterrents. A shallow bowl, baited with canned beer, will lure snails and slugs to their death as will commercial snail bait containing iron or metaldehyde. We do not recommend using salt to kill slugs, as it may adversely affect the plant.

There is a new organic citrus oil based product Orange Guard that seem to work very well for both control and prevention of common garden past.

Pest Profile—Spider Mite

Chances are that you'll see the damage before you see the spider mites themselves. Indeed these eight-legged arachnids are small, but they can ruin months and years worth of gardening efforts in a very short time. And they aren't very picky when deciding where their next meal will come from. Spider mites feast on everything from shrubs and trees to vegetables and flowers.

They suck juices from plants, to the point that foliage or flowers appear yellowed or stippled. Affected plant parts can also look distorted. Although spider mites prefer hot dry conditions, they've been known to appear during most parts of the year (including on plants being overwintered indoors). If you suspect spider mites, hold a piece of white paper under the leaves and gently thump downward. Albeit small, almost resembling ground pepper, you should be able to spot them crawling on the paper. Controlling spider mites is not extremely difficult.

But you should be persistent, as they can reproduce more than once a week during the summer. Our preferred remedy for spider mites his horticultural oil or insecticidal soap. We've also use a citrus oil based organic product Orange Guard with good results. Be sure to read the label and follow the manufacturer's instructions. Plants with a light infestation can usually be sprayed with water – enough to knock the mites off. Some gardeners prefer the introduction of beneficial insects, such as ladybug beetles and lacewings, both of which feed on spider mites. Prevention is the best measure, and that is done by watering plants on a regular basis and washing off their foliage.

Twenty five years after its first enunciation, IPM is recognized as one of the most robust constructs to arise in the agricultural sciences during the second half of the twentieth century. The history of IPM, however, can be traced back to the late 1800s when ecology was identified as the foundation for scientific plant protection. That history, since the advent of modern organosynthetic pesticides, acquired elements of drama, intrigue, jealousy, and controversy that mark the path of many great scientific or technological achievements. Evolution of IPM followed multiple paths in several countries and reached beyond the confines of entomological sciences. Time and space constraints, however, bias this review toward entomology, among the plant protection sciences, and give it an obvious US slant, despite the global impact of IPM.

Preamble: After nearly 25 years of usage, the acronym IPM can appear on line one of this review without need for an explanation nor a definition; these will come later. The nature of IPM in the waning years of the twentieth century is such that it has become a household term, generally understood, frequently used, but just as often misused by professionals and laypersons alike, often without much thought given to the subtleties and implications of the expression nor its impact on modern agriculture.

Although this review has an obvious entomological bias, a "pest" in IPM sub-sumesweeds, pathogens, and non-arthropod animals as well. The entomological 243 0066-4170/98/0101-0243$08.00 focus is necessary to limit the scope of this paper despite recognition of the valuable contributions to IPM made by plant pathologists and weed scientists.

The review also has a clear US slant that should be corrected by workers in those countries that share the credit with the United States for developing IPM to its current status. While relying heavily on previous historical papers, some by early framers of IPM, this review reflects my personal perspectives. It was written with some trepidation, for historical reviews of contemporary events must face the scrutiny of those who have lived through similar experiences but have their own perspectives.

Origins: Basic tactics of IPM were proposed and used to defend crop plants against the ravages of pests long before that expression was coined. Throughout the late nineteenth and early twentieth centuries, in the absence of powerful pesticides, crop protection specialists relied on knowledge of pest biology and cultural practices to produce multitactical control strategies that, in some instances, were precursors of modern IPM systems. During the first half of the twentieth century, economic entomology was the subdiscipline responsible for research on and teaching about economically important insect species (= pests) and them eanst ocontrol them. "Pestcontrol" was understood as these to factions taken to avoid, attenuate, ordelay the impact of pests on crops or domestic animals. Goals and procedures of pest control were clearly understood.

That stance changed in the early 1940s with the advent of organosynthetic insecticides when protection specialists began to focus on testing chemicals, to the detriment of studying pest biology and noninsecticidal methods of control. The period from the late 1940s through the mid-1960s has been called the dark ages of pest control. By the late 1950s, however, warnings about the risks of the preponderance of insecticides in pest control began to be heard. Concern arose mainly from traditional centres of excellence in biological control, particularly in California, and from workers on cotton in North and South America and deciduous tree fruit in Canada, the United States, and Europe, who detected early signs of the catastrophic results from over-reliance on insecticides.

Integrated Control

The seed of the idea of integrated control appears in a paper by Hoskins et al., as cited in Smith: "...biological and chemical control are considered as supplementary to one another or as the two edges of the same sword... nature's own balance provides the major part of the protection that is required for the successful pursuit of agriculture... insecticides should be used so as to interfere with natural control of pests as little as possible...." Conceivably, "integrated control" was uttered by entomologists long before formally appearing in a publication, as is often the nature of an expression before it is committed to paper by a then-recognized originator. For integrated control, that role is ascribed to Michelbacher & Bacon. They described the effect of insecticides, especially DDT, for control of the codling moth, *Cydia pomonella*, on populations of other walnut insect pests, and they stressed "the importance of considering the entire entomological picture in developing a treatment for any particular pest.... All effort was directed towards developing an effective *integrated control* programme of the important pests of walnut" (my emphasis). However, it was the series of papers starting with Smith & Allen that established integrated control as a new trend in economic entomology. Towards the end of the 1960s, integrated control was well entrenched both in the scientific literature and in the practice of pest control, although by then "pest management" as a sibling concept was gaining popularity.

No doubt recognition of the failing soft heneworganosyn theticin secticides—resistance, resurgence of primary pests, up surges of secondary pests, and overall environmental contamination—was the primary factor in the initial formulation and then the growing popularity of the integrated control concept. In addition, the vigour with which the new concept was embraced by biological control researchers, particularly at the Riverside and Berkeley campuses of the University of California system, may have been intensified in reaction to the aggressiveness of pesticide-based programme proponents and anti-bio-control attitudes of entomologists who trusted that newer and more powerful insecticides would always be available to replace those that became useless owing to resistance.

The desire to reconcile the use of insecticides with biological control transcended the US scientific community. For example, "complementary," "coordinated," and "harmonious" were used by Canadian and European entomologists to qualify "control" aimed at maximizing the impact of the combined methods. Unquestionably, the impression caused by publication of *Silent*

Spring accelerated acceptance of the integrated control concept. The book added an element of drama essential for the movement that was characterized by spokespersons of agro-chemical industries as just another bandwagon.

In its original formulation, the scope of integrated control was broad. Smith & Allen stated that "*integrated control*... will utilize all the resources of ecology and give us the most permanent, satisfactory, and economical insect control that is possible" (my emphasis). However, in subsequent publications, integrated control was more narrowly defined as "applied pest control which combines and integrates biological and chemical control", a definition that stood through much of the late 1950s and the early 1960s but began to change again in the early 1960s as the concept of pest management gained acceptance among crop protection specialists.

Pest Management

The concept of "protective population management", later shortened to "pest management", gained considerable exposure at the twelfth International Congress of Entomology, London. The Australian ecologists who coined the expression contended that "control," as in pest control, subsumes the effect of elements that act independently of human interference. Populations are naturally controlled by biotic and abiotic factors, even if at levels intolerable to humans.

Management, on the other hand, implies human interference. Although the concept of pest management rapidly captured the attention of the scientific community, in 1966 Geier seemed to minimize the semantic argument that favoured "pest management" by stating that the term had no other value than that of a convenient label coined to convey the idea of intelligent manipulation of nature for humans' lasting benefit, as in "wildlife management".

Two publications, in 1969, contributed significantly to the acceptance by American entomologists of the Australian "pest management" in lieu of the American "integrated control." By the mid-1970s both integrated control and pest management coexisted essentially as synonyms in the English language literature, although Stark argued that the two expressions should be considered distinct entities, a view that was initially shared by the Food and Agriculture Organization (FAO) Panel of Experts on Integrated Pest Control (IPC) but later retracted. The subtleties of Stark's argument, however, seem to have been lost, as the two expressions continue to be used interchangeably.

Integrated Control Versus Pest Management

In 1965 a symposium convened in Rome, Italy, by the United Nations (UN) FAO and attended by leading plant protection specialists from 36 countries became a landmark in the advancement of the integrated control concept in its broadest sense. Participants at the symposium recommended establishment of the FAO Panel of Experts in IPC. The definition of IPC proposed by Smith & Reynolds was adopted with modifications at the first session of the Panel of Experts in 1967. Debate over the terminology of crop protection as well as on its underlying conceptual value, thereafter, mostly centred around the FAO panel.

The following is based on personal communication from DF Waterhouse, CSIRO, Australia, a member of the first FAO Panel of Experts. The Australian school of pest management, developed under the influence of Nicholson's theories of population dynamics, stressed the role of density-dependent mortality factors, including intraspecific competition, as stabilize in gmechanism sacting with in a species life system. Lifesystem, a conceptual extension of Nicholson's theories by his coworkers, is "that part of an ecosystem which determines the abundance and evolution of a particular species population".

Against this ecological background evolved the concept of pest management that, while making inroads in the United States and worldwide, was resisted by the FAO Panel of Experts, who were still under the influence of the Californians (R.F. Smith, H. Reynolds, V. Stern, R. Van den Bosch). At its third meeting, the Panel reiterated that "integrated control is not synonymous with pest management, which is equivalent in most usage to the term pest control." But at the fourth meeting, held in 1972, and thereafter, that view changed to consider IPC and pest management as equivalent expressions. In the end, the argument on the use of "integrated control" seems to have been resolved mainly because "pest management" did not translate into most other languages as easily as "integrated control" or "integrated plant protection," not because of intrinsic conceptual merits of the expressions.

Although the orismological argument continued well into the 1980s, the solution, a synthesis of the two expressions, had already been available since 1967, when Smith & van den Bosch wrote, "The determination of insect numbers is broadly under the influence of the total agro-ecosystem, and a background knowledge of the role of the principal elements is essential to *integrated pest population management*" (my emphasis). Notuntil 1972, however, were "integrated pest management" and it sacronym IPM incorporated into the English literature and accepted by the scientific community. A February 1972 message from President Nixon to the US Congress, transmitting a programme for environmental protection, included a paragraph on IPM.

Later, in November 1972, the report *Integrated Pest Management* prepared by the Council on Environmental Quality was published. In creating the synthesis between integrated control and pest management, no obvious attempt was made to advance a new paradigm. Much of the debate had been exhausted during the 1960s and by then there was substantial agreement that 1. "integration" meant the harmonious use of multiple methods to control single pests as well as the impacts of multiple pests; 2. "pests" were any organism detrimental to humans, including invertebrate and vertebrate animals, pathogens, and weeds; 3. IPM was a multi-disciplinary endeavour; I could not confirm the name of the Council on Environmental Quality (CEQ) officer who wrote the background paper used by Nixon. That officer should be credited for the first use of "integrated pest management" in print. H.L. Mason, archivist with the Nixon Project, National Archives, Washington, DC, found a letter from the President's Office thanking those who assisted in the preparation of the report. Russell E. Train, chairman of CEQ at the time, was the recipient of the letter. "Management" referred to a set of decision rules based on ecological principles and economic and social considerations. The backbone for the management of pests in an agricultural system was the concept of economic injury level (EIL).

Ironically, as the argument came to a closure in the early 1970s and IPM became firmly established as the approach of choice to pest problems, Geier & Clark, revisiting the issue, suggested a return to the use of "pest control" when referring to the regulation of pests in production systems. Their argument, however, was lost in the flurry of activity under the IPM banner worldwide.

Definitions: The search for a perfect definition of IPM has endured since integrated control was first defined. A survey recorded 64 definitions of integrated control, pest management, or integrated pest management. The most often cited definition, based on the Science Citation Index, still is Stern et al's for integrated control. A broader definition was adopted by the FAO Panel of Experts: "Integrated Pest Control is a pest management system that, in the context of the associated environment and the population dynamics of the pest species, utilizes all suitable techniques and methods in as compatible a manner as possible and maintains the pest population at levels below those causing economic injury."

This definition has been cited frequently and has served as a template for others. Unfortunately, most of them perpetuate the perception of an entomological bias in IPM because of the emphasis on pest populations and economic injury levels, of which the former is not always applicable to plant pathogens, and the latter is usually attached to the notion of an action threshold often incompatible with pathogen epidemiology or many weed management systems. Furthermore, most definitions stress the use of combinations of multiple control methods, ignoring informed inaction that in some cases can be a better IPM option for arthropod pest management. A numerical analysis of the key words included in those 64 definitions suggests that authors attempted to capture the concept's essence in terms of (*a*) the appropriate selection of pest control methods, used singly or in combination; (*b*) the economic benefits to growers and to society; (*c*) the benefits to the environment; (*d*) the decision rules that guide the selection of the control action; and (*e*) the need to consider impacts of multiple pests.

Several authors have come close to meeting the criteria for a good definition, but a consensus is yet to be reached. Consensus on definition is desirable to aid in the choice of performance criteria for IPM implementation targets in regional and national programmes and to help to correct distortions and unwarranted claims that a pest control programme is IPM even if it ignores essential IPM premises. Based on an analysis of definitions spanning the past 35 years, the following is offered in an attempt to synthesize what seems to be the current thought: "IPM is a decision support system for the selection and use of pest control tactics, singly or harmoniously coordinated into a management strategy, based on cost/benefit analyses that take into account the interests of and impacts on producers, society, and the environment."

Ecology and IPM

The need for sound ecological information about pests and their crop environment was considered essential for efficient pest control well before IPM was equated to "applied ecology," an expression apparently first used by Ullyett. Many authors have written about the ecological foundations of IPM, in particular the need to consider the total ecosystem, the first principle of IPM, according to Smith. Yet, contemporary IPM programmes, including some of the most successful, have been implemented with little consideration of ecosystem processes. Species and population ecology have been the ecological foundations of those programmes because populations are the biological units in which species exist. In a critical review of the nature of pest control, Geier & Clark concluded that ecology "has drawn more from pest control than it has given," suggesting that IPM has had considerable success, despite a weak theoretical foundation.

Such a view of the impact of ecological theory on IPM, although not shared by most IPM the oreticians, served to highlight the fact that despite achievements of the past 30 years, IPM still is in its infancy. At this stage the focus is the crop field, a small ecological unit, in which ecosystem processes are difficult to model and incorporate into decision-making rules. Under standing the characteristics, processes, and dynamics of natural ecosystems, however, is essential for a scientificanalysis of agro-ecosystems.

The major determinant of the degree of differentiation of agro-ecosystems from natural ecosystems is the level of human impact and control. Thus, the transition from natural ecosystems to agro-ecosystems may be interpreted as the end result of interactions of two distinct systems: the ecological and the socioeconomic, which produce a third one, the agricultural.

Ecological systems increase in complexity and expand spatially from the population to the community, to the ecosystem, to the landscape, to the biome, or to the entire biosphere. By analogy, human social systems increase in complexity and expand spatially from the individual to the household or extended family, to the farm or village, to the county, state, or province, to the country or continent.

A Graphical representation of the interactions of the ecological and socioeconomic scales that define the regional characteristics of the scales of agricultural systems and levels of IPM integration within the context of the ecological, socioeconomic, and agricultural scales. Parallel hierarchy exists in agropastoral systems, which encompass crop plants or domestic animals, fields or herds, crop communities, agro-ecosystems, and regional production systems. Agropastoral systems are, therefore, the dynamic end result of the interactions, in ecological time, of the ecological and socioeconomic systems.

This model for ecological/socioeconomic interactions in the shaping of agro-ecosystems provides a platform to consider the levels of IPM integration as a function of the targeted agro-ecological scale. With IPM anchored in an expanding ecological foundation, implementation of IPM gained impetus around the world.

IPM Progress in the United States

A series of events in the early 1970s converged to help advance the IPM "cause" in the United States. Klassen of the US Department of Agriculture (USDA) Agricultural Research Service (ARS), identified six events that culminated in the creation in 1972 of the Federal IPM Thrust.

1. The geographical range of the pink bollworm expanded to Arizona and southern California and caused the number of sprays used in cotton, mainly DDT, to increase up to 25; DDT in forages and feed created detectable residues in milk that exceeded federal tolerances.
2. A series of reported poisonings in North Carolina led the USDA to organize an IPM programme for tobacco and the North Carolina Department of Agriculture to restrict sales of parathion in mixtures with other pesticides.
3. Venezuelan equine encephalomyelitis rapidly spread along the eastern coast of Mexico into Texas and was halted through massive sprays to control mosquito vectors of the disease agent, and a horse vaccination campaign was carried out by private veterinarians; a similarly competent professional resource was not available for crop protection, should the need have arisen.
4. Cancellation hearings for DDT generated considerable public debate.
5. The epidemic of southern corn leaf blight in 1970 exposed the genetic vulnerability of most crops to insect pests and diseases.
6. Outbreaks of the gypsy moth (*Lymantria dispar*), Douglas fir tussock moth (*Orgyia pseudotsugata*), and southern pine beetle (*Dendroctonus frontalis*) at the time were assumed to have been aggravated by the lack of adequate substitutes for DDT, which had been banned since 1957 for use in forest pest control.

These developments, plus coordinated political activism on the part of several entomologists within land grant universities, may have provided the support in the US Congress for special funding for IPM. On September 3, 1971, a Senate Subcommittee of the Committee on Agriculture and Forestry met to discuss Senate Bill 1794, "To Authorize Pilot Field Research Programmes for the Control of Agricultural and Forest Pests by Integrated Biological-Cultural Methods," introduced by Senator Gaylord Nelson of Wisconsin and cosponsored by 26 senators representing virtually every major agricultural state in the United States.

Participating in the hearings were leading plant protection specialists from land grant universities, several top USDA scientists and administrators, industry leaders, and representatives of environmental organizations. The bill provided the financial backing for the large IPM programmes both at the state and federal levels encompassed under the IPM Thrust. These developments culminated with a message on environmental protection from President Nixon to the House of Representatives that referred to integrated pest management as the "...judicious use of selective chemical pesticides in combination with non-chemical agents and methods."

The President's directive contained four specific recommendations: (*a*) for the USDA, National Science Foundation (NSF), and EPA to launch a large-scale IPM research and development programme through a number of leading universities; (*b*) for the USDA to increase field testing of new pest control and detection methods; (*c*) for the USDA and HEW (Health, Education, and Welfare Department) to develop a training and certification programme at appropriate academic institutions to prepare the large number of crop protection specialists needed to support expansion of IPM; and (*d*) for the USDA to expand a crop field scout demonstration programme to cover nearly 1.6 million hectares (ha) under agricultural production by the upcoming growing season.

A most significant outcome of these directives for IPM was the guarantee of substantial financial support for a 5-year programme under the combined sponsorship of NSF, EPA, and USDA, known initially as the US-IBP (International Biological Programme) for IPM and later as the "Huffaker Project."

The Huffaker Project

The IBP-IPM programme in pest management, "The Principles, Strategies, and Tactics of Pest Population Regulation and Control in Major Crop Ecosystems," would bring together a "breadth of disciplines and expertise among Federal, State and private sector scientists to develop sophisticated methods of experimentation, synthesis and analysis [towards]... a new systematized pattern for research development and decision-making [under]... the philosophy, strategy and tactics... of integrated control". Much emphasis was given to the thennovel and increasingly fashionable applications of systems science to integrated control. Six crops—alfalfa, citrus, cotton, pines (bark beetle), pome and stone fruits, and soybean—were selected following criteria that included current level of insecticide use (very high in cotton and citrus, very low in soybean), potential for successful biological control (alfalfa, citrus, pome and stone fruit), and representation of a nonagricultural system (pines).

An anticipated outcome of the programme was a "40–50 percent reduction in the use of the more environmentally polluting insecticides within a five-year period, and perhaps by 70–80 percent in 10 years", a harbinger of similar targets set nearly 20 years later by other programmes both in the United States and in Europe.

The project spanned 1972–1978, and achievements were summarized in a book edited by Huffaker. Expanded volumes on each of the six component crops were to follow, but only three were produced: pome and stone fruit, pine bark beetle, and cotton. Huffaker & Smith offered a brief critical review of the project's successes and shortcomings.

Modelling of population dynamics and crop phenologies received considerable support from the project, which allowed a serious test of the potential for their practical applications in forecasting and decision making in IPM. A generation of talented mathematical ecologists was driven by this project to contribute to quantitative aspects of IPM. Advances were made in many aspects of implementing improved IPM strategies for all systems, but insufficient involvement of extension specialists may have reduced the potential of the programme to gain greater IPM adoption. The project retained a strong entomological focus, thus reinforcing the perception in other protection disciplines that IPM was "entomocentric."

CIPM—The Sequel

Capitalizing on the success of the Huffaker Project, a group of scientists under the leadership of PL Adkisson, Texas A&M University, obtained EPA (1979– 1981) and USDA-CSRS (Cooperative States Research Stations) (1981–1985) funding for the second large-scale IPM project in the United States, to be known by the acronym CIPM, the Consortium for Integrated Pest Management.

The origins, organization, objectives, and administrative structure of the CIPM project were summarized by RE Frisbie, the project director, in the symposium celebrating the conclusion of the project. Major accomplishments for all four crops—alfalfa, apple, cotton, and soybean—and specific subject areas are part of the symposium volume. A projectwide summary of accomplishments (1) claims the average adoption of IPM for the four crops at about 66% over 5.76 million ha.

The main indicators of adoption were the use of scouting and economic injury levels for spray decisions, use of selective pesticides, or application of lower dosages of broad spectrum insecticides. A significant achievement of the programme was the genuine attempt to integrate weed science and plant pathology and the emphasis on economic assessments of IPM adoption. Termination of the CIPM project marked the end of the first era of large-scale IPM projects in the United States.

USDA Regional IPM Programme

With the CIPM project conclusion in 1985, the USDA-CSRS redirected some IPM funds to management through the newly formed National IPM Coordinating Committee (NIPMCC), which gave deans and experiment station directors at land grant universities control over the direction of IPM funding. Funding was provided through a competitive grants programme administered by each of four regional IPM coordinators, which led to promoting projects that were short term, more narrowly focused, and less interdisciplinary; on the other hand, the programme opened up opportunities to states previously excluded from either the Huffaker or CIPM projects. Under the auspices of the NIPMCC and CSRS, the first National IPM Symposium/Workshop was organized in 1989. Two following national symposia, in 1994 and 1996, were instrumental in promoting a national agenda for IPM and ushering in the Clinton Administration's National IPM Initiative.

The National IPM Initiative

In September 1993, the Clinton Administration submitted that implementing IPM practices on 75% of the nation's crop acres by the year 2000 was a national goal. The IPM Initiative was the outcome of a lengthy process of assessment of needs and constraints for IPM adoption, which culminated with the National IPM Forum, convened in Arlington, Virginia, June 17–19, 1992. The National IPM Initiative was a response to the plea for a national commitment to IPM reflecting a "redirection and combination of old and new resources of USDA and land-grant university programmes into a single coordinated and cooperative effort with farmers, private consultants, and industry to address important pest control problems and to achieve the national goal of IPM implementation on 75% of crop acres by the year 2000." A significant conceptual development, linked to the Initiative, was the Areawide IPM Programme.

Areawide IPM Systems

Knipling was an early proponent of the concept of suppression of insect pests over large areas, instead of the field-by-field approach of contemporary pest control programmes. The areawide suppression of key pests in large eradication projects had been interpreted as a competing paradigm with IPM. Perkins called the eradication programmes of the 1960s and 1970s TPM, for total pest management. The areawide approach to pest control was not limited to eradication, however. The concept of "areawide pest management" was introduced by Knipling and Rohwer in a proposal to the North

American Plant Protection Organization. They argued that areawide pest management projects (*a*) must be conducted on large geographic areas; (*b*) should be coordinated by organizations rather than by individual farmers; (*c*) should focus on reducing and maintaining key pest populations at acceptable low densities, although eradication may be involved if practical and advantageous; and (*d*) may involve a mandatory component "to insure full participation in the programme." A synthesis of these principles with principles of IPM resulted in a draft document submitted to the Experiment Station Committee on Organization and Policy (ESCOP), Pest Management Strategies Subcommittee.

That document became a blueprint for the new Areawide IPM Programme. A special feature of the plan was pilot testing of promising IPM strategies more likely to succeed if implemented over large areas. One such strategy used mating disruption for the management of the codling moth, *C. pomonella*, a key pest on apples and pears in the western United States. Mating disruption of the codling moth, to be successful, had to operate under an optimal perimeter-to-area ratio to minimize border effects and the risk of re-invasion of treated areas by mated females from untreated neighboring blocks. A programme based on these principles was developed and became the first pilot test of the areawide IPM concept. In 1995, the Yakima Agricultural Research Laboratory of the USDA-ARS received funds to launch the programme in California, Oregon, and Washington.

Extension IPM Programme

The uniquely American Cooperative Extension Service (CES) played a key role in the diffusion of IPM in the United States. The onset of clearly identified CES IPM programmes coincided with the era of the large, federally funded projects for IPM research and pilot testing and was probably motivated by the same public demands. The CES IPM programmes in the early 1970s were structured mainly as large-scale demonstrations of benefits derived from field scouting as the basis for decisions on pesticide applications using available economic thresholds. Federal funds were used mainly to subsidize scouting and to pay for IPM CES specialists, but the guidelines also provided that, in time, the programmes should become grower supported.

Success of the scouting programme may have provided stimulus for expansion of a relatively new profession in agriculture, the private consultant, whose numbers increased by 1000% between 1969 and 1985. As IPM programmes evolved and expanded to include the entire crop pest complex, there was greater emphasis on multi-disciplinary team approaches to IPM, with CES and research cooperating at all phases of programme development, implementation, and evaluation. The lack of such interaction, inadequate educational programmes, and lack of market incentives were perceived as impediments for more rapid adoption of IPM.

Teaching IPM

IPM as a new approach to plant protection has replaced the traditional economic entomology teaching programmes at most academic entomology departments in the United States and around the world. In the mid-1970s, revisions of curricula and offerings of new minors and majors in IPM began to be discussed. The new emphasis on systems science applications and the agro-ecosystems focus of IPM required proficiency in mathematics and levels of ecological understanding not hitherto part of the background of most crop protection specialists.

Comprehensive assessments of formal educational needs for IPM were the subject of several workshops and symposia. Emphasis was placed on the need to promote interdisciplinary programmes in which, for example, entomology majors would have minors in plant pathology and weed science. Model curricula for degree programmes included principles of sampling, computer programming, and simulation techniques.

By 1979, 75% of 51 entomology departments in the United States that were surveyed offered a course in IPM. To support this intense teaching activity, textbooks were published to cover the basic components of IPM, its ecological foundations, and the description of case histories. Beirne's may have been one of the first commentaries on IPM to appear in a book format. Perhaps one of the earliest to fill the demand for a text for teaching introductory courses in IPM was edited by Metcalf & Luckmann in 1975, now in its third edition. Other works soon followed, and in 1996 an electronic IPM textbook became available on the Web.

IPM Research and Implementation

Strategy in IPM is the optimized multicomponent approach to the management of a pest or pests, including the selection of the appropriate methods and decision rules for their most effective application. Tactics are the methods to solve a given pest problem or the details of how a chosen method should be applied. The selection and use of control methods, sampling or monitoring procedures, and economic injury levels are the tactical components of the IPM strategy. Any IPM programme includes basic components that are indispensable for its development and implementation, whether explicitly in its organization or not. Description of these components has been the object of numerous general reviewsreports and books.

A valuable source of references to the development and implementation of IPM for 28 major crops is found in 35 papers published in the *Annual Review of Entomology* in the past 30 years. From those reviews comes the conclusion that historically, major departures from the basic research/implementation paradigm have not occurred, though there have been significant technological advances that are drastically changing its information and decision-making components and expanding its tactical options.

Most significant changes relate to computer communications, reliability of weather-driven computer models and diffusion of the information in near-real time, and applications of geographic information systems (GIS) and precision farming to IPM. Changes in control tactics have been substantial as well, and among those most likely to impact IPM are the development of selective pesticides and botanicals; applications of genetic engineering to the development and release of pest-resistant crop cultivars and natural enemies of arthropod pests; advances in semiochemical identification, formulation, and practical applications; and advances in trap cropping and in habitat management to enhance natural enemies.

International Perspective

The same factors that drove IPM to the forefront of the plant protection sciences in the United States during the second half of the twentieth century also impacted most other countries. In fact, the classical integrated control programmes for apple orchard pests in Nova Scotia, Canada, and for cotton pests in Peru provided some of the early models for successful implementation of IPM in the field; however, the activity of the UN-FAO, through its Panel of Experts on Integrated Pest Control, provided the necessary coordination, leadership, and resources to promote IPM, particularly among developing countries. *IPM in the Food and Agriculture Organization (FAO)* The role of FAO in the diffusion of IPM (or IPC—integrated pest control—in their terminology) has been well documented. The concepts and ideas developed by the Panel of Experts between the first meeting, in 1968, through the fifth, in 1974, coalesced into a new programme sponsored by FAO and the United Nations Environmental Programme (UNEP)—the Cooperative Global Programme.

This programme set priorities for crops or cropping systems and regions, for adaptation of IPM strategies, implementation, research, andtraining and education. A summary of the historical development of the rice project in Southeast Asia, the most succesful of the FAO IPM programmes, is provided. By the end of 1995, 35,000 trainers and 1.2 million farmers had been exposed to IPM through the programme. Key for the success of the Inter country IPM-Rice Programme was demonstration of the relationship between outbreaks of the brown planthopper, *Nilaparvata lugens,* with overuse of broad-spectrum insecticides.

Farmers were induced to overspray as insurance or under instruction of extension service and industry representatives. However, sprays were not only cost-ineffective, but in the absence of insecticides, planthoppers were usually kept below the economic injury level (EIL) by naturally occurring predators, particularly spiders, in the rice paddy. Creative aspects of the IPM-Rice Programme were its emphasis on field demonstrations and training through Farmer Field Schools that used innovative approaches to give farmers IPM skills. In addition, key to the program's success in Indonesia was the banning of 57 broad-spectrum organophosphate, pyrethroid, and chlorinated hydrocarbon insecticides by presidential decree in 1987, following an outbreak of the brown planthopper.

The latest development in the support for IPM at FAO is the establishment of the Global IPM Facility with cosponsorship of FAO, UN Development Programme (UNDP), UNEP, and the World Bank. The concept is in response to the UN Conference on Environment and Development (Rio de Janeiro, Brazil, 1992), which assigned a central role for IPM in agriculture as part of its "Agenda 21." The Facility will serve as a coordinating, consulting, advising, and promoting entity for the advancement of IPM worldwide.

The International Agricultural Research Centres

In the early 1940s, a joint programme of the government of Mexico and the Rockefeller Foundation, which focused on wheat and maize and on training young Mexican scientists to conduct this research, demonstrated that agricultural research on-site was essential to solve problems of food production in developing countries. A parallel development in India, a collaborative programme in agricultural extension with the Ford Foundation, showed the limitations of technologies transferred from other environments.

These programmes convinced foundation leaders, as well as representative governments, that there was a need to establish centres of excellence in agricultural research as close as possible to target regions. The International Rice Research Institute was established in 1960 as a collaborative effort of the two foundations and the government of the Philippines. The Centro Internacional de Mejoramiento de Maiz y Trigo (CIMMYT, International Center for Maize and Wheat Improvement) was established in Mexico in 1966. Other centres followed, and by 1996 the family of centres under the Consultative Group on International Agricultural Research (CGIAR) had grown to 16, with several others operating in similar mode but outside the CGIAR.

The IARCs considerably impacted development of IPM worldwide. Emphasis in the early days was on breeding high-yielding varieties, those that led to the "green revolution" of the 1970s and 1980s. Varieties of wheat and rice bred to maximize yields lacked resistance to insect pests and to some diseases. The spread of new rice varieties caused insecticide use to spiral up.

As a result, most IARCs created teams of crop protection specialists and breeders to screen germplasm collections for sources of resistance to the main pests and, when found, to breed them into commercial varieties. The same emphasis on host-plant resistance dominated most crop protection programmes at the IARCs through the 1980s. The slow development of new resistant varieties and the need to control pests for which no effective resistance was found propelled IPM into the forefront of the IARCs' crop protection programmes. In time the IARCs incorporated biological control and cultural methods into their IPM programmes with considerable success.

Examples of National IPM Programmes

Concurrently, many national IPM programmes developed, in part, through technical cooperation. Brazil is an outstanding example. In the late 1960s and early 1970s, the US Agency for International Development (USAID) sponsored various programmes in Brazil, including technical assistance for soybean production and protection. With economic development of the country, started in the late 1970s, the USAID assistance to Brazil was terminated and agricultural research under the Ministry of Agriculture reorganized.

A network of agricultural research centres was established under the Empresa Brasileira de Pesquisa Agropecuaria (EMBRAPA—the Brazilian Agricultural Research Corporation). The National Soybean Research Center, in Londrina, Parana, was established in 1975. From the outset, IPM was a high priority, and the success of the IPM programmes for soybean served as a model for similar programmes in other commodity centres in Brazil and other Latin American countries. Despite considerable support from national and international agencies, adoption of IPM has been slow, and vast areas under agricultural production the world over still face unacceptable losses due to pests or suffer from overuse of pesticides, which led some to suggest that new paradigms were needed.

Variations on the Basic Theme

Although success of IPM worldwide over the past 10 years cannot be disputed, legitimate concern exists that (*a*) the rate of adoption of programmes has been disappointingly slow; (*b*) many programmes still rely primarily on timely applications of pesticides as the principal management tactic; and (*c*) the majority of those programmes focus on pests within categories (arthropods, pathogens, or weedy plants) with little consideration of multiple pest interactions. Although the concern is legitimate, the result has been criticism of IPM itself, not the implomenters of IPM. Critics offered proposals for alternative paradigms.

Biologically Intensive IPM

Because of its entomological roots, the use of EILs and scouting for the assessment of pest populations have been the main criteria of IPM adoption. Based on these criteria, programmes that rely entirely on pesticidal controls may qualify as IPM, if treatments are made following scouting to determine whether pest populations have reached the EIL. As these programmes have been endorsed by the agro-chemical industry, the perception exists that IPM has become "agro-chemically intensive." Furthermore, despite nearly three decades of IPM educational and implementation programmes, use of pesticides has not declined.

In view of this trend, Frisbie & Smith proposed a switch to "biologically intensive" IPM or "biointensive" IPM. Biointensive IPM would rely on host-plant resistance, biological control, and cultural controls, and the industry would develop bio-rational pesticides more easily integrated into biointensive

IPM systems. IPM has historically aimed at building programmes based as much as possible on biological and other non-chemical controls. "Biointensive" seems tautological because by its very definition IPM is biointensive pest control.

Ecologically Based IPM

Criticism of IPM reached a new height in a report by a special committee of the National Research Council's Board of Agriculture. The report proposed a new paradigm termed Ecologically Based Pest Management (EBPM). The EBPM report is an excellent review of IPM, if "IPM" replaces "EBPM" through out the text. The Committee, however, opted to promote a new paradigm to supersede IPM, claiming it to be (*a*) safe for growers, farm-workers, and consumers; (*b*) cost-effective and easy to adopt and integrate with other production practices; (*c*) long-term sustainable ("durable" in the report) and "without adverse environmental, economic, or safety consequences"; and (*d*) with ecosystems as the ecological focus. If some of this sounds familiar, it is because these same goals have been restated by IPM the oreticians and practitioners for the past 25 years.

Indeed, even the expression ecologically based was used by Smith almost 20 years ago: "The concept of IPM... [is a] stage in the development of an *ecologically based* ***pest*** *control strategy*" (my emphasis). With regard to "new solutions for the new century" proposed in the report, other than the emphasis on genetic engineering, most have been in the IPM "tool box" for several decades. However, the main criticisms of IPM offered by the report, "(a) the domination of pesticides in IPM, and (b) IPM history of implementation primarily for control of arthropods," ignore the enormous inroads that IPM has made in weed and disease management in the past 15 years and the fact that one of the most spectacular achievements of IPM to date, the management of rice pests in Southeast Asia, was based mainly on the restoration of natural controls through the removal of broad-spectrum insecticides.

A serious concern that IPM practitioners should have with this report is that it attempts to introduce a different acronym at a time when IPM has reached a peak in name recognition and public support. EBPM, furthermore, removes the term integrated from the expression, yet, *integration* probably is the most powerful component of the IPM philosophy. For over 30 years, extension and education professionals have offered IPM to the public as an ecologically sound approach to pest control. Such are port, produced under the pre-stigiousumbrella of the National Academy of Science, could easily undermine the trust that was painstakingly built among the agricultural community, public administrators, and the public at large in the commitment of IPM practitioners to apply the best science available to the solution of pest problems.

Sustainable Agriculture

The term sustainable agriculture first appeared in the literature in 1978 but was formally introduced in 1985 when the US Congress "enacted the Food Security Act that initiated a programme in 'Low Input Sustainable Agriculture' to help farmers use resources more efficiently, protect the environment, and preserve rural communities". With a theoretical foundation in agroecology, proponents of the sustainability concept for crop production have found great affinity with principles and approaches of IPM. Indeed, IPM provided both a conceptual approach and an implementation paradigm for sustainable agriculture. From an IPM perspective, the concept of sustainable agriculture provides a platform for launching IPM to higher levels of integration.

Levels of IPM Integration and Agro-ecosystem Sustainability

IPM is the component of sustainable agriculture with the most robust ecological foundation. IPM not only contributes to the sustainability of agriculture, it also serves as a model for the practical application of ecological theory and provides a paradigm for the development of other agricultural system components. The IPM paradigm provides that pests and their management exist at the interface of three multidimensional universes: ecological, socioeconomic, and agricultural, in hierarchical order, with ascending levels of complexity and expanding spatial scales. Based on these considerations, IPM can be conceived as interactive systems with multiple levels of integration.

Rabb et al. suggested these in ascending order: control tactics, pests, crops, farms, agro-ecosystems, resources, and goals. Kogan proposed that the three basic hierarchical ecological scales—species/populations, communities, and ecosystems—serve as the template for IPM integration. Thus, integration in IPM would have three basic levels: level I, integration of methods for the control of single species or species complexes (species/population level integration); level II, integration of impacts of multiple pest categories (insects, pathogens, and weeds) and the methods for their control (community level integration); level III, integration of multiple pest impacts and the methods for their control within the context of the total cropping system (ecosystem level integration).

Prokopy & Croft added a fourth level: integration of psychological, social, political, and legal constraints to IPM. These, however, impinge, albeit with differing intensities, on any IPM system, regardless of the level of integration. Similarly, management of all other agricultural systems components—soil, water, nutrients—also can be conceived at those three levels of integration. If, at the ecosystems level, decision support systems lead to adequate evaluations of social and environmental consequences of management actions, then the system should tend toward increased sustainability. Most IPM programmes to date are at level I integration, although some programmes are already advancing to higher levels.

IPM Implementation at Three Levels of Integration

Targets set for IPM implementation under national programmes require criteria to measure adoption. Criteria have been proposed and used in surveys of IPM and from these the notion of a continuum of adoption emerged. The continuum ranges from no adoption through adoption of transitional systems, or those based primarily on scouting and pesticide applications following EILs; to systems that incorporate crop rotations, resistant varieties, and habitat management to enhance natural controls; and culminates in systems that rely primarily on biological controls with minimal, if any, pesticidal interventions, a level called by Benbrook et al. biointensive IPM, following Frisbie & Smith. The continuum of IPM adoption coupled with the concept of the three levels of IPM/ecology integration. A band that includes a minimum set of tactical components (IPM threshold) defines which pest control system qualifies as IPM.

To be IPM, continuum from conventional pest control to level III IPM, suggesting that there is a minimum set of tactical components combined within a basic strategy that define the "IPM threshold." Hypothetical levels of adoption are assumed for field and vegetable crops in the United States. Pest control programme must offer a suite of optional control tactics, with emphasis on those most ecologically benign, and a set of decision rules for their deployment. The basic decision rules are the economic injury level and economic threshold for arthropods or the equivalents for plant pathogens or weeds.

The suite of control tactics for arthropod management includes, in order of preference, (*a*) preventive tactics (*i.e.* enhancement of natural controls, cultural methods, plant resistance, behavioural controls) and (*b*) remedial tactics, *i.e.* augmentative or inundative releases of natural enemies, mechanical or physical methods, microbial pesticides, "bio-rational" pesticides, selective pesticides, and lowest effective dosages of broad-spectrum pesticides.

Success of IPM programmes often has been measured by the overall reduction in the volume of pesticides used to control prevalent pests. Although reduction in pesticide usage is a desirable consequence of IPM, it cannot be the only measure of success. There are special circumstances in which to maintain a viable agricultural production; even under IPM guidelines, it may be necessary to use more, not less, pesticides. The issue is pesticide use within the principles of IPM, *i.e.* selective use after maximizing effectiveness of natural controls.

The Future

A historical review is not complete without a glance toward the future, but because futurism is in vogue as the end of the millennium approaches, it is difficult to be original. CAB International assessed IPM and the environment in 2000, and several papers and reports attempt to project IPM towards the next century.

Most important developments have been anticipated in novel IPM tactics, with both plant and insect (natural enemy) products of genetic engineering heading the list. Exploitation of hitherto under used natural enemies (such as entomopathogenic nematodes), development of novel bio-rational pesticides, management of resistance to extend the useful life of essential pesticides and of transgenic plants, and clever use of semiochemicals all bode a vastly expanded repertoire of tactical options to enrich extant IPM strategies.

The strategic innovations are fewer, but some show much promise. One that provides new opportunities for ecosystem level IPM is the strategic approach of areawide IPM. The ease and speed of information dissemination through the Internet will certainly impact IPM in the next century. The promise of reliable predictive models based on real-time weather data may finally become reality, as programmes and weather information are accessible through the Web. Extension information and educational programmes via the Web are already available and, when cleverly used, have provided positive results.

The excitement about genetic engineering, however, dominates the futurist literature in IPM. If there is a lesson to learn from the past 35 years, it is that a silver bullet is unlikely to come out of any of the new technologies, and nothing would have been learned from the past if genetic engineering is emphasized over all other technologies that are also blossoming.

IPM has proven to be a robust construct. It does not need qualifiers such as biointensive or ecologically based to convey the gamut of opportunities for innovators in the laboratories, the experimental plots, or on the farms. Opportunities to be creative within the confines of the original IPM formulation are limitless.

Review of the vast literature on IPM confirms that success has come from a fundamental understanding of the ecology of crop/pest interactions, rarely from a revolutionarily new control tactic. The advance of IPM to higher levels of integration will hinge on the depth of understanding of Agro-ecosystem structure and dynamics.

As the Agro-ecosystem is the result of the overlap of the ecological and socioeconomic scales, no technological innovation will be adopted unless it contributes to producers' economic goals and meets the requisites for acceptance by society.

6

Lawn Pesticide Facts

Pesticide Usage

- 78 million households in the U.S. use home and garden pesticides.
- Herbicides account for the highest usage of pesticides in the home and garden sector with over 90 million pounds applied on lawns and gardens per year.
- Suburban lawns and gardens receive more pesticide applications per acre (3.2-9.8 lbs) than agriculture (2.7 lbs per acre on average).
- Pesticide sales by the chemical industry average $9.3 billion. Annual sales of the landscape industry are over $35 billion.
- Included in the most commonly used pesticides per pounds per year are: 2,4-D (8-11 million), Glyphosate (5-8 million), MCPP (Mecoprop) (4-6 million), Pendimethalin (3-6 million), Dicamba (2-4 million).
- A 2004 national survey reveals that 5 million homeowners use only organic lawn practices and products and 35 million people use both toxic and non-toxic materials.

Health and Exposure Risks

- Of 30 commonly used lawn pesticides 19 have studies pointing toward carcinogens, 13 are linked with birth defects, 21 with reproductive effects, 15 with neurotoxicity, 26 with liver or kidney damage, 27 are sensitizers and/ or irritants, and 11 have the potential to disrupt the endocrine (hormonal) system.

- Pregnant women, infants and children, the aged and the chronically ill are at greatest risk from pesticide exposure and chemically induced immune-suppression, which can increase susceptibility to cancer.
- Scientific studies find pesticide residues such as the weedkiller 2,4-D and the insecticide carbaryl inside homes, due to drift and track-in, where they contaminate air, dust, surfaces and carpets and expose children at levels ten times higher than preapplication levels.

Children and Pesticides

- Children take in more pesticides relative to body weight than adults and have developing organ systems that make them more vulnerable and less able to detoxify toxins.
- The National Academy of Sciences estimates 50% of lifetime pesticide exposure occurs during the first 5 years of life.
- A study published in the Journal of the National Cancer Institute finds home and garden pesticide use can increase the risk of childhood leukemia by almost seven times.
- Studies show low levels of exposure to actual lawn pesticide products are linked to increased rates of miscarriage, and suppression of the nervous, endocrine, and immune systems.
- Exposure to home and garden pesticides can increase a child's likelihood of developing asthma.
- Studies link pesticides with hyperactivity, developmental delays, behavioural disorders, and motor dysfunction.
- Children ages children ages 6-11 have higher levels of lawn chemicals in their blood than all other age categories. Biomonitoring studies find that pesticides pass from mother to child through umbilical cord blood and breast milk.

Wildlife, Pets and Pesticides

- Studies find that dogs exposed to herbicide-treated lawns and gardens can double their chance of developing canine lymphoma and may increase the risk of bladder cancer in certain breeds by four to seven times.

- Of 30 commonly used lawn pesticides: 16 are toxic to birds, 24 are toxic to fish and aquatic organisms, and 11 are deadly to bees.
- Pesticides can be toxic to wildlife and cause food source contamination, behavioural abnormalities that interfere with survival, and death.
- Lawn and garden pesticides are deadly to non-target species and can harm beneficial insects and soil microorganisms essential to a naturally healthy lawn.

Pesticides in the Water

- Of 30 commonly used lawn pesticides, 17 are detected in ground-water, and 23 have the potential to leach.
- Runoff has resulted in a widespread presence of pesticides in streams and ground-water. 2,4-D, found in weed and feed and other lawn products, is the herbicide most frequently detected in streams and shallow ground water from urban lawns.
- Of the 50 chemicals on EPA's list of unregulated drinking water contaminants, several are lawn chemicals including herbicides diazinon, diuron, naphthalene, and various triazines such as atrazine.
- Runoff from synthetic chemical fertilizers pollutes streams and lakes and causes algae blooms, depleted oxygen and damage to aquatic life.

The Registration System and Pesticide Regulation

- The health data assessed by EPA for the registration of pesticides comes from the manufacturer of the pesticide. EPA is not obligated under the Federal Insecticide Fungicide and Rodenticide Act (FIFRA) to review peer-reviewed scientific literature.
- The U.S. GAO has told Congress on several occasions that the public is misled on pesticide safety by statements characterizing pesticides as "safe" or "harmless." EPA states that no pesticide is 100 percent safe.

- Pesticide testing protocol was developed before science fully understood the human immune and hormonal system. EPA still does not evaluate data for several neurological effects or disruption of the endocrine (hormonal) system.
- EPA does not evaluate the health and environmental effects of actual pesticide formulations sold on the shelf. Data submitted to the EPA also does not account for low-dose effects, synergistic effects with inerts or combined exposure to more than one pesticide at a time.
- Most states have preemption laws that prohibit localities from passing local pesticide-related ordinances that are stricter than the state policy.

Inert" Ingredients

- Pesticide products are made of an active ingredient and several inert, or other, ingredients. Inert ingredients are neither chemically, biologically nor toxicologically inert. Inerts are not disclosed to the public due to their status as "trade secrets".
- Active ingredients usually comprise only 5% of the actual product; the other ingredients make up the majority of a given pesticide product or formulation.
- Inert ingredients can be more toxic to humans than the active ingredient. Ethylene chloride, a nerve poison, is an example of an inert ingredient linked with damage to the heart, eyes, liver, and adrenal glands.
- 800 out of 1200 inerts are classified as "of unknown toxicity," 57 as highly toxic due to known carcinogenicity, adverse reproductive effects, birth defects, neurotoxicity and/or other chronic effects, and 64 as potentially toxic.
- 394 chemicals used as inert ingredients are listed as active ingredients in other pesticide products, and more than 200 inerts are considered hazardous pollutants and/or hazardous waste under federal environmental statutes.

Lawn Maintenance

Maintaining a healthy lawn involves using good maintenance practices throughout the growing season. These include proper mowing, fertility, irrigation, thatch control, integrated pest management, weed management and insect management. These techniques provide a dense, healthy, high quality lawn.

Mowing: The importance of good mowing practices is often overlooked but has a major influence on turf density, uniformity and aesthetic quality of a home lawn. It is the most repetitious and time-consuming maintenance practice and it is often done incorrectly.

Frequency and Height: Turf can be mowed frequently, provided no more than one-third of the grass blade is removed in a single mowing. Mow as high as possible. Lower mowing produces a shallow root system. Shallow grass roots cannot take up water and nutrients and make the lawn susceptible to drought stress.

Low mowing encourages broadleaf weed invasion and invasion from grassy weeds such as creeping bentgrass and annual bluegrass. It is best to mow a lawn when the leaves are dry. Dry grass cuts cleanly and clippings distribute more evenly.

Clippings: Leave clippings on. If they are excessively heavy, rake them up and remove them. Clippings contain nutrients and water, breakdown rapidly and do not contribute significantly to thatch. You can cut down your fertilizer (especially nitrogen) by 20%-35% by leaving the clippings on.

Mowers: Mowers need the capacity and power to handle the area being mowed. Consider weight, manoeuverability, ease in starting, ease of adjustment of height of cut and safety features. Keep mower blades sharp for a good quality cut. Select mulching type mowers that recycle grass clippings.

Fertility: Understanding and implementing a well-balanced fertilizer programme is one of the most important factors in maintaining an attractive healthy lawn. The three main nutrients required by lawns are:

- Nitrogen (N)
- Phosphorus (P)
- Potassium (K)

Nitrogen promotes dark green colour, leaf and blade development, and density of the turf. Phosphorus is important for good root and rhizome development and promoting plant maturity. Potassium contributes to the general vigour of the plant, promotes wear and drought tolerance and hardiness against winter injury.

Amount of Nutrients: The amount of nutrients required by a home lawn is best determined by soil testing. A soil test will provide levels of phosphorus, potassium, pH and lime requirements. There is no soil test for nitrogen. Generally, 1.5-2 kg/100 m^2 of actual nitrogen can be applied throughout the season, split into 2-4 applications. In the absence of a soil test, a 4-1-2 ratio (N-P-K) such as 20-5-10 is recommended. The three numbers on the fertilizer bag represent the amount of N, P and K in that order.

For example the 20-5-10 fertilizer ratio listed above contains 20% N, 5% P and 10% K. Nitrogen has to be applied every year, while phosphorus and potassium are relatively stable in the soil. If the lawn is on sandy soil, higher potash or more frequent applications may be required because it may leach. On newly established lawns, higher levels of phosphorus and potash may be required.

Fertilizers: Common turf nitrogen fertilizers and their properties are listed.

Application: An even application of lawn fertilizers is very important in achieving a uniform green lawn. If using a drop type spreader, operate it the long way of the lawn. First apply header strips at each end of the lawn to provide room for turning. Overlap one wheel's width when spreading the fertilizer and shut off the spreader when reaching the header strips. With a centrifugal type spreader, make two split (half rate each) applications at right angle to each other. Always make sure the spreader is properly adjusted, otherwise you could end up with striping or uneven colour.

Common Turf Nitrogen Fertilizers and Their Properties					
Type	Examples	Response	Problems	Water Solubility	Potential for burn
Inorganic	• ammonium nitrate • ammonium sulfate	• immediately available • quick green up	• readily leaches • causes lush growth	High	High to very high
Organic	• activated sewage sludge • animal by-products • plant by-products	• slow release • low leaching	• more expensive than inorganic forms	Low	Low
Synthetic	• IBDU • urea formeldehyde • sulfur coated urea • polymer coated urea	• slow release • low leaching	• release rate is dependent on temperature or moisture levels depending on the source	Very low	Low to very low

Irrigation

When normal rainfall does not provide enough moisture during the growing season grass goes dormant and turns brown. To ensure a high quality lawn the lawn must be watered. Signs that a lawn needs water include:

- footprints remain while walking across the lawn
- a slight change in colour to dark blue-green and grass blades folding inwards.

Frequency and Timing: Water in the early morning when there is little or no wind. This allows more even water distribution. Water before mid-day when the evaporation rate is the highest. Watering can be done in the evening, but this may encourage disease developing. Most disease-causing fungi require several hours of leaf wetness for infections and disease to occur.

Amount of Water: Too much water can cause thatch, fertilizer leaching, increased disease or grass weed problems such as creeping bentgrass, annual bluegrass or rough bluegrass. Too little water can cause shallow rooting of the turf, which makes the lawn susceptible to disease, drought stress or winter injury. Infrequent, thorough watering is best. When the lawn wilts, wet the entire area to a depth of 10-20 cm. The amount of water required to achieve this depends on soil characteristics. To measure how much water has been applied, place a straight-sided can or jar in the area being watered, and then check the water level in the can or jar. Approximately 2.5-4 cm of water in the can corresponds to an adequate irrigation of the lawn. Areas of the lawn needing more water include slopes, areas near buildings, curbs, sidewalks and light soils. Low lying areas, shaded areas and heavy soils may not need as frequent irrigation.

Dormant Lawns: During extended dry periods, a lawn may turn brown and go dormant. A lawn can survive from 4-6 weeks in a dormant state during summer dry periods. Once the rains return the lawn will green up in 7-10 days. If the lawn is dormant:

- Check regularly for insect pests
- Keep traffic off
- Stop mowing
- Do not fertilize

Irrigation Equipment: Hose watering is suitable for small areas only. A sprinkler attachment provides adequate coverage for an average size lawn despite the inconvenience in moving the sprinkler and a lot of water can be wasted. An underground irrigation system is the most expensive, but also the most efficient method, and may be considered for very large lawns or industrial properties.

Thatch

Thatch is a layer of organic matter made up of decaying grass leaves, stems and roots that build up in between the lawn and soil surface. It is a common problem on home lawns, particularly for lawns established for several years.

Identification: A thatchy lawn feels very spongy when walked on. Cut a triangular patch of lawn with a sharp knife and lift it back to measure the thickness of the thatch layer. More than 2.5 cm of thatch is too much.

Why is Thatch a Problem?: Thatch harbours insects and diseases. Thatch can restrict grass roots from growing into the soil root zone, resulting in a shallow rooted lawn. Thatch interferes with water infiltration.

Minimizing Thatch: Cultural practices that minimize thatch development are:

- frequent mowing
- proper watering
- proper ferilization

Excess thatch can be removed by vertical mowing or core aerating. Core aerate using a hollow steel tine core aerator which removes cores of soil. This physically breaks up the thatch, brings up beneficial soil micro-organisms that help break down the thatch and alleviates compaction.

Timing: Dethatch or aerate in spring and fall during periods of good growth, allowing for quick lawn recovery.

Overseeding: Overseeding is a method of thickening up a lawn that has become thin due to insects, disease or other types of damage. To insure success, add compost, peat or topsoil before overseeding. Overseed at double the seeding rate for establishing a new lawn. The best time to overseed a lawn is in the fall (mid-August to mid-September). Keep the overseeded area moist by watering several times a day. One week after seeding, reduce watering to twice a day until seedlings are established.

Integrated Pest Management

Try to manage pest problems in lawns by following the principles of integrated pest management. With integrated pest management prevention of pest problems is the best approach. Use good maintenance practices to promote a healthy lawn. It involves:

- Proper lawn planning and maintenance to prevent pests.
- Checking frequently for lawn pests.
- Proper identification of lawn pests.
- Treating with a pesticide only when a pest is present in large enough numbers to cause damage to the lawn.

The goal is to reduce pesticide use but still maintain healthy lawns.

Weed Management

A thick vigorous lawn is the best prevention against weed invasion. A dense stand of turf can compete successfully with weed seedlings for light and nutrients.

Weed Invasion: Problem weeds include both broad-leaved and grass weeds. They may occur when there are thin or damaged areas or heavily trafficked areas. Before attempting any weed control, weeds should be properly identified. Homeowners can consult nurseries, lawn care professionals, Publication 529, Weed Control in Lawns and Gardens or Publication 505, Ontario Weeds from the Ontario Ministry of Agriculture and Food or the Pest Diagnostic Clinic at the University of Guelph.

Control: Control problem weeds by:

- hand pulling
- hand raking
- mowing to prevent seed formation
- spot application of selective herbicides
- using a combination of the methods mentioned above.

Control a few weeds in a lawn by hand weeding or spot treating with a broad-leaved herbicide. If the weed infestation is too big to be handled with these methods, a broadcast herbicide may be required. Avoid using combination products containing herbicides and fertilizers unless the whole lawn is infested with weeds.

Most broadleaf herbicides available to home owners contain a combination of 2,4-D, mecoprop and dicamba. Weeds are easiest to control with herbicides when they are growing rapidly.

Herbicide Use: Spot treat whenever possible. Early spring or fall treatments are usually best. Younger weeds are more susceptible than mature weeds. Use the following precautions when applying herbicides:

- Do not apply during hot days because they may injure the lawn.

- Do not apply during the rain. Broad-leaved herbicides require 24 hours of dry weather to ensure good uptake by the plant.
- Delay mowing or irrigation for several days after application.
- Do not spray under windy conditions.
- Do not use 2,4-D or dicamba products on newly seeded lawns.

Preemergence herbicides are used to control weeds like crabgrass. To be effective, apply the herbicide before germination of weed seedlings. Only apply preemergence herbicides to areas with a history of a crabgrass problem. Read manufacturer's label for specific instructions on application and the required waiting period before re-seeding.

Insect Management

Insects that infest home lawns are generally difficult to notice and their presence goes undetected until significant damage has been done. Insect damage can often be mistaken for drought damage.

If the lawn remains brown or shows signs of thinning out despite watering, then closer examination for insects should be done. Regular inspection of the lawn including leaves, stems, roots, thatch and soil will help to determine if the problem is insect-related and catch the problem before extensive damage occurs. The most common lawn insect pests are:

- Hairy chinch bug
- Grubs
- Sod webworms
- European cranefly
- Bluegrass billbug
- Turfgrass Scale

Hairy Chinch Bug: Hairy chinch bug damage starts to become noticeable from mid-July to mid-August. It causes damage by sucking plant juice from the grass stems with its piercing and sucking mouth parts.

The first signs of damage are small fist sized sunken areas in the lawn. As the insects continue to feed these areas can grow very rapidly into large dead areas. Damaged areas are often taken over by weeds. Adults are very small (4 mm long) and their wings form an X on their backs.

One method of detecting chinch bugs is to cut the ends of a metal can to make a cylinder and force it into the ground. Fill the cylinder with water, chinch bugs will float to the surface if they are present in the lawn. If chinch bugs are found in a lawn apply one of the insect pesticides available from garden centres, etc. that are labelled to control hairy chinch bugs.

Grubs: Several species of grubs can cause damage by feeding on grass roots in home lawns. The most common grubs are:

- June beetle
- European chafer
- Japanese beetle

If animals such as skunks begin digging up the lawn or if small irregular patches of grass turn brown, it may indicate grubs present in the lawn. Check for grubs in late summer or early fall before damage is noticed. Lift a section of sod and soil with a spade, 10 cm square and look for white, C-shaped grubs in the soil.

Keeping the lawn well watered helps minimize grub damage. Insecticides that control grubs are available at local garden centres. Timing for grub insecticide treatments is late summer or early fall before extensive damage occurs. The insecticide must be watered in with 2.5 cm of water to be effective.

Sod Webworms: Sod webworms are caterpillars that feed in the thatch on home lawns. The adults are small tan moths that fly around lawns at night. The caterpillars grow to 2 cm and are tan in colour.

They have dark spots on their backs. They feed in the thatch causing damage that is similar to grub damage, where areas of turf can be lifted like a carpet. They also leave behind soft green fecal pellets in the areas they are feeding. The damage occurs in September. Use products containing carbaryl to control sod webworms.

Bluegrass Billbug: Bluegrass billbugs are in the weevil family. The adults are black and 5 mm long. Larvae are small white and legless with a brown head. Damage begins with small groups of plants turning yellow and dying. This occurs in mid-July to mid-August. Damage is usually spotty and rarely affects a whole lawn. Billbugs leave behind a sawdust-like excrement in areas they have been feeding. This is helpful in diagnosing the damage.

European Cranefly: The European cranefly is a relatively new pest to lawns in Ontario. The adult cranefly resembles a large mosquito. The larvae are known as leatherjackets. They are light greyish-brown with black specks. There is no visible head region. They range in size from 0.5-3.0 cm in length. Leatherjackets feed primarily on grass shoots during the evening and on grass roots during the day. Damage begins to show between early to mid-May and peaks by mid-June. Heavy infestations of leatherjackets can chew the grass down to the bare soil.

Turfgrass Scale: Turfgrass scale is a typical scale insect that resembles an egg cut in half lengthwise. It is brown with a yellow stripe in the middle. The immature stage is called a crawler and it is the size of the head of a pin. Typical damage is small patches of dead grass that do not green up in the spring. They are found mainly on sodded lawns and in general, do not cause much damage. During early July crawlers can be found on shoes when you walk through the lawn. There is no insecticide registered for use on turfgrass scale in Ontario.

Endophytes: One way to combat the damage caused by leaf feeding insects is to plant grasses that contain endophytes. Endophytes are fungi that grow inside the grass plant and make it taste bad. Lawn insects repelled by endophytes are hairy chinch bugs, bluegrass billbugs and sod webworms.

A summary of the major turf insect pests, how to identify them, the damage they cause and how to treat them can be found. Lawn species that may contain endophytes are perennial ryegrass, fine fescues and tall fescue. Consult your local garden centre or seed supplier about the endophytic grasses they sell.

Other Pests

Moss: Mosses are primitive forms of green plants that form tangled clumps that grow in amongst a lawn. Moss plants have a tremendous capacity to spread. They produce large numbers of spores, each of which can give rise to a new moss plant. Mosses are poor competitors with a healthy lawn and are only a problem when the lawn is weakened by poor growing conditions. The following conditions that weaken a lawn and promote moss invasion:

- poor aeration
- poor drainage
- low fertility
- high acidity
- heavy shade

Cultural methods can be effective in controlling moss. They are:

- Adequate fertility, especially nitrogen (2.0 kg per 100 m^2 of actual N).
- Control thatch by vigorous raking, aeration or vertical mowing.
- Reduce shade by pruning trees.
- Maintain a soil pH of between 6 to 7-apply lime if soil is acidic.
- Improve surface drainage.
- Reduce compaction and increase aeration by spiking slicing or aerifying with a mechanical aeifier.
- Do not over-water.
- Do not remove more that 1/3 of the top growth at one time when mowing and mow at a height appropriate for the grass species.

Disease Management

If integrated pest management practices are followed, disease problems in home lawns are minimal. Excessive fertility can cause succulent growth that is more susceptible to diseases. When establishing or renovating a lawn area, select varieties that are resistant to various diseases. Improper irrigation also contributes to lawn diseases. Make sure to water in the early morning to minimize the length of time that the lawn stays wet. A summary of common turfgrass diseases on home lawns. Outlines a sample integrated pest management programme for home lawns in Ontario. It can be used as a guideline for fertilizing, overseeding and aerating as well as for pest monitoring and treatment.

Pesticide Use

The two types of pesticides commonly used on lawns are herbicides for weed control and insecticides for insect control. Before applying a pesticide follow the steps of integrated pest management. Make sure that the pest is properly identified. When purchasing a pesticide make sure the label includes the pest you are trying to kill and that the pesticide lists lawns. Read the label carefully and follow the manufacturer's directions. Spot treat areas where possible and time applications correctly to avoid repeat application.

Landscape Introduction

Lawns, ornamental shrubs and trees, often poorly adapted to difficult urban conditions, have for many years dominated urban landscape design. To survive, these landscapes require high levels of maintenance, irrigation, fertilizers, herbicides and pesticides. These not only increase the cost of ownership, but pollute stormwater runoff and provide little or no habitat for local wildlife. Ecologically based landscape design can change this pattern.

It considers a region's water flows, climate, open spaces, native vegetation, wildlife and existing urban development. Understanding the ecology of the region helps when working with the needs of a specific site design, including its solar access, wind patterns, topography, rainfall and drainage patterns, the preservation of existing vegetation and unique features of the site.

In recent years the City of Santa Monica has promoted a more environmentally responsive approach to landscape design, particularly in water conservation. Through the City requirement to use drought-resistant plants, restrict the amount of lawn and the use of efficient irrigation systems, water consumption has dropped significantly.

The Required Practices focus on landscape design that conserves water and improves water quality. Outdoor water use accounts for approximately 35% of overall water consumption in Greater Los Angeles, of which half is used to irrigate gardens and landscaping. Planting drought-tolerant vegetation, minimizing lawn areas and using drip irrigation can reduce water use in the garden by 50% to 70% and overall water consumption by 20% to 25%. By managing stormwater runoff through on-site surface water retention and reducing the area of impermeable paving, fewer pollutants enter Santa Monica Bay.

The Recommended Practices address a broader range of environmental benefits gained through landscape design. These include improving the microclimate around buildings to reduce cooling energy consumption and improve occupant comfort, reducing glare, enhancing the appeal of exterior spaces, providing habitat for urban wildlife and creating opportunities for local food production.

Controlling Solar Gain and Improving Ventilation: Controlling solar gain in a building through planting on south, southwest and southeast sides of buildings is a very effective way to reduce cooling loads. In Santa Monica, where southwest-oriented building facades have the greatest solar heat gain, planting shade trees regulates heat gain and reduces air-conditioning needs. Trees and other vegetation can also shade paved areas and provide a canopy for pedestrians.

In addition to controlling solar gain, landscaping and landscape structures can enhance a building's natural ventilation and cooling by influencing wind flow. This requires the landscape design to respond to prevailing wind patterns and local wind flow variations, and strategically locating trees, hedges and shrubs to direct winds toward ventilation inlets and create low-pressure areas at outlets.

Dissipating turbulent, higher velocity winds in circulation areas around buildings can also be achieved by placing a multilayered planting of large trees and shrubs with dense foliage at the base and corners of buildings.

Air Quality and Wildlife Habitat: Ecologically based landscape design can improve local air quality by absorbing carbon dioxide, producing oxygen and filtering particulates. Landscaped parks and streets provide a "green lung" for the community. Building roofs and balconies can be deliberately designed to accommodate vegetation. Conventional roofs degrade air quality by replacing a site's original vegetative cover with an impervious surface that absorbs solar energy and contributes to the urban heat island effect. Planted roofs provide a living surface that cools and insulates the building, improves air quality and protects roof membranes from ultraviolet breakdown.

Landscape design can create important habitat for resident and migratory wildlife by providing food and shelter. Through mulching and composting green matter, ecologically-based landscaping can maintain and improve soil fertility, retain soil moisture, stimulate soil-based microbial activity and maintain the cycle of nutrients in the soil. In addition, the use of native and other ecologically appropriate plants reduces water consumption, maintenance requirements, and the use of pesticides and herbicides, and increases the area's suitability for wildlife.

Health Benefits of Ecological Landscaping: Finally, environmentally based landscape design practices can have direct financial and human health benefits. Capital and annual utility costs and regular maintenance requirements can be reduced, resulting in lower overall operating costs. Incorporating areas to grow food within developments encourages local food production and reduces monthly food expenses.

It can provide occupants with a secure source of organically grown, fresh produce. Opportunities to garden provide personal health benefits that can improve the quality of life, particularly for older people with leisure time to enjoy gardening.

Pests and Diseases of Roses

Roses *Rosa sp.* are susceptible to a number of pests, diseases and disorders. A large number of the problems affecting roses are seasonal and climatic.

Certain varieties of roses are naturally more resistant or immune than others to certain pests and diseases. Cultivation requirements of individual rose species and cultivars, when observed, often assist in the prevention of certain pests, diseases and disorders.

Pests

Pests are often considered to be the insects that affect roses:

- **Aphids** (Greenfly) (Order Hemiptera: Family Aphididae) *Macrosiphum rosae*

  Likely to be found on new shoots and buds, aphids are soft bodied insects 1-2mm long. Often green but occasionally light-brown, and sometimes with wings, they may cover (in a colony) the complete growing tip of the plant. Aphids are most active in spring and summer and multiply at a prodigeous rate feeding on the sap of the plant by piercing the plant cells via a proboscis. In large quantities they may seriously retard the growth of the plant and ruin buds. They are particularly damaging to the new shoots with subsequent damage to the emerging leaves which become malformed with much the same appearance as leaf-curl in peaches.
- **Two-spotted mite** (Spider-mites or Red spider mite) (Order Acari: Family Tetranychidae) *Tetranychus urticae*

Previously known as red-spider mite these arachnids prefer the underside of leaves and are difficult to see with an unaided eye. Evidence of their presence is silvering of leaves where the mites have destroyed individual leaf cells. Fine webbing and eggs on the undersides of leaves is further evidence of the presence of *Tetranychus urticae*.

- **Thrips** (Order Thysanoptera)

  Thrips are slim-winged insects 1mm in length, resembling fine black slivers of wood. Preferring light-coloured blooms and often appearing in plague numbers flowers are often left looking bruised and lustreless.

- **Caterpillars** (Order Lepidoptera) See also List of Lepidoptera which feed on Roses

  The tortryx (tortrix) moth *Lozotaenia forsterana* is a prominent pest of roses, although not the sole pest. The caterpillars are green, up to 15mm long, and can be found boring into buds or within curled leaves. When disturbed the caterpillars move swiftly, dropping to the ground on a fine thread. Damage is chewn leaves and flowers and buds with "shot holes".

- **Curculio beetles** (Family Curculionidae)
- **Scale** (Order Hemiptera)

Cottony Cushion Scale (Order Hemiptera : Family Coccoidea) *Icerya purchasi*

This scale infests twigs and branches. The mature female is oval in shape, reddish-brown with black hairs, 5 mm long. When mature the insect remains stationary and produces an egg sac in grooves, by extrusion, in the body which encases hundreds of red eggs. The insect causes little damage but produces copious honeydew (frass) that can cause damaging sooty mould.

California Red Scale (Order Hemiptera : Family Coccoidea) *Aonidiella aurantii*

A hard scale, orange to orange-pink, the female covering being less than 1.5mm across. Often in plague numbers this scale infests upper surfaces of foliage causing yellowing, leaf fall, and twig and branch dieback. Serious infestations can cause plant death.

Rose scale (*Order Hemiptera* : Family Coccoidea) *Aulacaspis rosae*

Mainly found on the stems and branches of the plant, lack of control will allow the pest to spread to flower stalks and petioles. At this point the plant would be stunted, spindly and with a white, flaky crust of scales on the bark. Female *Aulacaspis rosae*may live for 1 year and may lay 80 eggs each with several overlapping generations living within millimetres of the original parent.

- **Leaf cutting bee** (Order Hymenoptera : Family Megachilidae) *Megachile spp.*

  Leafcutter bees are 6-16mm long and mostly black with bands of light-coloured hair. They chew pieces from the edges of leaves. The pieces are regular in shape, circular or oval. Damage is not often significant.

- **Nematodes** (Eelworms) (Order Tylenchida: Family Heteroderidae)

Root-knot nematode *Meloidogyne spp.*

Root-knot nematode-symptoms of *Meloidogyne* infestation in roses is stunting, slow-growth, pale green leaves and wilting in mild weather.

- **Metallic flea-beetles** (Order Coleoptera: Family Chrysomelidae) *Altica* spp.

The small, shiny and metallic *Altica* beetles have thickened hindlegs adapted to jumping, similar to fleas. The insects are 3mm long and chew holes of irregular shapes in young leaves and buds. As the leaves enlarge so do the holes.

Diseases

Fungal, bacterial and viral diseases affect roses:

Fungal Disease

- **Black Spot** (Class Leotiomycetes: Family Helotiales) *Marssonina rosae* syn. *Diplocarpon rosae*

Marssonina rosae causes black spots on leaves. The spots, which may be as much as 12mm across, are generally circular and have an irregular edge often with a yellow halo. Leaves frequently turn yellow and fall early. Sometimes new leaves are produced, and these may also become affected.

Continual defoliation will cause weakness, die-back or death of the plant. Some very susceptible species may have stems affected with a considerable reduction in plant vigour.

- **Powdery Mildew** *Oidium* sp.

  Oidium produces a very fine, powdery coating on the surface of buds and leaves. Significant cases have stems and particularly thorns, infected. Attacks on young leaves and buds will cause deformity with retardation of growth. Infected buds will fail to open. The disease is likely in hot, humid weather, with fungal spores overwintering on the stems and fallen leaves.

- **Downy mildew** (Class Oomycetes : Family Peronosporaceae) *Peronospora sparsa*

  Peronospora causes purple-red to dark-brown spots on the leaves with irregular margins, however, often angular. Stems, petioles and flower stalks can split and spotted with purple marks. Buds, sepals, petals and calyces can be affected and will present purple spots. New growth affected will be deformed. The disease is spread by wind.

- **Rust** *Phragmidium mucronatum*

  Rose rust appears as yellow patches on the surface of leaves, with orange pustules of spores underneath the leaf. The fungus is spread by wind. Affected leaves fall prior to healthy ones and plants may be defoliated in serious infections.

- **Anthracnose** *Sphaceloma rosarum*

  Spots caused by this fungus originate from a point where leaves are watersoaked, ususally unnoticeable at first, until they turn black with a very distinct defined edge. As the spots enlarge the centre becomes gray and may fall out resulting in a shot-hole appearance. Defoliation may occur but is often not serious.

- **Grey mould** (Class Leotiomycetes: Family Sclerotiniceae) *Botrytis cineria*

  On roses grey mould is prmiarily a disease of the flowers and buds, leaves are infrequently attacked. Infected buds rot on the stem and infection may progress down the stem. On petals *botrytis cineria* produces pink rings.

- **Verticillium wilt** (Class Incertae sedis: Family Verticillium) *Verticillium dahliae*

- **Sooty moulds** *Alternaria* spp.

  Sooty mould appears as black, dry powder on leaves similar to chimney soot. Many sooty moulds grow on the honeydew (frass) produced by sap-sucking insect such as aphids and soft scales. *Alternaria* does no direct damage to plants but surface cover of leaves will reduce the plants capacity to photosynthesise and may create an unsatisfactory plant appearance.

- **Canker** *Leptosphaeria coniothyrium* and *Cryptosporella umbrina*

  Cankers present as small yellowish or reddish spots on bark slowly increasing in size. *Leptosphaeria coniothyrium* turns brown, increases in size, and may eventually girdle the stem. The tissue within the infection begins to dry out and shrink, presenting a shrivelled appearance. If the disease infects only part of the stem, growth above the canker will continue. If it girdles the stem, however, growth will cease and the stem will die.

Viral Disease

- **Rose Mosaic**

  This diesase is caused by a complex or viruses and is charaterised by yello patterns on the leaves. The patterns vary considerably, ranging between all-over fine blotches to patterns of lines in waves. The patterns may appear on a few or many leaves. Plants are infected by this virus at propagation using infected plant material.

- **Rose Wilt**

  Rose wilt is a complex of viruses and is referred to as *dieback* in some areas. The disease can be spread by vectors such as aphids. Symptoms are variable and range from stunted growth to curled young leaves. The soft tissue symptoms are more evident in spring and new leaves will reflex towards their own petioles. The affected leaves are brittle and easily fall from the plant. Fully formed leaves will 'wilt' as if the plant were water stressed.

Bacterial Disease

- **Crown gall rot** (Class Alpha Proteobacteria: Family Rhizobiaceae) *Agrobacterium rhizogenes*

  This disease is characterised by large lumps at the base of the plant stem or on roots. Galls may appear higher on stems as the disease progresses. Galls are soft compared to surrounding plant tissues. The pathogenic bacteria enter the plant via a wound. If the disease affects the plant whilst it is young the plant may be affected to the degree where it will not produce blooms. All affected plants wilt readily and grow poorly.

Environmental Disorders

- **Frost**

  Frost will destroy fresh growth causing stems and leaves to wilt, turn black and fall away from the plant. Timing pruning to promote growth after the threat of frost is a means to avoid frost damage.

- **Salinity**

  Salinity will present in roses as limp and light brown leaves with dry leaf margins. Soil may require testing to determine salinity levels. Symptoms will present if salinity is greater than 1200 parts per million.

- **Herbicide Damage**

Overspray or soil leaching of herbicidal sprays can present with several symptoms:

Prolonged exposure to overspray of glyphosatewill cause yellow leaves and new leaves will be small and elongated.

Hormone weedsprays (e.g. 24-D & 245-T) may cause grotesque new growth with thin twisted leaves and distorted buds. Plants may die in severe cases.

Pre-emergent herbicides contacting the plants' rootsystem via the soil will cause yellowing foliage. Effects of soil borne herbicide may take several years to clear.

Additives for Cut Flowers

Additives for cut flowers are substances added to water, intended to extend the viability of the flowers. Once flowers are removed from the plant they continue to grow slowly but have a diminished capability of receiving the nutrients that are vital for their survival.

That there are different techniques of insuring that fresh cut flowers remain alive for the longest amount of time.

Sterilization

According to James C. Schmidt, a horticulturist at the University of Illinois, originally putting cut flowers in a sterilized vase is important to extending the life of the flowers. Vases can be cleaned using a household dish detergent or a combination of water and bleach. Using these disinfectants insures that there will not be any bacteria growing within the vase that could potentially cause the plant to wilt and die at a faster rate. Schmidt also claims that cutting the flowers diagonally with a sharp knife under running water insures that they can immediately take up fresh and clean water. Re-cutting the stems periodically throughout the lifespan of the flowers will insure that there is a fresh surface from which the stems can take up water. This will allow the freshly cut flowers to last even longer.

Additives

According to the Brooklyn Botanical Garden, different additives can be used to prolong the lives of fresh cut flowers. Experiments were performed with various substances mixed with water, including aspirin, vitamin pills, vinegar, pennies, and flower food to test their effect on cut flowers' lifespans.

Each plant was put into the same environment and the same type of plant was used in each vase.

This research found that the best additive for flowers was the retailer-provided "flower food" that is usually given with a bouquet. Plants are known to thrive in an environment where there are little bacteria, there is plenty of food for energy, and water uptake is encouraged. Flower foods contain an acidifier which helps to adjust the water's pH. With a lower pH the water and food conducting system within the flower can work at maximum efficiency.

The sugar in the food will be used by the plant as an energy source, which had been lost when the flower was cut away from its root. With these nutrients the plant will be able to fully develop. Finally, there are stem unpluggers that will make sure that the flower can easily take up water and nutrients that can later be used to take care of the needs of the rest of the plant. This combination gives the fresh cut flowers everything that they need to survive longer.

Adventitious

Adventitious, in botany, refers to structures that develop in an unusual place, and in medicine, it refers to conditions acquired after birth. This article discusses adventitious roots, buds and shoots, that are very common in vascular plants.

Adventitious Roots

Root developing from any part other than the radicle is called adventitious root. Adventitious roots develop on stems, leaves and even old roots. The radicle or primary root and its lateral roots are the only nonadventitious roots. Many aerial stems naturally form aerial roots. There are two types of adventitious roots. Aerial stems often have preformed root initials at nodes that will develop into roots given the proper conditions. Other adventitious roots are termed wound roots, because they do not form until the stem, root or leaf is wounded.

In some species, adventitious roots form on aerial stems, grow down into the soil and help keep the stems upright, *e.g.* prop roots of maize, screwpine and banyan. Some vine stems cling to their supports using adventitious roots, *e.g.* English ivy and philodendron. Adventitious roots may also form naturally when an aerial stem contacts the soil, *e.g.* arching branches of forsythia, blackberry and weeping willow. Some trees, such as willow, naturally shed pieces of twigs, a phenomenon known as cladoptosis. The shed twigs are often transported via rivers and streams and can form new plants if they develop adventitious roots.

Virtually the entire root system is adventitious in many vascular plants, especially ferns, fern allies and most monocots, *e.g.* grasses. In most monocot species, the radicle never develops to any extent, and adventitious roots form at the base of the stem. Such adventitious root systems are also termed fibrous root systems.

Root systems of specialized underground stems (rhizomes, bulbs, tubers, corms) are all adventitious roots. The tap root systems of most dicots and gymnosperms develop from the primary root but even they often develop some adventitious roots when the old roots or lower stem is wounded. Horizontal, aboveground stems, termed stolons or runners, usually develop adventitious roots at their nodes, *e.g.* strawberry.

Adventitious Buds and Shoots

Adventitious buds develop from places other than a shoot apical meristem, which occurs at the tip of a stem. They may develop on stems, roots or leaves. Shoot apical meristems produce one or more axillary or lateral buds at each node. When stems produce considerable secondary growth, the axillary buds may be destroyed. Adventitious buds may then develop on stems with secondary growth.

Adventitious buds are often formed after the stem is wounded or pruned. The adventitious buds help to replace lost branches. Adventitious buds and shoots also may develop on mature tree trunks when a shaded trunk is exposed to bright sunlight because surrounding trees are cut down. Redwood (*Sequoia sempervirens*) trees often develop many adventitious buds on their lower trunks. If the main trunk dies, a new one often sprouts from one of the adventitious buds. Small pieces of redwood trunk are sold as souvenirs termed redwood burls. They are placed in a pan of water, and the adventitious buds sprout to form shoots.

Some plants normally develop adventitious buds on their roots, which can extend quite a distance from the plant. Shoots that develop from adventitious buds on roots are termed suckers. They are a type of natural vegetative reproduction in many species, *e.g.* many grasses, quaking aspen and Canada thistle. The Pando quaking aspen grew from one trunk to 47,000 trunks via adventitious bud formation on a single root system.

Some leaves develop adventitious buds, which then form adventitious roots, *e.g.* piggyback plant (*Tolmiea menziesii*) and mother-of-thousands (*Kalanchoe daigremontiana*). The adventitious plantlets then drop off the parent plant and develop as separate clones of the parent.

Coppicing is the practice of cutting tree stems to the ground to promote rapid growth of adventitious shoots. It is traditionally used to produce poles, fence material or firewood. It is also practised for biomass crops grown for fuel, such as poplar or willow.

Location of Origin

Adventitious roots and buds usually develop near the existing vascular tissues so they can connect to the xylem and phloem. However, the exact location varies greatly. In young stems, adventitious roots often form from parenchyma between the vascular bundles. In stems with secondary growth, adventitious roots often originate in phloem parenchyma near the vascular cambium. In stem cuttings, adventitious roots sometimes also originate in the callus cells that form at the cut surface. Leaf cuttings of the *Crassula* form adventitious roots in the epidermis.

Modification of Adventitious Root

Tuberous Roots: These are without any definite shape. *e.g.* Sweet Potato.

Fasciculated Root: In this type the tuberous root occur in clusters at the base of the stem e.g. asparagus, dahlia.

Nodulose Roots: This type of roots become swollen near the tips. *e.g.* turmeric.

Stilt Roots: These roots arise from the first few nodes of the stem. These penetrate obliquely down in to the soil and give support to the plant. *e.g.* maize, sugarcane.

Prop Roots: These roots give mechanical support to the aerial branches. The lateral branches grow vertically downward into the soil and acts as pillars. *e.g.* banyan.

Most second-generation moths emerge in mid-July. The second-generation larvae also attack nuts, but the loss is less because an individual PNC typically requires only one nut for its development. Third-generation moths emerge during late August and September, and larvae feed in the nut shuck at the base of the nut, on the shuck surface and, to some extent, on the leaves.

Description: Eggs are minute and change from white to pink as they incubate for three to nine days (an average of five days). Most are found near the flower end of the nut, on and beneath the calyx lobes. A larva has five pairs of prolegs and changes from olive-gray to gray-brown as it grows to measure one-half inch.

The head is reddish-brown, and the body is sparsely covered with fine, white hairs. The larval stage lasts from 25 to 33 days. Adult moths are slate-gray with a ridge of long, dark scales on the basal end of forewings. Moths are one-third inch long, with a wingspan of four-fifths of an inch.

Scouting and Control: The first generation is the most damaging, causing an average loss of 20 percent in unsprayed pecan orchards in southwest Missouri. Begin scouting for PNC eggs/larvae when all the catkins on native trees have fallen or when the tips of the nuts turn brown after pollination (approximately June 1 in southwest Missouri). You should inspect at least 200 nut clusters. When you find that 1 percent to 3 percent of the nut clusters have been damaged, apply an insecticide. During years of heavy nut set on native trees, you can delay spraying until 5 percent of the nut clusters sustain PNC damage.

The narrow window of time for insecticide application is a two-day to four-day period that varies each year, so controlling the PNC can be difficult. Properly timing insecticide means applying it early enough to kill PNC larvae that have not yet begun boring into nutlets, but late enough to destroy late-dispersing egg-laying females and their offspring. A single, properly timed insecticide application will control PNC. The optimal application dates for PNC control ranged from June 15 to June 22 during our four-year study in southwest Missouri.

Texas researchers currently are field-testing traps that use a recently identified PNC female sex pheromone. The pheromone traps capture male PNC moths and serve as an early warning of adult flight activity. Trap monitoring can help you know when to begin scouting for eggs/larvae. Timely scouting allows you to more reliably assess the need for insecticide. The PNC pheromone traps should be on the market in 1996.

Hickory Shuckworm (*Cydia caryana*)

Three generations of HSW exist in southwest Missouri. Mature larvae overwinter in pecan shucks found on the ground or the tree and emerge as moths in mid-May. Spring development of HSW coincides with that of native hickory trees, which set fruit two to three weeks earlier than pecans. First-generation moths oviposit on hickory nuts, phylloxera galls and on pecan foliage, although those larvae hatching on pecan foliage rarely survive.

Few pecan trees are infested with first-generation HSW because most moths die before pecan nut set. Second-generation larval feeding in the interior of the nut, which occurs from mid-July until shell hardening in mid-August, causes premature nut drop. In newly dropped nuts, you often can detect a chalky, white deposit at the larval entry point.

This deposit is the scales of the female moth, placed to protect and seal the egg to the shuck. The HSW larva creates a paper-thin "window" in the shuck before pupation, which protects the pupa and provides an easily torn exit hole for the adult moth.

The third-generation moths typically emerge in early August. After shell hardening, the larvae mine tunnels in green shucks, which attaches the injured portions of the shucks to the shell (sticktights). Such third-generation shuckmining also delays nut maturity and inhibits proper kernel development.

Description: Eggs are minute, white and flattened and usually are laid on the shucks. Larvae have five pairs of prolegs, are creamy-white with brownish heads and are three-eighths of an inch long when mature. Adult moths are dark-gray nocturnal flyers, three-eighths of an inch long with a wingspread of one-half inch. Pupae, dark-brown and up to one-third inch long, are found within the shuck.

Scouting and Control: Second-generation HSW rarely causes economic damage to native pecans. You should focus on controlling the third-generation moths, which often emerge at the same time as pecan weevils (early August). If PW emergence is delayed by drought conditions, you can apply an insecticide at the shell-hardening stage of nut development in mid-August. Adequate control of the third-generation often translates into lower HSW populations in subsequent years.

Nut Curculio (*Conotrachelus hicoriae*)

The adult NC attacks immature pecans from mid-July to mid-August. Females make shallow, crescent-shaped punctures with their beaks in the shucks of immature nuts, and they deposit a single egg in each nut. The eggs hatch in four to five days, and the larvae feed for 10 to 14 days. This puncture and the larval feeding cause a bleeding of brown sap on the nut shuck at the point of entry and also premature nut drop. The damaged nuts drop from the tree in late July to late August, and the larvae continue to feed in the fallen nuts for about two more weeks. The larvae exit through a one-sixteenth inch hole and enter the soil. The adult NC emerges four weeks later, from September to October, and overwinters in ground trash or other protected places. The NC produces one generation a year and rarely is economically damaging.

Description: Adults are dark-gray to reddish-brown and are three-sixteenths of an inch long, with the beak about one-third the body length. Larvae have no legs or prolegs and are creamy-white, three-sixteenths of an inch long and found within immature pecans.

Scouting and Control: People often confuse damage from the NC with that of the HSW. Usually trees adjacent to woody areas are prone to NC (and PW) attack because of the protection provided for overwintering sites. Insecticides applied for the control of third-generation HSW or PW also can reduce numbers of NC adults because their active periods coincide with these pests.

Pecan Weevil (*Curculio caryae*)

The adult PW typically emerges from the soil as early as July 25, frequently two to three days after a heavy rain. Adults cause two types of nut damage, depending on the stage of nut development during attack. Adults feeding on nuts before the gel stage (*i.e.*, in the water stage, usually before shell hardening) induce kernel shriveling and blackening and premature nut drop. You sometimes can recognize nuts damaged in this way by a tiny, dark puncture that extends through the shuck and unhardened shell and a tobacco-like stain around the feeding wound. The presence of a larva in the nut, prior to shell hardening, indicates damage by another insect, usually NC or HSW. PW grubs are not found in nuts with unhardened shells.

The second type of nut damage is caused by weevil grubs feeding in partially matured nuts. Females oviposit two to four eggs in separate pockets within each kernel, after the nuts have entered the gel stage (about mid-August) until shuck split. Damaged mature nuts neither bleed nor drop. PW grubs feed on the kernels for approximately 30 days and then exit through a one-eighth of an inch emergence hole beginning in late September.The PW remains in the larval stage for one to two years in earthen cells 4 to 12 inches underground. They pupate in early autumn and metamorphose into adults in about three weeks. These adults remain in the soil until the following August. The complete life cycle requires two to three years.

Description: Adults are light-brown to gray and about one-half inch long. The beak of the male is half the length of the body, and the beak of the female is slightly longer than the body. Larvae have no legs or prolegs and are creamy-white, C-shaped grubs with reddish-brown heads measuring up to one-half inch long.

Scouting and Control: The PW is considered to be the most serious late-season pecan pest. Pecan varieties differ widely in their susceptibility to attack. Early ripening varieties that enter the gel stage in early August are most commonly infested. Ordinarily, weevils do not move far from the tree under which they emerge from the soil (provided there is a crop of nuts on that tree). Consequently, certain trees may be infested year after year while other adjacent trees of the same variety may not be attacked. You can spray pecan trees that have a history of PW damage with an insecticide at gel stage and then spray again 10 to 14 days later.

Cone-shaped emergence traps are the best way to detect first emergence of PW adults. Place the PW traps (four per tree, near the drip line) under suspected "weevil trees" by July 25. The economic threshold is five PW per trap when the nuts have reached the gel stage.

Pecan Phylloxera (*Phylloxera devastratrix*)

Three species of phylloxera are pecan pests, but only the PP causes economic damage in certain years. The pecan leaf phylloxera and the southern pecan leaf phylloxera feed primarily on the foliage, whereas the PP attacks the foliage, shoots and fruit and is therefore the most damaging. The PP is a small, aphid-like insect that is rarely seen, but the galls it produces are prominent and easily noticed. Severe infestations cause malformed, weakened shoots that finally die; such infestations can destroy entire limbs.

The PP overwinters as eggs located inside the dead body of a female adult, which is in protected places on the branches of pecan trees. Soon after budbreak, the eggs hatch and the young insects migrate to opening buds or leaf tissue to feed on expanding new growth. The individuals that hatch from the overwintering eggs are known as stem mothers. Feeding by the stem mothers stimulates the development of galls, which enclose the stem mother in a few days. Inside the gall, the stem mother matures, lays her eggs and dies. Eggs laid by the stem mother hatch within the gall, and these nymphs feed within the gall until they mature.

In early July, the galls split open and the mature nymphs emerge as winged, asexual adults. These adults migrate to other trees or other parts of the same tree and lay eggs that are of two sizes. The smaller eggs hatch into male sexuals, and the larger eggs hatch into female sexuals. Male and female sexuals do not feed; their sole purpose is to mate and produce the overwintering egg. After mating, female sexuals seek out sheltered places on a tree, where they die with a fertilized egg inside them, protected for the winter.

Description: The adults and nymphs are small, one-eighth inch long, soft-bodied and cream-colored. They resemble aphids without cornicles (the protruding tubes located on the dorsal end of aphids). You'll need a hand lens to observe and identify them.

Scouting and Control: Because the galls are seen easily, PP infestations often appear worse than they are. Only when galls occur on large numbers of shoots or nuts should you consider insecticides for the next season. Timing of control is critical, and you must target insecticide applications toward the stem mothers. Apply sprays from budbreak to one inch of new growth. Once the galls appear, it is too late to control PP for the season. Often only the trees that were infested the previous year will need treatment, not the entire orchard. Certain native trees and grafted varieties within an orchard become more heavily infested than other trees. Spraying or even removing these trees can prevent economic infestations from spreading throughout the entire orchard.

Major Pecan Diseases

Pecan scab (PS) is the only economic disease found in Missouri orchards. Nut losses on unsprayed susceptible varieties can reach 50 percent to 100 percent in a year. In addition, unsprayed trees prematurely defoliate, which negatively affects next season's nut crop. Two other diseases commonly seen on many varieties, but not at levels to cause economic losses, are anthracnose (*Microspheara penicillata*) on the nuts. Fungicides applied to control scab also control anthracnose and powdery mildew.

Pecan Scab (*Cladosporium caryigenum*)

The scab fungus overwinters as a small, tight mat of fungal material called a "stroma" on shucks, leaf petioles and stems infected the previous season. With warmer temperatures and rainfall in the spring, fungal spores are produced on the stroma.

Dew and rain spread spores locally within a tree, and the wind spreads them over long distances to adjacent trees or orchards.

Description: PS first appears as small, circular, olive-green spots that turn to black on the newly expanding leaves, leaf petioles and nut shuck tissue. All tissues are most susceptible when young and actively growing. Lesions expand and may coalesce. Old lesions crack and fall out of the leaf blade, giving a shot-hole appearance. Nut infections cause the greatest economic damage. Early infections may cause premature nut drop but more commonly cause the shuck to adhere to the nut surface, causing sticktights. Late infections can prevent nuts from fully expanding and decrease nut size.

Control: Resistant varieties offer the first line of defence against PS because pecan varieties vary greatly in their susceptibility to PS. Some varieties are resistant, but many grafted varieties are susceptible. Producers should keep in mind that most commercial varieties were at one time resistant to PS and have now become susceptible because of genetic changes in fungus virulence. Native pecan trees in Missouri exhibit a high degree of genetic variability in resistance to scab. Some trees are resistant, but some are moderately susceptible. The grafted varieties 'Brewster,' 'Colby,' 'Giles,' 'Hirschi,' 'Neosho,' 'Osage,' 'Pawnee,' 'Peruque,' 'Ridgeway,' 'Shoal' and 'Stark's Hardy Giant' are susceptible to PS. 'Hirschi' is highly susceptible to PS and will be defoliated and suffer severe nut loss without protective fungicide sprays.

Apply the first spray (Orbit at 4 fluid ounces or Enable 2F at 8 fluid ounces) at three-fourths to one-inch growth after budbreak. Follow the first spray by two applications (of Super Tin 4L at 6 fluid ounces plus Benlate 50 WP or Topsin M 70W at 0.5 pound) at 14-to 21-day intervals.

On native trees or moderately susceptible cultivars, you often can delay the first fungicide spray until the first-generation PNC insecticide treatment and follow it by a second application 21 days later. The first spray is the most critical and often the most overlooked because the lesions are so small. However, remember that PS is difficult to control once infections of the foliage and young nuts occur.

9

Post Harvest Pest Management

Georgia is one of the main fruit and vegetable producing states in the eastern United States, with shipments going throughout the eastern United States and Canada. Growers and handlers must be aware of issues concerning the shelf life and shipping requirements of produce to ensure quality and minimize loss.

Temperature, humidity and ethylene production affect internal quality, the tendency of fruit to rot, and dehydration. Some products will generate ethylene, potentially damaging other products in the same load.

So load compatibility is an important consideration when shipping produce. Many of the products listed are not grown in Georgia but may be part of a load if the trucking company handles shipments from different areas. In addition, Groups 1 and 2 have the same environmental conditions but are listed separately because they have storage incompatibility concerning ethylene.

Many commodities may be handled differently than suggested in this publication. For example, onions may be handled differently because of onion type or level of maturity. Shallots may be top iced, causing higher relative humidity, then listed in Group 3.

For a more complete description of storage conditions for a particular commodity, consult the USDA publication The Commercial Storage of Fruits, Vegetables, and Florist and Nursery Stocks.

Postharvest shelf life, optimum temperature, humidity and top ice requirements				
Item	Shelf Life (days)	Optimum Temperature (degrees F)	Relative Humidity (%)	Top or Package Ice
Apples	90-240	32-34	90-95	No
Artichokes	10-16	33-38	95-100	Yes
Beans, Snap	7-14	40-45	95	No
Beans, Lima	7-14	37-41	95	No
Beans, Pole	7-14	37-41	95	No
Blackberries	7-14	32	90-95	No
Blueberries	10-21	32	90-95	No
Broccoli	10-14	32	95-100	Yes
Cabbage	90-180	32	98-100	Yes
Cantaloupe	10-14	35-40	90	No
Carrots, topped	28-180	32	98-100	Yes
Cauliflower	14-21	32	90-98	No
Chinese Cabbage	60-90	32	95-100	Yes
Corn, Sweet	4-10	34-38	85-90	Yes
Cucumbers	10-14	45-50	90-95	No
Cucumbers, seedless	10-14	50-55	85-90	No
Daikon	120	32-34	95-100	Yes
Eggplant	10-14	46-54	90-95	No
Elephant Garlic	90-210	32-34	65-75	No
Endive/Escarole	14-21	32	90-95	Yes
Figs	7-10	32	90-95	No
Garlic	90-210	32-34	65-75	No
Grapes, Bunch	56-180	32	95	No
Grapes, Muscadine	7-21	32	95	No
Honeydew*	14-21	45-50	90-95	No
Kale	10-14	34-36	95-100	Yes
Kiwifruit	90-150	32	90-95	No
Leeks	60-90	32	95-100	Yes
Lettuce	14-21	34-36	98-100	Yes
Melons, mixed	14-21	50	90-95	No
Mushrooms	5-7	34-38	85-90	No
Okra	7-10	43-45	85-95	No
Onions, Dry Bulb	30-180	32	65-70	No
Onions, Green	7-10	32	95-100	Yes
Peaches	14-28	31-32	90-95	No
Pears, Asian	150-180	34	90-95	No
Pears, European	60-90	32	90-95	No
Peas, English	7-10	32-35	85-95	Yes
Peppers, Bell	14-21	45-50	85-90	No
Peppers, Hot	14-21	38-44	60-70	No
Persimmon	35-84	48-50	90-95	No
Plums	14-28	32	90-95	No
Potatoes, Early	10-14	45-50	90	No
Potatoes, Late	56-140	45-50	90	No
Pumpkins	84-160	50-60	50-75	No
Quince	60-90	31-32	90	No

Fact Sheet 100/January, 2004

The University of Georgia and Ft. Valley State University, the U.S. Department of Agriculture and counties of the state cooperating. The Cooperative Extension Service, the University of Georgia College of Agricultural and Environmental Sciences offers educational programmes, assistance and materials to all people without regard to race, colour, national origin, age, sex or disability.

An Equal Opportunity Employer/Affirmative Action Organization Committed to a Diverse Work Force: Issued in furtherance of Cooperative Extension work, Acts of May 8 and June 30, 1914, The University of Georgia College of Agricultural and Environmental Sciences and the U.S. Department of Agriculture cooperating.

Radicchio	14-21	32-34	95-100	No
Radish	10-21	32	95-100	Yes
Romaine	14-21	32	95	Yes
Rutabagas	120-180	32	98-100	No
Satsumas	56-84	37-39	85-90	No
Shallots	180-240	32	95-100	Yes
Spinach	10-14	32	95-100	No
Squash, Summer	7-14	41-50	95	No
Squash, Winter	30-180	50-55	70-75	No
Strawberries	7-14	32	95	No
Sweetpotato	120-210	55-60	85-90	No
Tomato, mature-green	21-28	62-68	85-88	No
Tomato, pink	4-7	62-68	85-88	No
Tomatillos	21	55-60	85-90	No
Turnip greens	10-14	34-36	95-100	Yes
Turnip roots	120	32	90-95	No
Watermelon	14-21	50-60	90	No
*Treated with ethylene.				

Easier Transportation

Transportation cost of fruits and vegetables often make up a large percentage of their retailing price. Some fruits and vegetables needs to be transported with refrigeration, some need to be transport by air, and some, by any means, could not stay fresh for more than a few days. (*e.g.* tomatoes and strawberry).

Fruits and vegetables that are genetically engineered for easier transport do not decompose this fast. They lowered transportation cost as well as minimized wastage due to decomposition

Tomatoes have a short shelf life and can quickly go mouldy. Much of the tomatoes produces are wasted because they are spoiled during the process of transportation or retailing. Twenty years ago, scientists first started to study the ripening of the tomato. They identified and enzyme called pectin, which helped ripening by breaking down the pectin which holds the plant cell walls together, allowing the fruit to soften. By removing the gene, cutting a bit off, and then replacing the gene, they were able to stop the enzyme form working. The altered tomato ripened slower, remained firm, was easy to handle during transport and there was much less wastage.

Gene Therapy

Gene therapy refers to the process of changing human genetic material to repair or compensate for the effects of a mutation or abnormality. For example, a gene therapy for a single gene disorder might aim to replace the mutated copy of the gene with a normal one. Because gene therapy aims to alter only some cells in an individual (those affected by the genetic condition), and because it seeks primarily to relieve the suffering of disease, there are generally less ethical objections.

The challenge facing genetic medicines is daunting. First, they must somehow deliver their genetic payload into enough cells to do some good. Retroviruses seemed well suited for this task, because these kinds of viruses normally infect cells by copying part of their DNA into the genetic code of a host cell. Most early trials of genetic medicines therefore co-opted retroviruses, replacing their harmful parts with genes intended to help treat a disease, such as cystic fibrosis or brain cancer. But viral drugs can take effect only if they can slip past the multilayered defences of the human immune system.

First comes an onslaught of antibodies soon after any familiar virus is detected in the bloodstream. These antibodies quickly bind up the virus and can also cause side effects such as inflammation. Viral particles that make it to target cells face a second obstacle: a tough membrane shielding the cell's DNA from attackers. Finally, those retroviruses that are lucky enough to make it past the immune defences and to infect cells do so in an unpredictable manner; they typically will insert the therapeutic gene at a random position in the cell's DNA. The new gene might interrupt an important sequence, actually harming the cell. Even in the best case, new genes often end up in dormant stretches of DNA where they do not get switched on frequently enough to make much of a difference to the patient.

Produce load compatibility			
Group 1. Temperature 32-36 degrees F, Relative Humidity 90-95%*			
Apples	Figs[b]	Mushrooms	Pomegranates
Apricots	Grapes[c]	Nectarines	Prunes
Asian Pears	Horseradish	Oranges[d]	Quinces
Beets, topped	Kohlrabi	Parsnips	Radishes
Berries[a]	Leeks	Peaches	Rutabagas
Cashew apples	Longans	Pears	Turnips
Cherries	Loquats	Persimmons	
Coconuts	Lychees	Plums	
Group 2. Temperature 32-36 degrees F, Relative Humidity 90-95%			
Amaranth	Cauliflower	Jerusalem artichoke	Radishes
Anise	Celeriac	Kiwifruit	Rhubarb
Artichokes	Celery	Kohlrabi	Rutabagas
Bean sprouts	Cherries	Leeks[e]	Scorzonera
Beets	Corn	Lettuce	Salsify
Belgian endive	Daikon	Lo bok	Snow peas
Berries[a]	Endive	Mushrooms	Spinach
Bok choy	Escarole	Parsley	Turnips
Broccoli	Grapes[c]	Parsnips	Water chestnuts
Brussel sprouts	Green onions[f]	Peas	Watercress
Cabbage	Greens	Pomegranates	
Carrots	Horseradish	Radicchio	
Group 3. Temperature 32-36 degrees F, Relative Humidity 65-75%[g]			
Garlic	Onions	Shallots	
Group 4. Temperature 40 degrees F, Relative Humidity 90-95%			
Cactus pears	Clementines	Lychees	Tamarillos
Caimito	Cranberries	Mandarins[d]	Tangelos[d]
Cantaloupe	Kumquats	Oranges[d]	Tangerines[d]
Cassavas	Lemons	Pepino melons	Uniq fruit[d]
Group 5. Temperature 50 degrees F, Relative Humidity 90-95%[h]			
Beans	Eggplant	Okra	Squash
Calamondin	Haricot vert	Peppers	Tamarindos
Chayotes	Kiwanos	Potatoes	Taro root
Cucumbers	Malangas	Pummelos	
Group 6. Temperature 55-60 degrees F, Relative Humidity 85-90%[h]			
Atemoyas	Cherimoyas	Lemons[d]	Potatoes, new
Avocados	Coconuts	Limes[d]	Pumpkins
Babaco	Feijoas	Mamey sapote	Rambutan
Bananas	Ginger root	Mangoes	Santol
Bitter melons	Granadillas	Mongosteen	Soursop
Black sapotes	Grapefruit	Melons[i]	Sugar apples
Boniato	Guavas	Papayas	Tomatillos
Breadfruit	Jaboticabas	Passion fruit	Tomatoes, ripe

Canistel	Jackfruit	Pineapple	Winter squash
Carambolas	Langsat	Plantains	
Group 7. Temperature 65-70 degrees F, Relative Humidity 85-90%			
Jicama	Sweetpotato[j]		Watermelon[j]
Pears (for ripening)	Tomatoes, mature-green		White sapote
* Items in this group can produce high levels of ethylene that can be detrimental to items in Group 2. [a] Except cranberries. [b] Not with apples. [c] No sulfur dioxide. [d] Citrus treated with biphenyl may develop odors that other produce can absorb. [e] Not with figs or grapes. [f] Not with grapes, figs, mushrooms, rhubarb or corn. [g] High moisture will damage these items. [h] Sensitive to chilling injury. [i] Except cantaloupes. [j] Not with pears or tomatoes.			

Research in gene therapy is moving forward, and there are many promising new approaches being investigated. They are all theoretical or experimental at this time, and have not been proven clinically. While the future will likely bring some successful ways of treating disease by fixing mutated genes or compensating for their dysfunction, the lesson of years of research is that it is extremely difficult to alter human genetic information, even in very limited ways.

The current state of technology makes gene therapy still an evolving hope for the future. This does not mean that the ethical questions raised by genetic engineering and gene therapy are not worth discussing. Rather, we are fortunate to have the opportunity to explore these issues and, hopefully, form thoughtful policies and beliefs regarding gene therapy and genetic engineering, before technology makes these procedures a reality. However, it is also important to remain calm and informed about the difference between science fiction and science fact.

Increase Food Production

Current population growth is already straining the earth's resources. One of the few certainties of the future is that the world's population will nearly double, reaching almost 10 billion inhabitants by the year 2030. According to Ismail Serageldin of the World Bank, "Biotechnology will be a crucial part of expanding agricultural productivity in the 21st century. If safely deployed, it could be a tremendous help in meeting the challenge of feeding an additional three billion human beings, 95% of them in the poor developing countries, on the same amount of land and water currently available."

Biotechnology, which allows the transfer of a gene for a specific trait from one plant variety or species to another, is one important piece of the puzzle of sustainable development. Experts assert that biotechnology innovations will triple crop yields without requiring any additional farmland, saving valuable rain forests and animal habitats.

Vaccines and Hormones

Traditionally vaccines are manufactured using animals. Weakened or dead bacteria that cause diseases are injected into an animal. The animal's immune system produces defensive chemicals called antibodies, which are later, removed as a vaccine for human use. As you can see, this method the costly and low in productivity.

With GE, vaccines can be made quickly, cheaply, in large quantities and without the need to use animals. By the GE method, DNA is removed from the bacterium that causes the disease, and the gene that carries the code for a protein is cut out and inserted into the DNA of yeast cells. The yeast cells produce the proteins, which can then be used in the vaccine.

Growth Hormones

Throughout our lives, tiny amounts of human growth hormone are released by the pituitary gland in the brain. It travels in the blood to muscles and bones, where it causes cells to divide and grow. A person who does not produce enough of this hormone is much shorter than normal, often less than 1.2m in height. Unfortunately, growth hormone taken form other animals does not work in humans. So the only way doctors could obtain hormone to treat their patients was by extracting it from the pituitary gland of dead people. Since each gland only contains a minute amount, this process was very time consuming and extremely expensive. It took 650 glands to produce just 2 or 3 grams of the hormone. At one time, human growth hormone was much more expensive than gold gram for gram. Now by GE it could cheaply produced and the cost of treatment has fallen dramatically.

New Organ Donors

Every year thousands of people die while they are waiting to receive a new heart or liver. Even more patients with kidney failure have to go through painful dialysis for year just because they are waiting for a suitable healthy kidney. The main problem is a severe shortage of donor organs, and this situation is unlikely to improve very much (unless there's laws making donation of all organs after death compulsory). The only way round the problem is either to find a source of artificial organs, or use animal organs.

The main problem making a suitable match of organ so hard is rejection. The patient's body recognizes that the new organ is "foreign", and so the immune system produces antibodies which attack the foreign organ and destroy it. Unless the patient is given drugs (which are literally poisons) to suppress the immune system, then new organ will be rejected. The suppressing of the patient's immune system will reduce their resistance to infection, so they catch diseases quite easily. They also have to take low doses of these drugs for the rest of their lives.

With GE, there is a possibility to get organs from pigs. Pig is chosen because they have very close gene structures to humans and they are widely available. (Some scientist uses monkeys too) This is achieved by first altering the DNA of the pig making it a transgenic pig.

The transgenic pig grows organs which are covered by human proteins. When these organs are used in transplants, known as xeno-transplantation, the human body is tricked into accepting the new organ, even though there are pig cells inside it. The first of these genetically engineered pigs have already been produced into monkeys.

There has yet been any successful surgery with organs from other spices. Quite a portion of the population are opposing doing this because of the step of inserting human genes into pigs and the possibility of virus transmission between species.

Reduce Agricultural Input

Pesticides: Pesticides are widely used in today's agricultural farms to kill insects that feed on the crops. However, increased usage not only kills other harmless organisms, but also lead to the evolution of pesticide resistance pests. By GE it is possible to reduce the need of input for chemical pesticides. This is done by making the crop to make it's own pesticides or fertilizers. The most common ways reduce a crop's need of pesticides is by inserting a gene from a common soil bacterium, called Bacillus thurengiensis or Bt. The gene causes the plant to produce a protective protein which is poisonous to pest but harmless to human. This is because human's stomach uses acidic hydrochloride acid during digestion, while most pests' digestive channels are alkaline. The Bt protein only became poisonous when meet an alkaline medium.

Fertilisers: The reduce usage of fertilizers benefits the environment. The excessive use of fertilizers today often cause fertilizers to escape into the natural habitats, encourage the over growth of fungi and eventually kills organisms living in ponds or rivers. Genetically modified crops will require less fertilisers.

Land: As the population on Earth grows, land becomes scarce. It is more difficult for farmers to find land to grow crops. With genetic engineering, we can produce crops that are able to grow in harsh conditions, such as desserts, and mountain tops. Thus, flat land can be saved for recreational, residential or industrial purposes.

Conclusion: The reduced in input brought about by genetic engineering will reduce the cost of production and thus the cost of food. This will indirectly solve the problem of hunger as food will be cheaper and more poor people can afford to buy them.

Bibliography

Abbot, A.J., Atkin, R.K.: *Improving Vegetatively Propagated Crops*, Academic Press, London, 1987.

Altieri, M.A.: *Agroecology, the Scientific Basis of Alternative Agriculture*, Westview Press, California, 1987.

Alvin, P.D.T.; Kozlowski, T.T.: *Ecophysiology of Tropical Crops*, Academic Press, New York, 1977.

Charudattan, R., and H.L. Walker: *Biological Control of Weeds with Plant Pathogens*, John Wiley & Sons, New York, 1982.

Coats, J.R.: *Insecticide Mode of Action*, Academic Press, New York, 1982.

Cobley, L.S.: *Introduction to the Botany of Tropical Crops*, English Language Book Society, London, 1976.

Dasgupta, S.: *Diffusion of Agricultural Innovations in Village in India*, Wiley Eastern Limited, New Delhi, 1989.

Desai, V.: *Issues in Agriculture and Forestry*, Himalaya Publishing House, Bombay, 1984.

Dover, M.; Talbot, L.M.: *Feed the Earth: Agro-Ecology for Sustainable Development*, World Resource Institute, U.S.A., 1987.

Edens, T.C., Fridgen, C. and Battenfield, S.L.: *Sustainable Agriculture and Integrated Farming Systems*, Michigan State University Press, Ann Arbor, 1985.

Edwards, C.A. and Heath, G.W.: *The Principles of Agricultural Entomology*, Chapman and Hall, London, 1964.

Edwards, C.A.: *Environmental Pollution by Pesticides*, Plenum, London, 1973.

Edwards, R. and A.E. Mill.: *Termites in Buildings: Their Biology and Control*, Rentokil Ltd. W. Sussex, 1986.

Farr, E.; Henderson, W.C.: *Land Drainage*, Longman Group Limited, London, 1986.

Follett, R.H., Murphy, L.S. and Donahue, R.L.: *Fertilizers and Soil Amendments*, Prentice Hall, NJ, 1981.

Francis, C.A.: *Multiple Cropping Systems*, New York, MacMillan, 1986.

Frankel, R.: *Heterosis: Reappraisal of Theory and Practice*, Springer Verlag, Berlin, 1983.

Free, J.B.: *Insect Pollination of Crops*, Academic Press Inc., London, 1970.

Hagin, J.; Tucker, B.: *Fertilization of Dryland and Irrigated Soils*, Springer Verlag, Berlin, 1982.

Harris, D.R.; Hillman, G.C.: *Foraging and Farming: The Evolution of Plant Exploitation*, Unwin Hyman Ltd., London, 1989.

Havlicek, J. Jr., Edwards, C.A.: *Profit Potentials of Sustainable Lower Chemical Input Agriculture*, Farm Income Enhancement Conference, Columbus, 1989.

Hawkes, J.G.: *Diversity of Crop Plants*, Harvard University Press, Cambridge, 1983.

Hegde, M.S.; Hegde, M.: *Effect of Rainfall Variability and Lift Irrigation on Rice Yield in U.K: A Case Study of Unchagi Village*, Centre for Ecological Sciences IISc., Bangalore, 1987.

Horn, D.J.: *Ecological Approach to Pest Management*, Elsevier Applied Science Publishers, London, 1988.

Howes, K.M.W.; *Rummery, R.A.: Integrating Agriculture and Forestry*, Natraj Publishers, Dehra Dun, 1984.

Jaiswal, W.; Wadhwani, A.M.: *Handbook of Agriculture (Facts and Figures for Farmers Students and All Interested in Farming)*, (ICAR) Indian Council of Agricultural Research, New Delhi, 1984.

Jenkins, D.: *Agriculture and the Environment*, Lavenham Press, Suffolk, 1984.

Jenkyn, J.F. and Finney, M.E.: *Fertilizers, Fungicides and Saving Date*, Blackwell, Oxford, 1981.

Kennedy, J.O.S.: *Dynamic Programming: Applications to Agriculture and Natural Resources*, Elsevier Applied Science Publishers, London, 1986.

Kogan, M.: *Ecological Theory and Integrated Pest Management Practice*, John Wiley and Sons, New York, 1986.

Kotschi, J.: *Ecofarming Practices: For Tropical Smallholdings*, Verlag Josef Margraf Scientific Books, Germany, 1990.

Kowalski, R. and Visser, P.E.: *Nitrogen in a Crop-pest Interaction: Cereal Aphids*, British Ecological Society, Oxford, 1979.

Kumar, R.: *Insect Pest Control: With Special Reference to African Agriculture*, English Language Book Society, Edward Arnold, 1984.

Lal, R.: *The Role of Mulching Techniques in Tropical Soil and Water Management*, I.I.T.A. Technical Bulletin, Ibadan, 1975.

Lisansky, S.G.: *Biological Pest Control*, Butterworth, London, 1981.

Martin, F.W.: *Handbook of Tropical Food Crops*, CRC Press Inc., Bocaraton, 1984.

Miller, D.A.: *Forage Crops*, MacGraw Hill Book Company, New York, 1984.

Newbury, P.A.R.: *Geography of Agriculture*, Longman Scientific & Technical, London, 1980.

Norman, M.J.T.; Pearson, C.J.; Searle, P.G.E.: *Ecology of Tropical Food Crops*, Cambridge University Press, Cambridge, 1984.

Norton, G.A., and C.S. *Holling: Proceedings of an International Conference on Pest Management*, New York: Pergamon Press, 1976.

Olson, G.W.: *Field Guide to Soils and the Environment: Applications of Soil Surveys*, Chapman and Hall, New York, 1984.

Palanisami, K.: *Irrigation Water Management: The Determinants of Canal Water Distribution in India: A Microanalysis*, Agricole Publishing Academy, New Delhi, 1984.

Park, J.R.: *Environmental Management in Agriculture: European Prespectives*, Belhaven Press, London, 1988.

Peltz, P. and M. Rossol.: *Safe Pest Control Procedures for Museum Collections*, Center for Occupational Hazards, New York, 1983.

Perkins, J.H.: *Insects, Experts and the Insecticide Crisis: The Quest for New Pest Management Strategies*, Plenum Press, New York, 1982.

Pfadt, R.E.: *Fundamentals of Applied Entomology*, MacMillan Publishing Company, New York, 1985.

Pimentel, D.: *Handbook of Energy Utilization in Agriculture*, CRC Press Inc., Boca Raton, 1980.

Pinniger, D. B.: *Insect Pests in Museums*, Archetype, London, 1994.

Querol, D.: *Genetic Resources: Our Forgotten Treasure. Technical and Socio-economic Approaches*, Third World Network, Penang, 1992.

Radosevich, S.R., and J.S. Holt: *Weed Ecology: Implications for Vegetation Management*, John Wiley & Sons, New York, 1984.

Rosenthal, S.S., D.M. Maddox, and K. Brunetti: *Biological Methods of Weed Control*, Thomson Publications, Fresno, 1984.

Rossol, M.: *The Artist's Complete Health and Safety Guide*, Allworth Press, New York, 1994.

Ruthenberg, H.: *Farming Systems in the Tropics*, Clarendon Press, Oxford, 1980.

Shafi, M.; Raza, M.: *Dryland Agriculture in India*, Rawat Publications, Jaipur, 1987.

Simmonds, N.W.: *Evolution of Crop Plants*, Longman Group Ltd., London, 1976.

Singh, R.S.; *Sitaramaiah, K.: Handbook of Economic Nematology*, Cosmo Publications, New Delhi, 1993.

Smith Jr., R.J.: *Integration of Micobial Herbicides with Existing Pest Management Programs*, Wiley, London and New York, 1982.

Story, K.O.: *Approaches to Pest Management in Museums*, Smithsonian Institution, Washington, D.C., 1985.

Thomson, J.R.: *Introduction to Seed Technology*, Leonard Hill, Glasgow, 1984.

Vandermeer, J.: *Ecology of Intercropping*, Cambridge University Press, Cambridge, 1989.

Vanderplank, J.E.: *Host Pathogen Interactions in Plant Disease*, Academic Press, New York, 1982.

Ware, G.: *Complete Guide to Pest Control-With and Without Chemicals*, Thomson Publications, California, 1980.

Youngberg, G.: *Alternative Argiculture in the United States: Ideology, Politics and Prospects*, Van Nostrand Reinhold, New York, 1984.

Zimdahl, R.L.: *Weed-Crop Competition: A Review*, Oregon State University, Corvallis, 1980.

Zohary,D.; *Hopf, M.: Domestication of Plants in the Old World: The Origin and Spread of Cultivated Plants in West Asia, Europe and the Nile Valley*, Clarendon Press, Oxford, 1988.

Index

D

E

F

G

H

I

K

L

R

S

T

❑❑❑